# FIREWAGON HOCKEY

## THE GAME IN THE EIGHTIES

Enjoy blad !

Love Sally Dove

+

Kelsey

June 18/2006

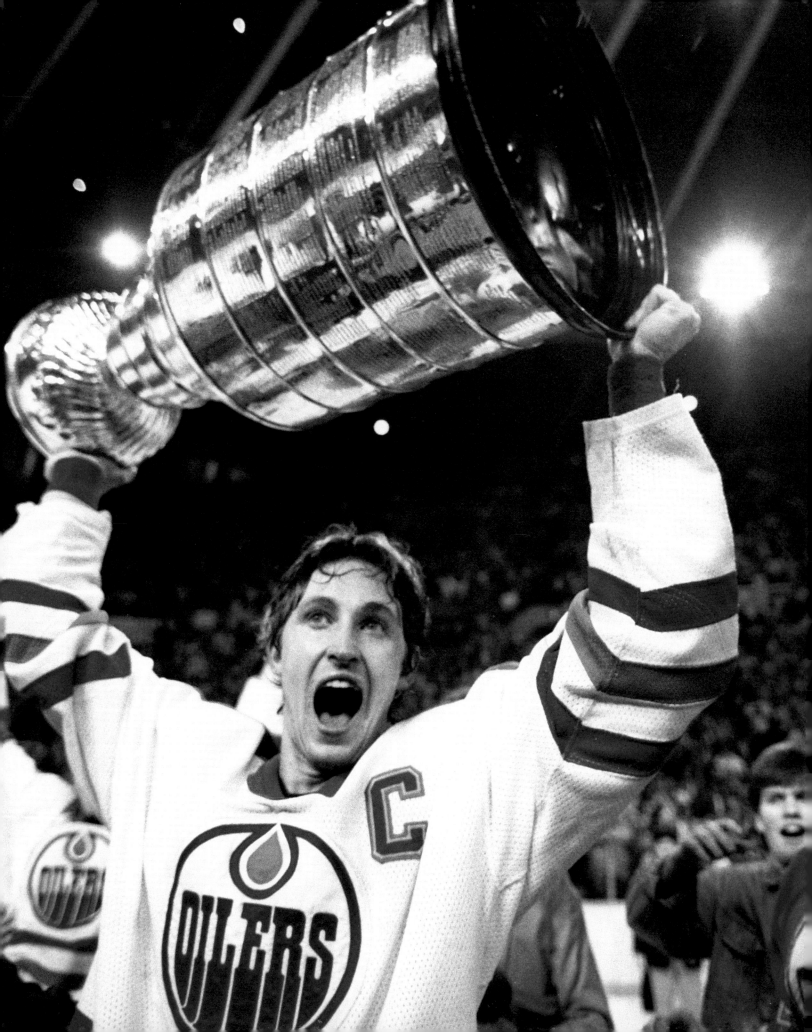

# FIREWAGON HOCKEY

## THE GAME IN THE EIGHTIES

# HOCKEY

## MIKE LEONETTI

FIREFLY BOOKS

# A FIREFLY BOOK

Published by Firefly Books Ltd. 2004

First printing

Publisher Cataloging-in-Publication Data (U.S.)
Leonetti, Mike, 1958-
    Firewagon hockey : the game in the eighties / Mike Leonetti.—1st ed.
[192] p. : col. photos. ;   cm.
Summary: Retrospective on the National Hockey League of the 1980s,
organized by season, including game highlights, statistics and player pro-
files.
ISBN 1-55297-911-3  (pbk.)
1. Hockey — North America — History.  2. National Hockey League —
History.  I. Title.
796.962/64/097 21     GV847.8.N3.L46 2004


Library and Archives Canada Cataloguing in Publication
Leonetti, Mike, 1958-
    Firewagon hockey : the game in the eighties / Mike Leonetti.
    ISBN 1-55297-911-3
    1. National Hockey League—History.  2. National Hockey League—
History—Pictorial works.  I. Title.
GV847.8.N3L458 2004          796.962'64'09048          C2004-
903415-4


Published in the United States in 2004 by
Firefly Books (U.S.) Inc.
P.O. Box 1338, Ellicott Station
Buffalo, New York 14205

Published in Canada in 2004 by
Firefly Books Ltd.
66 Leek Crescent
Richmond Hill, Ontario L4B 1H1

Cover and interior design by Kimberley Young
Printed in Canada

*The Publisher acknowledges the financial support of the Government of
Canada through the Book Publishing Industry Development Program for
its publishing activities.*

page 2: *Philadelphia's Tim
Kerr (#12) had four straight
50-goal seasons between
1983–84 and 1986–87.*

page 4: *A three-time 50
goal scorer in the eighties,
Toronto's Rick Vaive
celebrates a marker against
the New York Islanders.*

title page: *Wayne Gretzky
holding the Stanley Cup was
a familiar sight in the eighties.*

# Table of Contents

# Introduction
## Goals, Dynasties, and Gretzky

HOCKEY IN THE 1980S IS BEST DESCRIBED AS A MIX OF speed, youth, goals, goals, and more goals. As the new decade began, all National Hockey League teams had attack on their minds, and they worried about defense later, if at all. The style of play was reminiscent of the record-setting Montreal Canadiens of the fifties, who dominated the NHL during hockey's Golden Era. The Flying Frenchmen played an all-out offensive brand of "firewagon hockey," and in the eighties it was back in vogue. The action would come fast and furious, and if you went to the concession stand, you might miss more than one goal. The best players racked up plenty of points, especially in the first half of the decade, and if a team did not have a couple of 50-goal scorers, or at least a few players pushing toward that standard, they likely weren't in contention. A 40-goal season was not extraordinary, and a 20-goal scorer could be easily replaced. Scores like 7–5, 10–6, and 12–7 were not unusual, even in games involving the better teams.

Anyone who needs proof that it was a wild and crazy era that brought a cascade of goals can pick up the *NHL Guide and Record Book*. The Edmonton Oilers, the most attack-oriented team in hockey history, scored a record 446 goals in 1983–84, an average of 5.6 per game. The next four teams on the all-time list are also Edmonton clubs from the eighties — they topped 400 goals every year from

*Bryan Trottier (#19) of the New York Islanders keeps a close watch on Bobby Clarke (#16) of the Philadelphia Flyers. The two teams met for the Stanley Cup in 1980 and combined to set an NHL record 21 power-play (15 by the Islanders, six by the Flyers) in one playoff series. Trottier had four goals and four assists in the finals while Clarke had four goals and three assists in the six game series.*

1981–82 to 1985–86. The Oilers were also involved in one of the highest-scoring games ever when they defeated the Chicago Blackhawks 12–9 on December 11, 1985. The combined 21 goals tied an NHL record established in 1920 by the Montreal Canadiens and the Toronto St. Patricks. Edmonton was also a part of two other 20–goal shootouts — they beat Minnesota 12–8 on January 4, 1984, and lost 11–9 to the Toronto Maple Leafs on January 8, 1986.

The Buffalo Sabres set an NHL record with nine goals in one period when they clobbered the Leafs 14–4 on March 19, 1981. The Calgary Flames went from November 12, 1981, to January 9, 1985, without being shutout — they tallied at least one goal in 264 consecutive contests. The Pittsburgh Penguins set the mark for most power-play goals in one season when they scored 119 times with the extra man in 1988–89. Even with a man short there was no lack of offense. The Oilers set the top four marks for most short-handed goals in one season, starting with the 1985–86 season when they scored 36. Lists of teams with the most 50-, 40-, and 30-goal scorers in one season are all pockmarked with teams that played in the wildest scoring decade – the eighties.

The 1981–82 season saw the NHL's goals-per-game average go to eight, the highest mark in the modern era — contrast that with the game in the late nineties and beyond, where the average was around five. Even less than superstar players like Warren Young, Walt Poddubny, Troy Murray, Sylvain Turgeon, Mike Bullard, Wayne Babych, Jacques Richard, Tony McKegney, Paul MacLean, Geoff Courtnall, and Ron Duguay all had 40 goals in at least one season, and some scored 50 or more. Speedy forwards who owned a wicked shot and would charge to the net were in great demand. Checking was a dirty word, and players like Montreal's Bob Gainey or Boston's Steve Kasper, known primarily for their defensive efforts, were few and far between. Quality goaltending may have been at its lowest point in NHL history during the early eighties, just as firewagon hockey was emerging. However, there was also a lack of quality defensemen, and some coaches didn't even bother putting together a checking line. Plenty of defensemen recorded 20 or more goals in a season during the eighties — Paul Coffey, Paul Reinhart, Phil Housley, Denis Potvin, Ray Bourque, Reed Larson, Larry Murphy, and Al MacInnis led the goal production from the blueline — and these "defenders" were often ahead of many forwards on their teams' scoring lists. Who had time for defense when there were goals to be scored?

Opposite: *New York Islander captain Denis Potvin accepted the Stanley Cup on four occasions (1980, 1981, 1982 and 1983) during the eighties. A top playoff performer, Potvin recorded 164 points in 185 postseason games over his entire career.*

From 1980–81 to 1989–90, players reached 50 or more goals in season 75 times, and equaled or passed the 100-point barrier on 118 occasions. In addition, there were 15 games that featured a five-goal performance by one player (compared with only seven in the nineties), eight games that saw someone record eight points, and another nine games where an individual player logged seven.

While many offensive records were set during the eighties, the 10-year stretch was by no means without similarities to other decades in NHL history. Hockey's greatest team dynasties were rooted in the forties (Toronto), the fifties (Montreal and Detroit), the sixties (Toronto and Montreal), and the seventies (Montreal), and the eighties added two teams to that special list. The New York Islanders and the Edmonton Oilers both met the standard by which dynasties are measured — at least three Stanley Cups, won consecutively, or at least over a short time span — and a list of Hall of Fame players that, at least in the Oilers' case, is yet to be completed.

The Islanders were built the old-fashioned way by general manager Bill Torrey. By carefully making the most out of their high draft choices starting in 1972, New York was ready to challenge for the Stanley Cup by the late seventies, winning their first championship in 1980. The Islanders boasted an impressive group of stars, with Denis Potvin, Bryan Trottier, Mike Bossy, Clark Gillies, and goaltender Billy Smith. Add gritty performers like Bob Nystrom, John Tonelli, Ken Morrow, Brent Sutter, Duane Sutter, Bob Bourne, and Wayne Merrick and the Isles could play any type of game the opposition demanded. The acquisition that put the Islanders over the top was the trade that netted Butch Goring from Los Angeles. After premature playoff exits in 1978 and 1979 prepared them mentally, the Isles finally got to the finals in 1980 and defeated the Philadelphia Flyers in six games. That victory spurred them to reel off four straight Cups, defeating four different teams in the finals (Minnesota, Vancouver, and Edmonton were the others). The Islanders made it to a fifth straight final in 1984, but lost to the rising power in the NHL.

The Edmonton Oilers debuted in the NHL at the start of the 1979–80 season, when four teams from the upstart World Hockey Association joined the established league. (Hartford, Quebec, and Winnipeg were the others.) When they were in the WHA, the Oilers played a fast-tempo offensive style of game, and they did not change their approach when they moved to the NHL. Edmonton coach and

*Wayne Gretzky accepted the Stanley Cup as captain of the Edmonton Oilers on four occasions during the eighties and also took the Conn Smythe trophy twice.*

Opposite: *New York's Denis Potvin (#5) keeps track of Mark Messier (#11) of Edmonton. The Islanders and the Oilers met twice for the Stanley Cup in the eighties (1983 and 1984) with each side winning once. The rivalry between the two clubs was quite bitter but the Oilers finally dethroned the Islanders in 1984 when Messier won the Conn Smythe trophy.*

general manager Glen Sather was influenced by the style of hockey played in Europe, and by the Winnipeg Jets (with their European-laden roster), who played a similar game in the WHA. The Oilers got their NHL history off to a good start when they were able to keep Wayne Gretzky as one of their priority protected players (Gretzky was never drafted by an NHL team, even though he was eligible), while many other WHA stars went to established NHL teams or were put into the entry draft. Like the Islanders, the Oilers made the most of the draft in their early years, selecting Mark Messier, Grant Fuhr, Glenn Anderson, Kevin Lowe, Paul Coffey, and Jari Kurri. Sather was good at making deals — he acquired Mike Krushelnyski, Geoff Courtnall, Ken Linseman, Adam Graves, and Craig Simpson in various trades during the decade — and bringing in free agents like Charlie Huddy,

Craig MacTavish, Craig Muni, and Randy Gregg to help round out his club. The team had its share of grinders — Pat Hughes, Kevin McClelland, Dave Lumley, to name a few — but make no mistake: it was Gretzky who was the driving force behind the Edmonton Oilers.

By the time his incredible career was over, Wayne Gretzky owned just about every significant scoring record in the regular season and the playoffs. Most of those records were either set in the eighties or had their roots planted in that exceptional 10-year period when the 'Great One' ruled the NHL. His four highest point totals for one season (215, 212, 208, and 205) were all set in the eighties. His four best goal-scoring seasons (92, 87, 73, and 71) also came during this decade, as did his best four assist totals (163, 135, 125, and 121). As an individual, Gretzky pushed his totals into the stratosphere, and as a captain he led his team to four Stanley Cups in five years. There might have been more had the Oilers been more alert in 1982, when they were upset by the lowly Los Angeles Kings, and again in 1986, when a fluke goal by the Calgary Flames ended their playoff year suddenly. There might also have been more if Gretzky had not moved to Los Angeles in a shocking trade just after the Oilers won their fourth Cup in 1988. Philadelphia, Boston, Montreal, and Calgary were the best of the other teams in the eighties, with the Canadiens (1986) and Flames (1989) winning Stanley Cups as well.

As much as offense, dynasties, and Gretzky were the stories of the eighties, other noticeable trends developed in the NHL. The league got younger, as many teams added first-round draft choices to their rosters without sending them back to junior hockey. Prime examples included Steve Yzerman of Detroit, Wendel Clark of Toronto, Pierre Turgeon of Buffalo, and Mario Lemieux of Pittsburgh, who would eventually dethrone Gretzky for the Art Ross Trophy as the NHL points leader. Quality players like Rick Middleton of Boston, Darryl Sittler of Toronto, and Clark Gillies of the Islanders were forced to retire in their mid-30s, as they looked slow in this younger and speedier NHL, which during the 1980s would add rookies like Barry Pederson (Boston), Dale Hawerchuk (Winnipeg), Steve Larmer (Chicago), Luc Robitaille (Los Angeles), and Joe Nieuwendyk (Calgary).

The composition of the league was also changing as more and more Europeans began careers in the NHL. At the start of the decade, 82.1 percent of the NHL was made up of Canadian-born players, but by the end that number had declined to 75.5 percent. Many Europeans

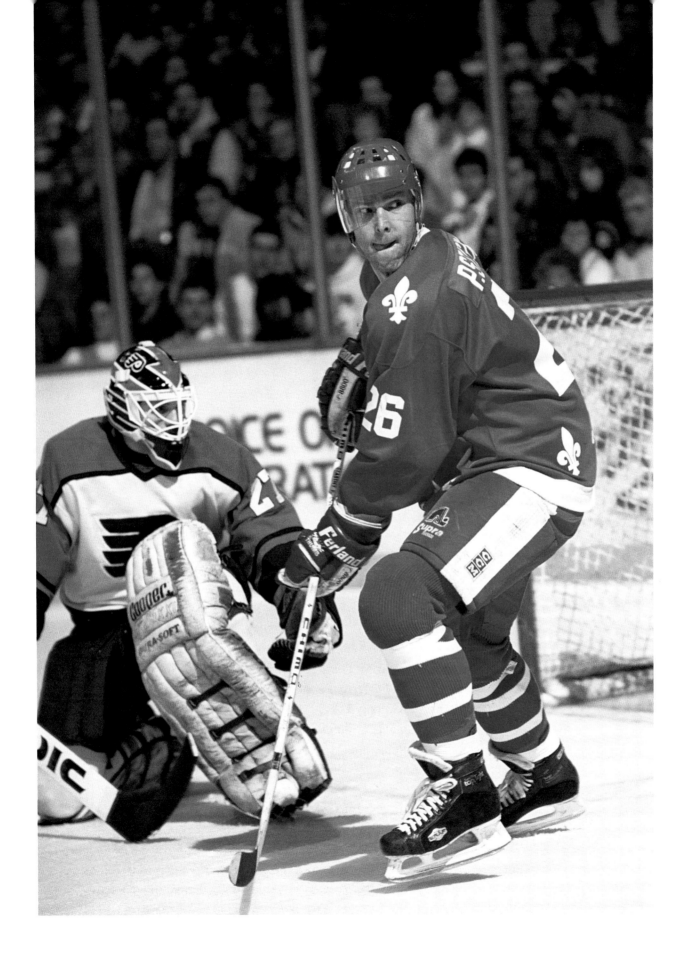

*Boston Defenseman Raymond Bourque (#77) had five seasons of 20 or more goals in the eighties including a career high 31 in 1983–84.*

who joined the NHL made quite an impact, led by Peter Stastny of the Quebec Nordiques. Starting in 1980–81, Stastny recorded seven seasons of 100 or more points, making him the second-best point producer of the decade after Gretzky. Other top European imports included Kent Nilsson, Hakan Loob, Mats Naslund, Pelle Lindbergh, Tomas Steen, Tomas Gradin, Tomas Sandstrom, Patrik Sundstrom, Petr Klima, Esa Tikkanen, and two other Stastny brothers, Marian and Anton, who also played for Quebec. Russian players started to appear on NHL rosters in the late 1980s — some with Soviet government approval and other via defections to the West — with Sergei Makarov,

Igor Larionov, and a young Alex Mogilny among the top names that first played in the 1989–90 season.

Americans were also on the rise in the eighties, as the U.S. gold medal in the 1980 Olympics spawned new interest in the game, at both the college and high-school level. Many players on that 1980 squad went on to productive NHL careers — Neal Broten, Mike Ramsey, Dave Christian, Mark Johnson, for example — and other Americans, including Bobby Carpenter, Phil Housley, Ed Olczyk, Mark Howe, Pat LaFontaine, and Chris Chelios, each starred on their respective clubs. Late in the decade, Jeremy Roenick, Jimmy Carson, Brian Leetch, and Mike Modano were examples of up-and-coming American-born talent. Coaches Herb Brooks, Bob Johnson, and Ted Sator also came from the U.S. college system, and all had good success in the NHL. Perhaps the biggest step forward for Americans came when two players — Brian Lawton in 1983 and Modano in 1988 — were selected first overall at the entry draft. Yet another important development was the advent of satellite television, which made the game available on local and national cable systems in the United States. (Canadian viewers, too, would get to watch more games than ever before.)

The NHL was remarkably stable in the eighties. The league remained at 21 teams for 10 seasons, with only one franchise moving — the Colorado Rockies shifted to New Jersey in 1982. It took time for the league to absorb the four WHA teams and get them to be competitive — Winnipeg struggled in the early years, while Quebec was good for most of the eighties, then in a shambles by the end — but once that happened, the NHL provided a high-powered, offense-oriented brand of hockey at a relatively low cost to fans. Million-dollar contracts were nonexistent for most of the decade, and player movement was generally about building better hockey teams, not economics. The Canadian clubs could compete with their U.S. counterparts, because their buildings were usually sold out and the value of the dollar was not an issue. As well, there were no strikes or lockouts like those experienced by Major League Baseball and the National Football League. The cozy relationship between the head of the Player's Association, Alan Eagleson, and NHL president John Ziegler kept the players quiet for the greater part of the decade, but as the eighties came to a close, labor unrest was starting to simmer. It would boil over in the nineties.

There were three Canada Cup tournaments during the decade (1981, 1984, and 1987), which even some ardent hockey fans consid-

*Mario Lemieux (#66) won his first Art Ross trophy for the 1987–88 season when he had 70 goals and 168 points. It marked the first time that someone other than Wayne Gretzky had won the award since 1980–81.*

ered too many. The gathering of hockey nations seemed like a good idea, considering the NHL now included players from around the world. But it was really Eagleson who pushed for these tournaments, supposedly for the benefit of the players' pension funds — history would also show many of the proceeds ended up in the wrong hands under Eagleson's direction. Still, there was some excellent hockey played in these tournaments, and the '87 competition was the highlight, as Canada and the Soviets played a three-game final ended in classic style by Wayne Gretzky and Mario Lemieux.

If these international games represented hockey at its finest, the NHL could still bring fans a dose of cold reality with bench-clearing brawls, attacks on referees, and ugly stick incidents that were painful reminders of the game in the seventies. NHL disciplinarian Brian O'Neill was tough on transgressors, but it did not stem the tide of stick work and brawling. Heavy suspensions were imposed to stop players from leaving the bench (this is one rule change that has worked well for years), but they were not enough to prevent individual incidents such as the one on January 6, 1988, when Minnesota's Dino Ciccarelli took his stick to the head of Toronto's Luke Richardson. Ciccarelli was suspended for 10 games, charged with assault by Toronto police, and given a one-day jail sentence. The vicious attack was played over and over again on television, and the court case was more poor exposure for the game that is still seen as too violent at times, especially in the American media.

As the decade ended, most NHL games found a better balance between offense and defense. The Gretzky trade meant the best team in the NHL was no longer able to dominate as it once had — although the Oilers did win one more Cup in 1990 — and better goaltending added an element that had gone missing. Patrick Roy made a sterling debut in 1986 and reminded hockey fans just how valuable and exciting a top netminder can be. Tom Barrasso, Ron Hextall, John Vanbiesbrouck, and Mike Vernon also became award winners or Stanley Cup champions like Roy. The great influx of Europeans and Russians also helped balance the league, and the ridiculous playoff system — whereby the top four teams in each division made the playoffs, regardless of the point totals of teams in other divisions — created bitter rivalries. Teams often tightened up during these hard-fought divisional games, and that brought a measure of defense back to the NHL.

A good number of Hall of Fame careers came to an end in the eighties, including those of Bobby Clarke, Tony Esposito, Darryl Sittler, Brad Park, Gilbert Perreault, and Denis Potvin. Many more Hall of Famers launched or made their careers in the decade: Denis Savard, Bernie Federko, Mike Gartner, Pat LaFontaine, Rod Langway, Clark Gillies, Grant Fuhr, Michel Goulet, Dale Hawerchuk, Peter Stastny, Joe Mullen, Jari Kurri, and of course, Gretzky and Lemieux. Others such as Raymond Bourque, Patrick Roy, and Mike Vernon will also be elected to the Hall of Fame in due time.

In this book, we have tried to recapture the excitement of the eighties with season-by-season accounts and captivating photography. Colorful action shots from photographers Bruce Bennett, Dennis Miles, and Paul Bereswill dominate this book, and they help tell the story of an electrifying era in the NHL — a time when firewagon hockey was the norm, and those who played it rewrote the record book.

# 1980–81

Gretzky wins his first scoring title, the Stastnys take Quebec, and Cherry picks a new role

AS the 1979–80 season came to an end, a number of coaching changes were in the works. The Boston Bruins hired former netminding great Gerry Cheevers, whose only previous experience behind the bench had come after Don Cherry was tossed during the third period on March 3, 1979. In his laid-back style, Cheevers led the Bruins to a 37–30–13 record in 1980–81, good for second place in the Adams Division. Other new coaches were Roger Neilson in Buffalo, Keith Magnuson in Chicago, Ted Lindsay in Detroit, former journeyman defenseman Bryan Watson as co-coach in Edmonton, Eddie Johnston in Pittsburgh, and Maurice Filion in Quebec (where he was also general manager). A young Gary Green began his first full year in Washington, but it would be a season to forget for the Capitals, who went 26–36–18 and finished last in the Smythe Division.

### Cherry Goes to TV

Don Cherry made his debut on *Hockey Night in Canada* in 1980, after the Colorado Rockies practically destroyed his reputation as a coach. The Rockies had dismissed him following a 19-win season in 1979–80 and then released to the media a six-page indictment of Cherry. "They had more charges against me than Charles Manson," the bombastic Cherry told *The Hockey News.* "I couldn't believe it. When I finished reading it, I didn't even like me!" Cherry was never a

*After another great season in 1980–81 (68 goals, 119 points), Islanders winger Mike Bossy (#22, shown here trying to score against Mike Liut and the St. Louis Blues) was even better in the playoffs, with 35 points in 18 games. The Blues finished on top of the Smythe Division with 107 points in 1980–81.*

25

*The 1980–81 season was Darryl Sittler's last full year as a Maple Leaf. He performed to his usual standards, scoring 43 goals and adding 53 assists. The Leafs were a very poor team and Sittler, worn down from fighting with management, wanted out by the middle of 1981–82. Sittler was dealt to Philadelphia in a trade that saw the Leafs get Rich Costello, Ken Strong, and a draft choice used to select Peter Ihnacak. The Maple Leafs got very little for their all-time scorer (916 points) and future Hall of Famer.*

head coach again in the professional ranks. He made a not-so-successful return behind the bench many years later for a junior team he partly owned, but his real calling was his gig on Canada's most-watched television show. Cherry has made himself into a broadcasting icon with a style — including outrageous jackets and ties — and flair unrivaled in sports television. On his regular "Coach's Corner" segments, Cherry will tackle any topic, and his politically incorrect opinions are the stuff of water-cooler discussions and, most importantly, high ratings. In 1980–81, Cherry provided color commentary during some games, but soon realized he was best suited to providing analysis during intermissions and at the end of the game.

Other notable off-ice happenings involved two of hockey's greatest legends. Bobby Orr quit as the special assistant to National Hockey League president John Ziegler, saying he was given nothing to do, and Gordie Howe became director of player personnel for the Hartford Whalers after ending his illustrious — and very long — playing career. Howe had been restless after retiring as a Detroit Red Wing in 1971, and he had taken a meaningless job in the front office for the Motown club. Now he would be able to watch his talented son Mark play defense for the Whalers, while another son, Marty, was also in the Hartford organization.

The NHL also instituted a new rule, whereby all players not involved in a fight had to retreat to a designated area — the home team to its own bench, and the visitors to the opposite side of the ice. Under the leadership of Phil Esposito, 85 percent of the players' association (NHLPA) voted against overtime in the regular season.

## The Hockey Circus at Maple Leaf Gardens
The circus that was the Toronto Maple Leafs continued, although there was a gesture of peace when owner Harold Ballard returned the captaincy to Darryl Sittler. (A year earlier, Sittler had torn the coveted C from his jersey in what Ballard called an "act of treason.") It was the first tangible sign that the ailing Punch Imlach was not going to be general manager of the Leafs for much longer. The former Leaf legend (four Stanley Cups in the sixties) was brought back to manage the team in 1979, an ill-advised hiring, but Ballard was prone to changing his mind almost daily. If this latest move was intended to smooth over the tremendous turmoil the year before, it didn't work out very well. The Leafs barely squeaked into the playoffs on the final night of the

# RANDY CARLYLE

Toronto chose 30th overall in the 1976 draft and selected defenseman Randy Carlyle, a native of Sudbury, Ontario. But before Carlyle could officially become a Leaf, he had to reach an out-of-court settlement with the Cincinnati Stingers of the WHA, who had a claim on him. (Carlyle insisted he had signed only a letter of intent with the Stingers.) With that out of the way, he played in 45 games as a Toronto rookie in 1976–77, and another 49 the next year, notching 15 points. At the age of 22, it appeared Carlyle had a secure future as a Leaf, but he was abruptly traded to Pittsburgh along with George Ferguson for another defenseman, Dave Burrows. At the time, Leafs coach Roger Neilson commented that Carlyle might one day be as good as Burrows, if not better. That day was not far off, and in 1980–81 Carlyle won the Norris Trophy as the NHL's top blueliner (no Leaf has ever won the award). Carlyle scored 16 goals and added 67 assists that year, and also found time to serve 136 penalty minutes. Interestingly, Carlyle was cut from Team Canada for the 1981 Canada Cup and soon found his way out of Pittsburgh as well. He was dealt to Winnipeg in 1984 and was a reliable defender with the Jets for eight seasons. He scored in double digits eight times, and the last goal of his career came against the Maple Leafs.

**CAREER STATS:** 1,055 games played; 148 goals; 499 assists; 647 points; 1,400 penalty minutes.

*Lanny McDonald scored 35 goals and 46 assists for the sad-sack Colorado Rockies in 1980–81. By the end of the following season, McDonald was in Calgary playing for the Flames, while the Rockies became the New Jersey Devils.*

season with a mere 71 points (based on a 28–37–15 record). On November 18, 1980, Maple Leafs founder Conn Smythe passed away at the age of 85. The proud Smythe would at least not have to watch the franchise — which he had built from nothing into a league power — become the worst team of the eighties.

The first firing of the season did not take long — Fred Shero was dismissed as bench boss after a slow start by the New York Rangers. The Rangers were the third-worst team in the league at the time, but the firing was still something of a surprise considering Shero's reputation. After winning two Stanley Cups with the brawling Philadelphia Flyers, Shero jumped to the Big Apple for the 1978–79 season, taking the Rangers all the way to the finals before losing to Montreal. The next season saw the Rangers out in the first round of the playoffs, and when they stumbled early in '80–'81, Shero was gone and would never return to the NHL. The Rangers handed the reins to Craig Patrick, and he turned the Blueshirts into a 30–36–14 club that would pull off a couple of upsets in the postseason. In addition to Shero, Watson, Lindsay, and Filion would all be replaced in short order as their teams struggled in the early going.

## Young Oilers Start to Develop

Glen Sather felt he was the best choice to coach the developing Edmonton Oilers, even though he was also the team's general manager. In just their second year in the NHL, the young Oilers were an emerging force, with Wayne Gretzky leading the way. The splendidly talented center led the league with a record 164 points (surpassing the mark of 152 held by Phil Esposito), and shattered Bobby Orr's record for most assists in a season when he tallied 109. Gretzky clearly proved his performance in 1979–80 was no fluke, and

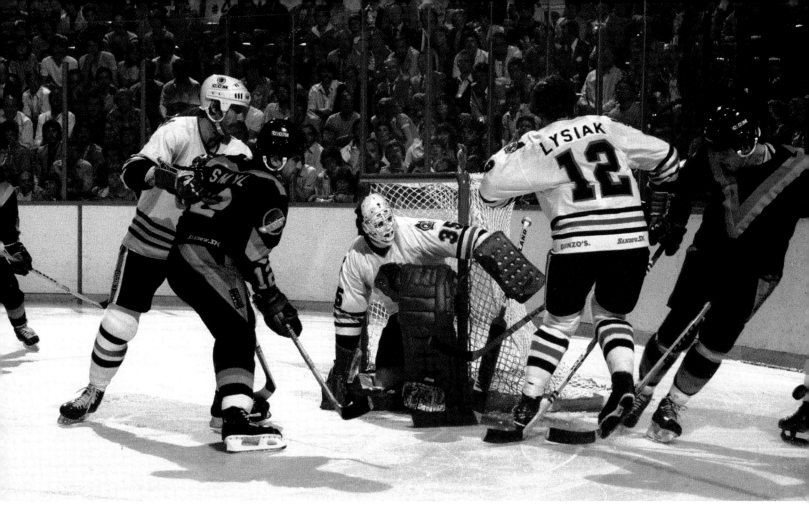

was named the NHL's most valuable player. Mark Messier and Kevin Lowe were already in place, and the '80–'81 campaign saw Glenn Anderson, Paul Coffey, Charlie Huddy, and Andy Moog (who took over in net during the playoffs) make their debuts in the NHL. Huddy was a surprising addition — the defenseman was never drafted by any NHL team, and was a signed as a free agent. He would make a splash in his first NHL game with two goals and one assist. The ability to find gems like Huddy, a five-time Cup winner, is a large part of what made Sather so successful as boss of the Oilers. Even with Ron Low and Ed Mio tending goal during the regular season, the club put together a 29–35–16 record, and set off fireworks in the playoffs.

## Flames Across the Border

The Oilers were not the only team in the province of Alberta as the new season began. The Atlanta Flames could no longer make a go of it in the Deep South and headed to Canada — a very different scenario from the one years later, when Quebec and Winnipeg were forced to leave for Denver and Phoenix respectively. Keeping the Flames nickname, the new team was forced to play in the Calgary Corral, where the arena capacity was only 6,492. Manager Cliff Fletcher helped build a strong foundation

*Goaltender Tony Esposito (#35) appeared in a league-high 66 games in 1980–81, winning 29 games for the Blackhawks with a 3.75 goals-against average. He tied another 14 games, but for the only time in his career, Esposito did not record a single shutout.*

# KENT NILSSON

The Calgary Flames record book is still filled with references to greatness of center Kent Nilsson. He holds the mark for most points (131), most assists (82), and most short-handed goals (9) in one season, as well as most career hat tricks (13). The slick Swede was known as the Magic Man for his superior puck handling and clever playmaking abilities — and also because he seemed to disappear during some games. He began his career in North America with the Winnipeg Jets of the World Hockey Association, where his style was perfectly suited to the freewheeling squad. He earned rookie-of-the-year honors in the WHA and helped Jets to the Avco Cup, but his rights were reclaimed by the Atlanta Flames (who originally drafted him in 1976) during the 1979 expansion draft. The Jets clearly erred in not protecting Nilsson, who scored 40 goals and added 53 assists during his one season in Atlanta, and when the team moved to Calgary, Nilsson became the star. He finished 1980–81 with 49 goals and 82 assists, and his 131 points was third-best in the NHL. Nilsson added 12 points in 14 games in the '81 postseason, and the Flames won two series for the first time in their history. He was with the Flames for four more years (including a 104-point effort in 1982–83) but his act wore thin and he was dealt to the Minnesota North Stars in 1985 for two draft choices (which turned out to be Joe Nieuwendyk and Stephane Matteau, a good deal for Calgary). Nilsson won a Stanley Cup with Edmonton in 1987 before his career was done.

**CAREER STATS:** 533 games played; 264 goals; 422 assists; 686 points; 116 penalty minutes.

for the club, and the surprise of the season was Kent Nilsson. The Swedish center scored 49 goals and finished third in the league with 131 points. Right winger Willie Plett scored a career-high 38 goals, while Guy Chouinard (83 points), Bob MacMillan (73 points), Paul Reinhart (67 points), and Eric Vail (28 goals) were also big contributors during this first year in Western Canada, which saw the Flames go 39–27–14 during the regular season.

Not all teams in Western Canada were enjoying a great year in '80–'81. The sophomore Winnipeg Jets would win all of nine games, while losing 57. The Jets defeated Chicago 6–2 on October 17 and then did not win again until December 30, when they beat the Colorado Rockies. The 30-game winless streak established an NHL record, and the victory over the lowly Rockies seemed like winning the Stanley Cup. The Jets' 32-point total was the worst in the league, and they went through three coaches — Tom McVie, Bill Sutherland, and Mike Smith. The fact that this team gave up a league-worst 400 goals meant there was much work to be done. At least their last-place finish gave the Jets first pick in the 1981 entry draft, and they were able to select

*Los Angeles netminder Mario Lessard (#1) tries to stop Toronto sniper Rick Vaive in front of the net, with Kings defenseman Larry Murphy (#5) looking to help out. Lessard led the NHL with 35 wins in 1980–81 and earned a spot on the Second All-Star Team. He played a total of six seasons with the Kings between 1978 and 1984 and posted a record of 92–97–39. Murphy was a rookie in '80–'81 and had 16 goals and 76 points.*

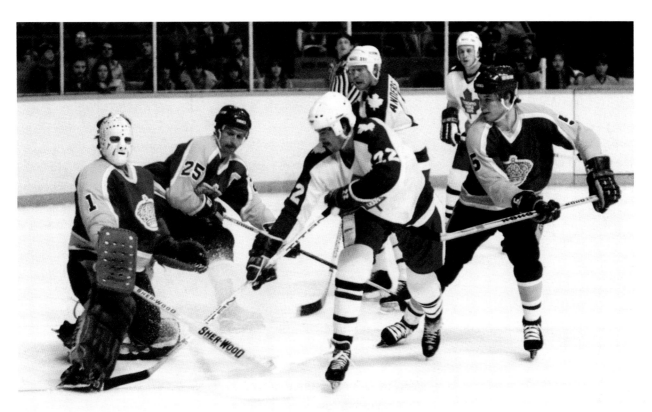

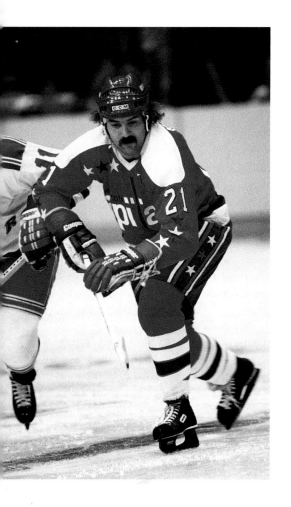

*Dennis Maruk was supposed to be too small (five-foot-eight and 175 pounds) to be a center in the NHL, but he proved the critics wrong with a 50-goal performance for the Washington Capitals in 1980–81 (he also added 47 assists). He showed it was no fluke by scoring 60 the following season and totaling 136 points — both are still club records.*

Dale Hawerchuk from the Cornwall Royals of the Ontario Hockey League (OHL). Dave Christian, Dave Babych, and Tomas Steen (who would join the club in '81–'82) gave the Jets some hope for the future.

**Islanders Still League Power**

One of the emerging stories of the season was New York Islanders winger Mike Bossy's pursuit of a very old record held by Maurice "Rocket" Richard. In 1944–45 Richard became the first player to score 50 goals in one season, and he accomplished the feat in 50 games, the length of the entire schedule. Bossy needed two goals to match Richard when he suited up for his 50th game, against the Quebec Nordiques on January 24. He scored once in the second period, but late in the third it looked like Bossy would miss the mark. Then, with less than two minutes left, he snapped one of his patented shots from just inside the blue-line, beating goalie Ron Grahame between the pads for the magic half-century mark. Bossy danced on his skates in celebration, and the New York crowd went wild. (He would finish the year with 68 markers to lead the league.) Of course, Islanders fans had lots to cheer about in '80–'81, with their team finishing first overall with 110 points (48–18–14). The Islanders were right in the middle of their dynasty, and this was likely their best team. No one would stop them as they romped through the playoffs, losing just three games on their way to a second straight championship.

Bossy was not the only player to top 50 goals in the '80–'81 season. Charlie Simmer of Los Angeles scored 56, and would have scored more but he broke his leg early in March. Teammate Marcel Dionne scored 58, while Gretzky and Rick Kehoe of Pittsburgh each had 55. Wayne Babych became the first member of the St. Louis Blues to reach the milestone with 54, while Jacques Richard (long considered a bust as a first-round draft choice) scored 52 for Quebec. Denis Maruk, a small but highly skilled center, scored 50 with Washington, the first Capital to do so. In addition, 13 players scored 100 or more points, while Dionne, Guy Lafleur, and Bobby Clarke all recorded their 1,000th career point during the season as well. Thirteen teams scored 300 or more goals, while the fewest goals allowed was 232 by the Montreal Canadiens, who finished third overall with 103 points.

**Success Comes Out of the Blue**

Perhaps the most surprising team in the NHL was the St. Louis Blues.

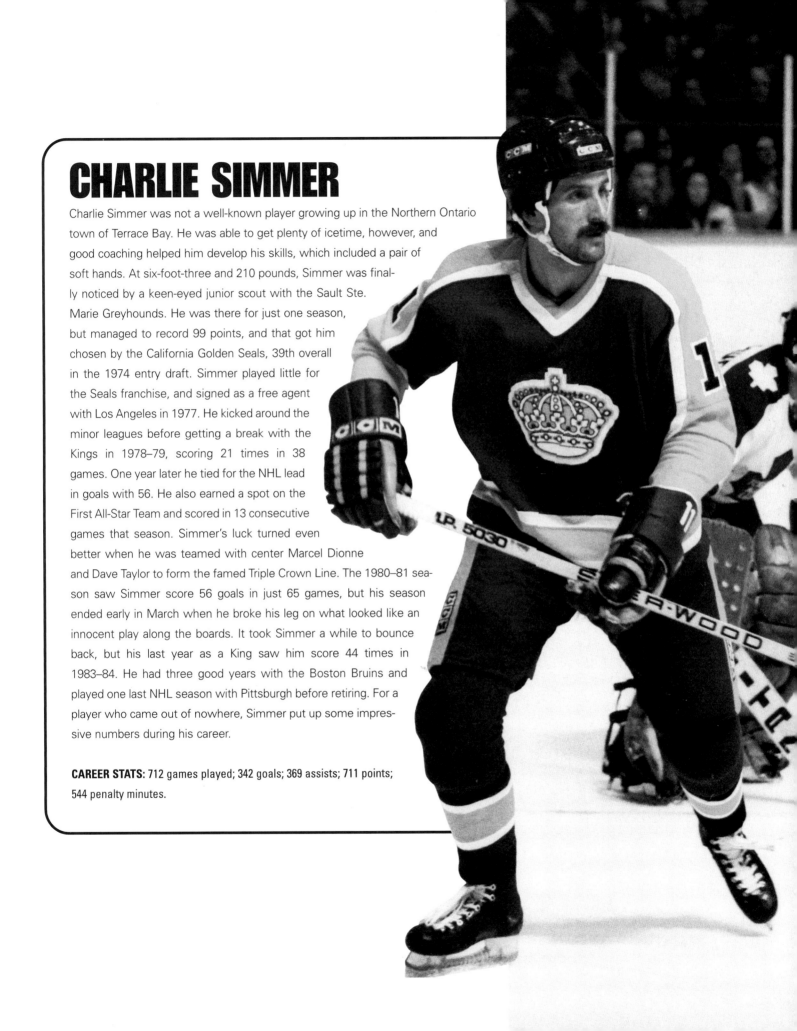

# CHARLIE SIMMER

Charlie Simmer was not a well-known player growing up in the Northern Ontario town of Terrace Bay. He was able to get plenty of icetime, however, and good coaching helped him develop his skills, which included a pair of soft hands. At six-foot-three and 210 pounds, Simmer was finally noticed by a keen-eyed junior scout with the Sault Ste. Marie Greyhounds. He was there for just one season, but managed to record 99 points, and that got him chosen by the California Golden Seals, 39th overall in the 1974 entry draft. Simmer played little for the Seals franchise, and signed as a free agent with Los Angeles in 1977. He kicked around the minor leagues before getting a break with the Kings in 1978–79, scoring 21 times in 38 games. One year later he tied for the NHL lead in goals with 56. He also earned a spot on the First All-Star Team and scored in 13 consecutive games that season. Simmer's luck turned even better when he was teamed with center Marcel Dionne and Dave Taylor to form the famed Triple Crown Line. The 1980–81 season saw Simmer score 56 goals in just 65 games, but his season ended early in March when he broke his leg on what looked like an innocent play along the boards. It took Simmer a while to bounce back, but his last year as a King saw him score 44 times in 1983–84. He had three good years with the Boston Bruins and played one last NHL season with Pittsburgh before retiring. For a player who came out of nowhere, Simmer put up some impressive numbers during his career.

**CAREER STATS:** 712 games played; 342 goals; 369 assists; 711 points; 544 penalty minutes.

Not expected to be among the elite of the league, the Blues rode the hot goaltending of Mike Liut to the second-best record overall, chalking up 45 wins and 17 ties for 107 points. Liut's performance included 33 wins and a 3.34 goals-against average, and he finished second to Gretzky in balloting for the Hart Trophy. (Liut did win the Pearson Award for most valuable player as voted by the NHLPA.) Center Bernie Federko led the team with 104 points, Blake Dunlop tallied 83 points (and won the Masterton Trophy), Jorgen Petterson scored 37 goals, and a 25-year-old Brian Sutter added 69 points. In spite of a great season under Red Berenson, named coach of the year, the Blues were upset in the second round of the playoffs and would not be a factor again until 1985–86.

If the Blues were the best team story of the season, the Quebec Nordiques provided the most intrigue. After a cloak-and-dagger operation got Peter and Anton Stastny out of Czechoslovakia, the brothers proved to be worth all the fuss. Peter would be the better of the two (over the short and long term) and took the Calder Trophy as the NHL's best rookie with 39 goals and 109 points. Hardly a true rookie at 24 when he entered the NHL, Stastny was a center who could do it all, especially on the attack. Anton had 83 points of his own, and the Nordiques could hardly wait for another brother, Marian, to arrive next year. As a team, however, the Nordiques were just average at 30–32–18, but they had a promising future considering that winger Michel Goulet was on the verge of stardom, a quality goaltender in Dan Bouchard was newly acquired from Calgary, and the fiery Michel Bergeron had just stepped behind the bench. The Nordiques would also be fuelled by a provincial rivalry with the Montreal Canadiens.

A near-tragic incident threatened to mar the entire year. Hartford defenseman Mark Howe crashed into the net after a check on the Islanders' John Tonelli, and was pierced through the upper thigh by a spike in the back of the goal. The wound was five-and-half inches deep and came within half an inch of his spine. Luckily, Howe was able to recover and returned to play during the season, but in the future nets would be redesigned to eliminate the dangerous point.

*Minnesota's Bobby Smith (#15) had 93 points for the North Stars during the 1980–81 season in just his third full year in the NHL. He added 25 points in 18 playoff games, helping his team to the finals, where they lost to the New York Islanders.*

# PETER STASTNY

Peter Stastny first came to prominence as a 19-year-old when he played in the World Hockey championships for his native Czechoslovakia. It was unlikely that the highly skilled Stastny would be allowed to leave the Iron Curtain nation, so along with brother Anton he defected and joined the Quebec Nordiques at the age of 24. The 1980–81 season was Stastny's first in the NHL, and he scored 39 goals — the first coming against Tony Esposito of Chicago — and totaled 109 points. Considering Stastny had to learn two new languages (French and English), plus his worries over the family he had left behind, his performance was astonishing. He had good size at six-foot-one and 200 pounds, and could set up a play from just about anywhere on the ice. In his first year, he and his brother each scored a hat trick in a 9–3 win over Vancouver on February 20, 1981. Stastny second season saw him record 139 points, as he and linemate Michel Goulet began terrorizing goalies throughout the league. He recorded six straight seasons of more than 100 points before playing in only 64 games in

The Stastny brothers (left to right): Peter, Marian, and Anton.

1986–87 and picking up 77 points. Stastny rebounded to record 111 points the following year, but despite the impressive numbers (only Wayne Gretzky had more points in the eighties), the Nordiques could never get beyond the semi-finals in the postseason. His greatest moment with Quebec may have come in the 1985 playoffs, when he scored the overtime winner in the Forum to oust archrival Montreal in the seventh game of the second round. He was dealt to New Jersey in 1990 and played for the Devils until 1993. He was elected to the Hockey Hall of Fame in 1998.

**CAREER STATS:** 977 games played; 450 goals; 789 assists; 1,239 points; 824 penalty minutes.

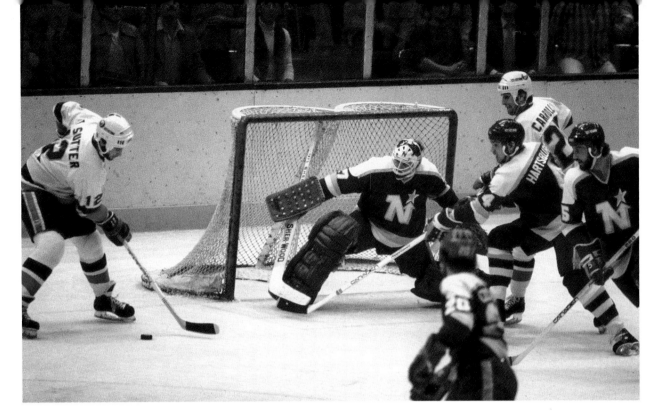

# The **PLAYOFFS**

The Stanley Cup playoffs started off with a best-of-five preliminary round, and the upstart Edmonton Oilers provided the biggest upset. Facing a solid Montreal club, the Oilers won the first two games in the Forum by scores of 6–3 and 3–1. Edmonton returned home and were not about to let the Habs off the hook, whipping them 6–2 with Moog in goal for the Oilers. Gretzky scored three times in the final contest, and Paul Coffey commented that the Oilers win over the once-mighty Habs was "like *Fantasy Island*." The New York Rangers (74 points in the regular season) knocked off the Los Angeles Kings (99 points) in four games, while Minnesota wiped out the Boston Bruins in three. The Calgary Flames won their first-ever playoff series by sweeping Chicago, and the Islanders humiliated Toronto in three lopsided games, using the Maple Leafs for practice fodder.

The Oilers put up a strong fight in the second round, but the champion Islanders were just too experienced and took the series in six games. The other three series all provided upsets, as Minnesota knocked off Buffalo in five games, Calgary stayed on a roll by beating heavily favored Philadelphia in seven (taking the last contest on the road), while the Rangers shocked the Blues in six games. But the next round saw the Islanders roll over the Rangers in just four games, and the North Stars ended Calgary's hopes in six. Minnesota was emerg-

*Minnesota's Gilles Meloche (#27) tries to stop New York's Duane Sutter during the Stanley Cup finals. Meloche played in 788 games, but his only appearance in the finals came with the North Stars in 1981, when he won eight of his 13 appearances in the postseason. Sutter won four Cups with the Islanders between 1980 and 1983.*

*Opposite: Dino Ciccarelli (#20) helped lead the North Stars to the Stanley Cup finals against the New York Islanders. Ciccarelli joined Minnesota for 32 games in 1980–81 and scored 18 goals. He was amazingly strong in the playoffs with 14 goals and 21 points in 19 games, setting scoring marks for rookies in the postseason that are still in the record book.*

# JOHN TONELLI

Left winger John Tonelli began his professional career with Houston Aeros of the WHA in 1975, when he was just 18. He played three seasons in Houston before he joined the New York Islanders, who had drafted him 33rd overall in 1977. His first year with the Isles saw him score 17 times in 73 games, and he had just 14 goals in 1979–80, but in the finals that year he set up the Stanley Cup winner by Bob Nystrom, hitting his streaking teammate with a perfect pass. In 1980–81, Tonelli scored 20 goals, five of them in one game against the Toronto Maple Leafs on January 6. A grinder in the corners with plenty of determination and energy, Tonelli scored 35 goals and 93 points in 1981–82, and in the playoffs he scored to even the fifth and deciding match of a series against Pittsburgh, then notched the winner in overtime. After being named MVP of the 1984 Canada Cup tournament, he had his best year with New York in 1984–85, when he recorded an even 100 points (42 goals, 58 assists). His style was unorthodox and he never considered himself a star, but he was a valuable member of the Islanders dynasty. He also played for the Calgary Flames and the Los Angeles Kings before making brief stops in Chicago and Quebec.

**CAREER STATS:** 1,028 games played; 325 goals; 511 assists; 836 points; 911 penalty minutes.

*New York Islanders captain Denis Potvin holds up the Stanley Cup, with the bearded Butch Goring watching from his right. Goring was a perfect acquisition for the New York Islanders, who got him from Los Angeles in 1980. During the 1980–81 season, he scored 23 goals and 37 assists and was even sharper in the play-offs when he had 10 goals and 10 assists in 20 games. He earned the Conn Smythe Trophy to go along with the Masterton and the Lady Byng trophies he won in 1978.*

ing as the story of the playoffs, using many youngsters in Craig Hartsburgh, Tom McCarthy, Steve Payne, and Bobby Smith were all key performers under the age of 23. (The North Stars also had key veterans like goalie Gilles Meloche, Fred Barrett, Al MacAdam, and Tim Young in the lineup.) Coach Glen Somnor seemed to get the best out of everyone, and the future seemed boundless. It was an unexpected turnaround for Minnesota, who just three years earlier finished last overall and had merged with the Cleveland Barons. However, the team was far too inexperienced to deal with the Islanders club they faced in the 1981 final.

The Stanley Cup final was never in doubt, as the Islanders won it easily in five games. A number of Islanders could have been named winner of the Conn Smythe Trophy, but it went to Butch Goring (10 goals and 10 assists in 18 playoff games), who recorded a hat trick in the third game of the final, a 7–5 win in Minnesota. A 4–2 North Stars win at home in the fourth game forced the Islanders to delay the celebration, but on May 21 a 5–1 victory on home ice ended the hopes of the Cinderella North Stars and sent Islanders fans home happy for the second year in a row.

# 1981-82

*The Leafs fall, the Canucks surge to the finals, and Gretzky scores 92*

**BEFORE** the 1981–82 season began, the best hockey nations competed for world supremacy in the second Canada Cup, held in September. The tournament did not have the luster of the 1976 gathering, but hockey fans were interested in seeing the top players compete for their countries, since NHLers were not yet allowed in the Olympics, nor were they all available for the World Championships, played each year in Europe. As expected, Canada played the USSR for the championship in a one-game showdown at the Montreal Forum. To the shock of Canadians, the Soviets won an 8–1 rout, with top players like Guy Lafleur and Mike Liut looking very ordinary in the lopsided defeat. Igor Larionov, a future NHL player, scored twice for the Russians, who tried to scurry out of the Forum with the Canada Cup trophy in a duffle bag. Alan Eagleson had the police stop their hasty exit and took the nickel-plated trophy back to the residence of Canada's governor-general, where it would sit until the next tournament in 1984.

The National Hockey League decided to realign itself geographically, and the Toronto Maple Leafs somehow ended up in the Norris Division with Minnesota, Winnipeg, St. Louis, Chicago, and Detroit. Leafs owner Harold Ballard said he agreed to take his team out of the Adams Division (where Boston, Buffalo, and Montreal resided) because the Red Wings and Blackhawks insisted they needed their

---

*Mike Bossy (#22) of the New York Islanders puts in another goal against the Vancouver Canucks in the Stanley Cup finals. Bossy scored seven goals in the finals and was named winner of the Conn Smythe Trophy.*

ancient rival in the Norris. It would mean more extensive travel for the Leafs, but perhaps an easier path to the playoffs, and therefore more postseason revenues. Four teams in each division would make the playoffs, with first place battling fourth in a best-of-five preliminary round. The second round would be a best-of-seven, with the division winners then meeting in a conference final to see who would play for the Stanley Cup. The Prince of Wales Conference now had virtually all of the eastern teams, while the Clarence Campbell Conference was made up of western clubs, except for Detroit and Toronto.

### Gretzky's Greatest Year

Once play began in the regular season, the NHL became the Wayne Gretzky show. No other player in the history of the NHL has ever had a season like the Great One did in '81–'82, when he notched an incredible 212 points, including a record 92 goals. In his race to become the fastest player to score 50, he went into his 39th game of the campaign against the Philadelphia Flyers on December 30 with 45 goals. He wound up scoring five times — the last one into an empty net — to eclipse the old mark by 11 games. Gretzky averaged 1.15 goals and 2.65

*Edmonton Oilers winger Glenn Anderson (#9) recorded 105 points (38 goals, 67 assists) in 1981–82, placing him 11th in the NHL scoring race. Anderson would record 100 or more points three times in his career.*

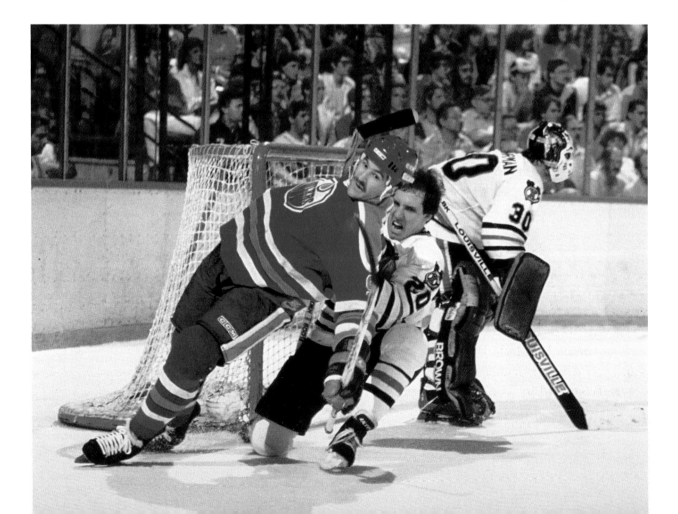

points per game, and won the Art Ross Trophy by 65 points over his nearest rival (Mike Bossy had 147). He was so consistent throughout the year that he recorded a point in 72 of 80 games played. On January 26, 1982, Gretzky agreed to a new contract with Edmonton owner Peter Pocklington that would pay him $20 million over the next 15 years. His base salary was reported to be between $650,000 and $800,000 per year, which put him ahead of Marcel Dionne of the Los Angeles Kings who was earning about $600,000.

The Oilers recorded 111 points (going 48–17–15) in '81–'82, the second-best total in the NHL after the defending champion New York Islanders, who managed 118 points (54–16–10). In addition to Gretzky, several other Oilers had great seasons, including Glenn Anderson (105 points), Mark Messier (50 goals), Paul Coffey (89 points), Jari Kurri (86 points) — plus a couple of virtual unknowns in Dave Lumley (42 assists) and Risto Siltanen (48 assists). An offense-minded team that wanted to play the entire game on the attack, the Oilers scored a whopping 417 times to lead the NHL (the Islanders were next with 385). But somehow Edmonton was unprepared for the playoffs.

### Jets Soar

One of the league's more interesting hires was Tom Watt, who was named as head coach of the Winnipeg Jets. Watt had been a highly successful mentor for the University of Toronto Blues, where his 14-year record included 378 wins in 503 games, with nine championships. After one year as an assistant with the Vancouver Canucks, Watt was given the reins of the young Jets, who had rookie Dale Hawerchuk in the lineup. In an unprecedented turnaround, Watt made the Jets an 80-point team (33–33–14) after they had recorded only 32 the year before. Hawerchuk was all he was advertised to be with a 103-point performance, including 45 goals, on his way to winning the Calder Trophy. Morris Lukowich also had a career year with 43 goals

*Mark Messier (#11) whoops it up after another Edmonton Oilers goal. In 1981–82, Messier scored 50 goals for the only time in his career and totaled 88 points in what was the first of many great seasons in the NHL.*

# RICK MIDDLETON

When New York Rangers center Phil Esposito bellowed to management that he wanted former teammate Ken Hodge on his wing in the Big Apple, the Boston Bruins could not have been happier. They quickly dispatched the aging Hodge to the Rangers and gleefully took right winger Rick Middleton in return. After he was a first-round draft choice of the Rangers in 1973 (14th overall), Middleton was sent to Providence of the American Hockey League for seasoning. He recorded 84 points in just 63 games and made it to the big team for the 1974–75 season and potted 22 goals in 47 games. He followed that up with 24 goals in 72 games the next year, but that still wasn't enough for the Rangers, who shipped him to Beantown. From 1976–77 to 1986–87, Middleton was one of the most consistent players in the NHL, putting up five straight seasons of 40 or more goals during that stretch. He tallied 103 points in 1980–81, and then a career high 51 goals in 1981–82. By the 1983–84 campaign the man known as Nifty was back among the league's top scorers with 105 points (47 goals, 58 assists). He credited Bruins coach Don Cherry with making him a solid two-way player. Middleton had a strong knack for getting into the right spots and could give a backpedaling defenseman fits, especially in one-on-one situations. He also owned incredibly soft hands, and his picture-perfect goals could lift fans out of their seats.

**CAREER STATS:** 1,005 games played; 448 goals; 540 assists; 988 points; 157 penalty minutes.

and 92 points, while Paul MacLean (36 goals) and Willy Lidstrom (32 goals) made noteworthy contributions. General manager John Ferguson was able to talk former Montreal great Serge Savard into playing for Winnipeg, and the team gained from his veteran savvy. However, the Jets were quickly disposed of in the playoffs and the team was never the same under Watt again. He soon became known as something of a disaster specialist, taking over bad clubs and turning them around for brief periods before they would slip backwards again. Watt was a capable assistant, but his head coaching record was a poor 176–252–62 (admittedly with three mediocre teams) but in '81–'82 he won the Jack Adams Trophy as coach of the year. It was not all great for the Jets, though — on the night of November 11, the Minnesota North Stars thrashed them 15–2!

If things were hot in Edmonton and improving in Winnipeg, they were downright awful in Toronto, where the Leafs won all of 20 games and earned just 56 points (only Detroit with 54 and Colorado with 49 were worse). The lone bright spot was Rick Vaive, who scored 54 times and was named team captain in January (an honor the young winger was not ready for) when Darryl Sittler was traded to Philadelphia. The Leafs were coached by an inept Mike Nykoluk, a former Flyers assistant during their glory days, who had lobbied for the job while he was a radio color commentator. He proved to be a poor choice to coach such an important team — his record with the Leafs was a horrid 89–144–47, but he had little help from general manager Gerry McNamara, whom Harold Ballard had appointed during the '81–'82 season. Among their many problems, the Leafs had little in the way of goaltending and few prospects on defense, allowing 380 goals, the most in the NHL. Leafs fans could only cheer Vaive on his quest to become the first Toronto player to hit 50, and he made history by scoring against Mike Liut of the St. Louis Blues on March 24. The other highlight for the Leafs was defenseman Borje Salming recording 56 points in 69 games, including his first hat trick on the opening night of the season in a 9–8 win against Chicago.

## Big Deals
The Maple Leafs were involved in one of the more notable trades of the year when they sent burly 40-goal winger Wilf Paiement (a player they had acquired for future Hall of Famer Lanny McDonald in 1979) to Quebec for Miroslav Frycer, a Czech winger who scored a hat trick

against Toronto early in the season. Frycer would never be as productive for the Leafs as they had hoped, and eventually caused more trouble on and off the ice than he was worth (although he did score 32 goals in 1985–86). Toronto also gave the once promising first-round draft choice Laurie Boschman to Edmonton for Walt Poddubny.

Buffalo and Detroit hooked up for the biggest transaction of the year when they completed a six-player swap. The Sabres shocked their fans by sending favorites Danny Gare and Jim Schoenfeld along with Derek Smith to the Red Wings for Dale McCourt, Brent Peterson, and Mike Foligno on December 2. Buffalo general manager and coach Scotty Bowman wanted to shake up his team, which had never won a Stanley Cup, but the trade certainly did not make him well-liked in Western New York. The Sabres, however, went on to post a fine 39–26–15 record for 93 points. Bowman's tenure as Sabres GM was not the highlight of his illustrious career, but he won this deal by nabbing Foligno, who scored 247 goals for a team he would one day captain. In the playoffs, the Sabres were knocked off by the Boston Bruins in the first round in four games. Bowman's other problem was that he could not stay away from the coaching role, trying Roger Neilson, Jim Roberts and Schoenfeld in the job during the eighties, but always firing his recruits and replacing them with himself.

*Boston defenseman Raymond Bourque was named to the First All-Star Team for the second time in his career in 1981–82 when he recorded 66 points (17 goals, 49 assists) in 65 games.*

Yet another important deal involved the Calgary Flames, who sent two quality players in Don Lever and Bob MacMillan to Colorado for Lanny McDonald. The Rockies were going nowhere (they won only 18 games) and probably felt two starting players for one was a good deal, even though the pair they received for McDonald were not nearly the caliber of the right winger with the ridiculous mustache. Unshackled from the bonds of a terrible hockey team, McDonald returned to his native province of Alberta and scored 34 goals in just 55 games for the Flames to close out the '81–'82 campaign. Calgary was stunned in three straight games by Vancouver in the first round of the playoffs, but the trade would have long-term benefits for the Flames. The Rockies, meanwhile, would be sold and out of Colorado by the start of the next season.

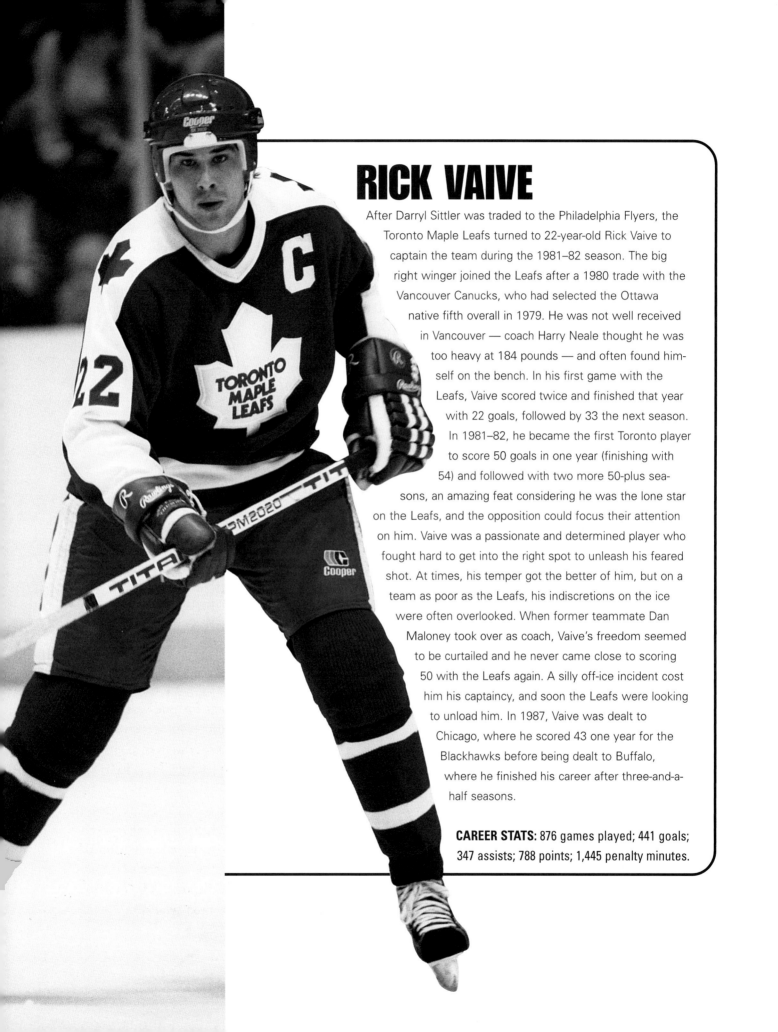

# RICK VAIVE

After Darryl Sittler was traded to the Philadelphia Flyers, the Toronto Maple Leafs turned to 22-year-old Rick Vaive to captain the team during the 1981–82 season. The big right winger joined the Leafs after a 1980 trade with the Vancouver Canucks, who had selected the Ottawa native fifth overall in 1979. He was not well received in Vancouver — coach Harry Neale thought he was too heavy at 184 pounds — and often found himself on the bench. In his first game with the Leafs, Vaive scored twice and finished that year with 22 goals, followed by 33 the next season. In 1981–82, he became the first Toronto player to score 50 goals in one year (finishing with 54) and followed with two more 50-plus seasons, an amazing feat considering he was the lone star on the Leafs, and the opposition could focus their attention on him. Vaive was a passionate and determined player who fought hard to get into the right spot to unleash his feared shot. At times, his temper got the better of him, but on a team as poor as the Leafs, his indiscretions on the ice were often overlooked. When former teammate Dan Maloney took over as coach, Vaive's freedom seemed to be curtailed and he never came close to scoring 50 with the Leafs again. A silly off-ice incident cost him his captaincy, and soon the Leafs were looking to unload him. In 1987, Vaive was dealt to Chicago, where he scored 43 one year for the Blackhawks before being dealt to Buffalo, where he finished his career after three-and-a-half seasons.

**CAREER STATS:** 876 games played; 441 goals; 347 assists; 788 points; 1,445 penalty minutes.

*Drafted 210th overall by the Los Angeles Kings in 1975, right winger Dave Taylor had his second consecutive season of more than 100 points in 1981–82 when he scored 39 goals and 67 assists. Taylor would go on to play 1,111 games for Los Angeles, scoring 431 goals, 638 assists, and 1,069 points, all of which rank third on the Kings' all-time list.*

The Detroit Red Wings also had a miserable season with only 21 wins, and there was talk of the team being sold. The Wings had the highest payroll at the time (an estimated $3.88 million) while their best-paid player, Vaclav Nedomansky at $288,000, was playing for their farm team in Glen Falls, New York! Eventually the Norris family, which had owned the Red Wings for the past 50 years, decided to sell their interest in the club to pizza magnate Mike Ilitch for a reported $9 million.

## Ugly Incidents

The regular season reached some new levels of on-ice nastiness during the 1981–82 season. It started with Philadelphia's Ken Linseman being fined a grand total of $200 for "attempting to kick an opponent," and

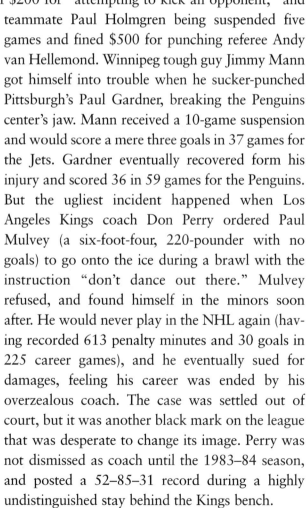

teammate Paul Holmgren being suspended five games and fined $500 for punching referee Andy van Hellemond. Winnipeg tough guy Jimmy Mann got himself into trouble when he sucker-punched Pittsburgh's Paul Gardner, breaking the Penguins center's jaw. Mann received a 10-game suspension and would score a mere three goals in 37 games for the Jets. Gardner eventually recovered form his injury and scored 36 in 59 games for the Penguins. But the ugliest incident happened when Los Angeles Kings coach Don Perry ordered Paul Mulvey (a six-foot-four, 220-pounder with no goals) to go onto the ice during a brawl with the instruction "don't dance out there." Mulvey refused, and found himself in the minors soon after. He would never play in the NHL again (having recorded 613 penalty minutes and 30 goals in 225 career games), and he eventually sued for damages, feeling his career was ended by his overzealous coach. The case was settled out of court, but it was another black mark on the league that was desperate to change its image. Perry was not dismissed as coach until the 1983–84 season, and posted a 52–85–31 record during a highly undistinguished stay behind the Kings bench.

In another legal battle earlier in 1982, Detroit's Dennis Polonich was awarded $850,000 for injuries suffered four years earlier as a result of his fight with Wilf Paiement. (Polonich had been struck in the face with Paiement's stick.) It was the first civil lawsuit against the NHL — but not the last, as Mulvey would prove — and it could have been settled prior to trial for a mere $50,000, but the league's insurance company refused.

Philadelphia decided to fire Pat Quinn as coach and named Bob McCammon as his replacement on March 19, 1982. The move was surprising, considering Quinn had led the team to the finals in 1980, rolling out an unbelievable 35-game unbeaten streak that same season. However, in '81–'82 the Flyers finished with a 38–31–11 mark and suffered a quick exit at the hands of the New York Rangers in first round of the playoffs. Quinn would rebound from his dismissal to coach (and sometimes manage) three other NHL teams — Los Angeles, Vancouver, and Toronto.

*Vancouver's Tomas Gradin had a great season for the Canucks in 1981–82 when he recorded 86 points (37 goals, 49 assists). The talented Swede also added 19 points in 17 playoff games, helping the Canucks to the finals. He played eight seasons for Vancouver before joining the Boston Bruins in 1986–87.*

Meanwhile in Vancouver, the Canucks were going through an eventful season under coach Harry Neale when he was abruptly suspended for 10 games — five in the regular season and the first five of the playoffs. During a donnybrook in Quebec City, Neale went after a fan in the stands, and assistant coach Roger Neilson was forced to take over as bench boss. It was supposed to be a temporary fix, lasting only the length of the suspension, but events in the playoffs would change that quickly. The Washington Capitals also axed coach Gary Green after the team lost 12 of its first 13 games, replacing him with Bryan Murray, who guided the Caps to a 25–28–13 record the rest of the year.

**Magic Moments**

Dave Keon played his final NHL season — his 22nd year as a professional — with the Hartford Whalers, who named him captain for the '81–'82 campaign. The much-decorated native of Noranda, Quebec, scored eight goals and had 19 points while playing in 78 contests. It brought his career totals in the NHL to 396 goals and 986 points in 1,296 games. He was the last member of the 1967 Stanley Cup–winning Maple Leafs team to retire.

Buffalo Sabres great Gilbert Perreault recorded his 1,000th career point on April 3, 1982, when he earned an assist during a 5–4 win over

# DOUG WILSON

Prior to the 1981–82 season, defenseman Doug Wilson was dedicated to getting into top shape, both mentally and physically. Up to that point in his young career, Wilson had not reached his potential, even though he had racked up 61 points in 1979–80, and 51 points in 1980–81. He knew he was not as consistent as he could have been, and when a blood condition was rectified with a change in his diet, Wilson was ready to dominate. Blessed with great skating skills and a wicked drive from the point, the Chicago blueliner scored 39 times in 1981–82, the most goals by a defense-man since Bobby Orr's 46 in 1974–75. Wilson was especially effective on the power-play, and he made the Blackhawks a feared team with the extra man. Wilson had actually started playing hockey as a goaltender, but decided that position was too dangerous — ironic, since he rarely wore a helmet during his NHL career. He was a top junior with the Ottawa 67s of the Ontario Hockey Association (OHA) and was selected sixth overall by Chicago in 1977. It was one of the Blackhawks best choices ever, as Wilson would retire as Chicago's all-time scoring leader among defenseman (779 points). His terrific performance in 1981–82 (85 points) earned him his only Norris Trophy. He was a member of the Blackhawks until 1991–92, when he was dealt to San Jose and named the first-ever captain of the Sharks. After his retirement, he returned to San Jose to work in the Sharks front office, and in 2003 was named general manager.

**CAREER STATS:** 1,024 games played; 237 goals; 590 assists; 827 points; 830 penalty minutes.

the Montreal Canadiens. The former Calder and Lady Byng Trophy winner had another good season with the Sabres, notching 31 goals and 73 points in 62 games. The Stanley Cup would prove elusive for the pride of Victoriaville, Quebec, and his name popped up in trade rumors, but he would eventually finish his Hall of Fame career in Buffalo.

Five-goal games during the '81–'82 season would be restricted to Gretzky, Grant Mulvey of Chicago, Brian Trottier of the Islanders, and Willy Lidstrom of Winnipeg. Defenseman Ian Turnbull, who had requested a trade out of Toronto after the Leaf fans got on him, scored four goals in one game when his Los Angeles Kings beat the Vancouver Canucks 7–5 on December 12, 1981. (Turnbull still holds the NHL record for most goals in a game by a defenseman, having put five past two Detroit goalies in a 1977 contest.)

Mike Bossy scored his 250th career goal during the season (in just his 315th game) and was rewarded for his outstanding play with a $4.5-million contract over seven seasons. That worked out to $640,000 a season and would make the 24-year-old sharpshooter one of the three highest paid players in the NHL. Bossy was one of 15 players to record 100 or more points in 1981–82, a list that included Mike Rogers of the Rangers (103), Dino Ciccarelli of Minnesota (106), and Denis Maruk of Washington (136). Chicago's Doug Wilson was named the top defenseman when he scored 39 goals and added 45 assists, while Bruins winger Rick Middleton took the Lady Byng with a 51-goal season to go along with just 12 penalty minutes. Islander netminder Billy Smith became the first goalie to win the Vezina Trophy under the new criteria — the recipient was now voted best goalie, instead of having the lowest goals-against average — when he won 32 games while losing only nine. Boston's Steve Kasper won the Selke Trophy as the best defensive forward. Kasper normally performed his checking duties cleanly (although he did record 72 penalty minutes), as noted by none other than Gretzky, a frequent target of Kasper's diligence.

The career of Buffalo Sabres sniper (384 goals in 685 games) Rick Martin was brought to an end at the age of 30 by recurring knee troubles. The Sabres had traded Martin to Los Angeles in March 1981 for two draft choices, one of which was a first-round selection the Sabres used to

*Philadelphia center Ken Linseman displays the Cooperall pants the Flyers wore during the 1981–82 season. Linseman, not-so-affectionately known as "the Rat," scored 92 points in 1981–82 while recording 275 penalty minutes. In spite of his performance, he was traded after the season.*

*Buffalo Sabres superstar Gilbert Perreault recorded his 1,000th career point on April 3, 1982, when he notched an assist during a 5–4 win over the Montreal Canadiens. Perreault played his entire career in Buffalo and totaled 1,326 points in 1,191 games.*

take goaltender Tom Barrasso. Considering Martin participated in just four games for the Kings, the Sabres got a great deal in return for a damaged player. It would take years for Martin to successfully sue the Sabres for the way doctors treated his injured knee, but it was worth it to him to right a wrong. Prior to the start of the 2002–03 season, Martin would be named as an assistant coach in Buffalo.

# The PLAYOFFS

The first round of the playoffs produced a shocking upset, with the Edmonton Oilers on the wrong end of the score. The Los Angeles Kings, who finished 45 points behind the Oilers during the regular season, shocked Edmonton if five games, winning the deciding contest 7–4 on the road. However, it was the third game that proved to be the most memorable. The Oilers appeared comfortably ahead 5–0 when the Kings responded with five straight tallies to tie the score, including a goal by Steve Bozek with just five seconds left in regulation. At 2:25 of overtime, rookie winger Daryl Evans drilled a shot past a startled Grant Fuhr in the Edmonton net, setting off a wild celebration in the Fabulous

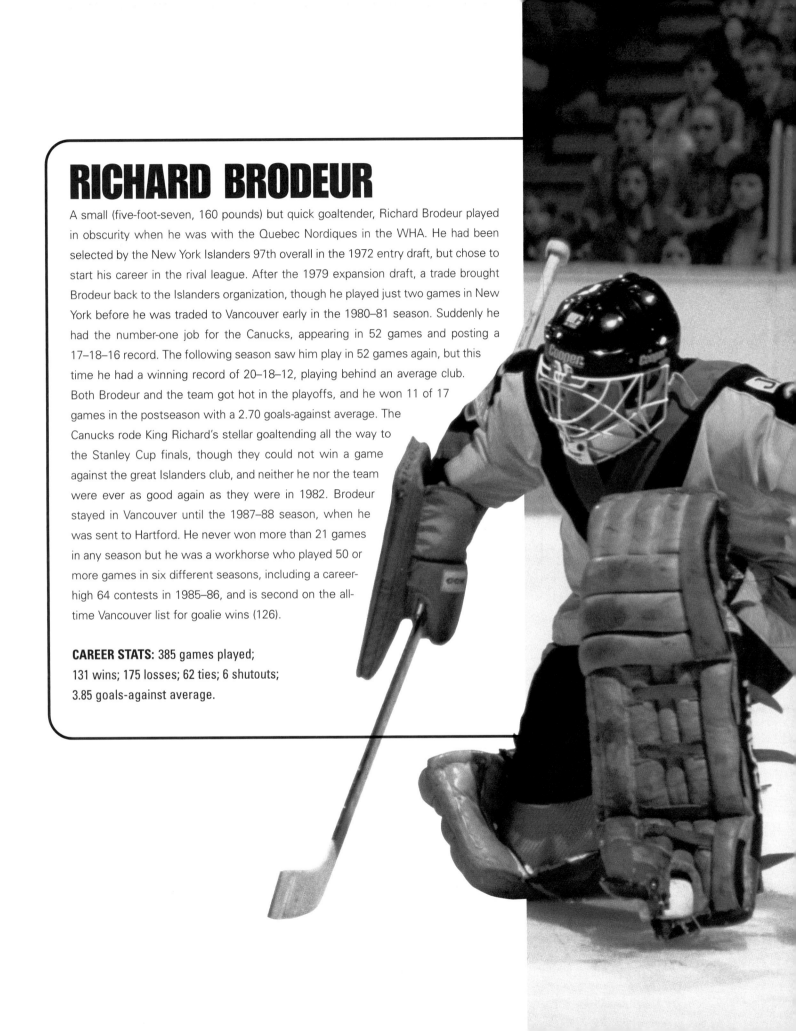

# RICHARD BRODEUR

A small (five-foot-seven, 160 pounds) but quick goaltender, Richard Brodeur played in obscurity when he was with the Quebec Nordiques in the WHA. He had been selected by the New York Islanders 97th overall in the 1972 entry draft, but chose to start his career in the rival league. After the 1979 expansion draft, a trade brought Brodeur back to the Islanders organization, though he played just two games in New York before he was traded to Vancouver early in the 1980–81 season. Suddenly he had the number-one job for the Canucks, appearing in 52 games and posting a 17–18–16 record. The following season saw him play in 52 games again, but this time he had a winning record of 20–18–12, playing behind an average club. Both Brodeur and the team got hot in the playoffs, and he won 11 of 17 games in the postseason with a 2.70 goals-against average. The Canucks rode King Richard's stellar goaltending all the way to the Stanley Cup finals, though they could not win a game against the great Islanders club, and neither he nor the team were ever as good again as they were in 1982. Brodeur stayed in Vancouver until the 1987–88 season, when he was sent to Hartford. He never won more than 21 games in any season but he was a workhorse who played 50 or more games in six different seasons, including a career-high 64 contests in 1985–86, and is second on the all-time Vancouver list for goalie wins (126).

**CAREER STATS:** 385 games played;
131 wins; 175 losses; 62 ties; 6 shutouts;
3.85 goals-against average.

*Mike Bossy of the New York Islanders scored in overtime to give his team a 6–5 win over the Vancouver Canucks in the first game of the finals. It was the first victory of a four-game sweep for the Islanders.*

Forum. The game became known as the Miracle on Manchester (the location of the Los Angeles rink), though Kings owner Jerry Buss was not around to see the ending, having left the arena earlier with actress Cathy Lee Crosby on his arm.

Other surprises in the opening round included Chicago knocking off Minnesota and the Nordiques taking the Battle of Quebec by eliminating the Canadiens in overtime of the deciding fifth game right in the Montreal Forum. Quebec won another round when they beat Boston in a seven-game series, but that would be all for them. The upstart Canucks pulled off a slight upset of their own when they took out Calgary in three straight, and then knocked off Los Angeles in the next round. The Vancouver magic under Roger Neilson — who remained behind the bench even after Neale's suspension ended — was still evident in the next round, when they beat the Blackhawks in just five games to reach the finals for the first time in team history. The Canucks only defeat in the semi-final came in the Chicago Stadium, and during the game Neilson decided he'd had enough of referee Bob Myers. He told his team to "surrender" by putting white towels on their sticks and raising them into the air. Neilson was ejected (he and the team were later fined $11,000), but he had made his point. The Canucks, backed by the superlative goaltending of Richard Brodeur and a legion of towel-waving fans, won the next three games to close out the Blackhawks.

In the finals, the surging Canucks would meet an impenetrable wall in the New York Islanders. The Isles rolled through the postseason again, after an initial scare by the Pittsburgh Penguins in the first round. The

Long Island club squeaked through with a 4–3 overtime win in the deciding contest and then took on their state rivals, the New York Rangers. That series went six games, but the Islanders were simply too strong for the Rangers, who had at least salvaged something of their season by taking out Philadelphia in the previous series. The Islanders just kept getting stronger, and the Nordiques were no match for them in a semi-final that ended in a sweep. The final was much the same, except for the first contest, which went into overtime. Vancouver defenseman Harold Snepsts gave the puck away to Mike Bossy, who made no mistake in giving the Islanders a 6–5 win. Losing the game in this fashion seemed to unnerve the Canucks, who never recovered and lost the next three games as well. Mike Bossy was rewarded with the Conn Smythe Trophy (an award he felt he had deserved the previous year) after scoring 17 goals and 27 points in 19 games. Teammate Bryan Trottier lead all playoff scorers with 29 points.

The Canucks really had no business being anywhere near the finals. Despite wearing the most garish uniforms in the league, they deserve credit for taking the opportunity that presented itself when the Oilers were eliminated early. They got career performances in the playoffs from many marginal NHLers, such as Gary Lupul, Neil Belland, Ron Delorme, Lars Molin, Gerry Minor, and Marc Crawford, who years later would become Vancouver's head coach.

*Bryan Trottier of the New York Islanders holds up the 1982 Stanley Cup, the third straight championship for his team.*

# 1982–83

Peeters shines in Beantown, New Jersey welcomes the Devils, and the Islanders win their fourth straight Cup

SOME big off-season events had major impacts on the 1982–83 campaign. It started on August 19 with the Philadelphia Flyers acquiring defenseman Mark Howe in a three-team deal involving the Hartford Whalers and the Edmonton Oilers. The Whalers foolishly gave up Howe and a 1983 third-round draft choice (used by the Flyers to select Derrick Smith) to Philadelphia in return for Ken Linseman, Greg Adams, and two draft selections. The Flyers then immediately sent Linseman and Don Nachbaur to Edmonton for Risto Siltanen and Brent Loney. Ironically, the team that need the most help, the Whalers, got the least, while Howe and Linseman went onto to make solid contributions to their new teams.

Another big defenseman moved on September 9, when the Montreal Canadiens completed one of the biggest trades in team history. They sent rugged blueliner Rod Langway along with Brian Engblom, Doug Jarvis, and Craig Laughlin to Washington in exchange for Rick Green and Ryan Walter, both former first-round draft choices by the Capitals. The Habs were forced into the trade because Langway, citing Canada's higher taxes, insisted on going to an American team. Montreal GM Irving Grundman was vilified for the trade, but he really had little choice. (The Habs were furious because Langway had been pleased to sign a six-year deal just a season earlier, and they threatened to let the big defenseman sit. It would not be

*Edmonton's Kevin Lowe (#4) tries to stop the Islanders' Bryan Trottier (#19) from checking Wayne Gretzky (#99) during the 1983 Stanley Cup finals. New York won the Cup in four straight games with Trottier recording four points (one goal, three assists) in the finals. Gretzky also had four assists in the series, but no goals.*

57

# ROD LANGWAY

The Montreal Canadiens were looking to make changes after being ousted from the playoffs by the Quebec Nordiques in 1982, but they surprised everyone when their best defensive pair — Rod Langway and Brian Engblom — suddenly found themselves in Washington. It was Langway who pushed for a trade when he realized he was taking far too little money home to the United States in the off-season (he was quoted as saying that he was "financially discriminated against"). Langway's impact was felt immediately in Washington, as he gave his new team a commanding presence on the blueline and got them into the playoffs. At six-foot-three and 210 pounds, he was smart, skilled, and his leadership ability won him the captaincy in his first season with the Capitals. Langway was never a big scorer (11 goals was his career best) but he did record 20 or more assists four times with the Capitals, and twice had 34 helpers as a member of the Habs. He won the Norris Trophy with his all-around play in 1982–83, when he had three goals and 29 assists, and again in 1983–84 when he scored nine and added 24 assists. The four-time All-Star spent the rest of his career with the Capitals, retiring after the 1992–93 season. In 2002, Langway became the only native of Taiwan (he was raised in the United States) to be elected to the Hall of Fame.

**CAREER STATS:** 994 games played; 51 goals; 278 assists; 329 points; 849 penalty minutes.

the only time Canadian clubs would hear similar complaints, especially the two based in Quebec.) The howls got worse when Langway went on to win the Norris Trophy that season, but time would prove that the Habs had not made such a bad deal after all.

## Devils Make Their First Appearance

In May 1982, Dr. John McMullen, a former partner in the New York Yankees, purchased the Colorado Rockies and moved the franchise to East Rutherford, New Jersey. (He would have to pay in the neighborhood of $30 million for territorial indemnity fees to the New York Islanders, New York Rangers, and the Philadelphia Flyers.) The team was renamed the Devils, and played its first game in the Brendan Byrne Meadowlands Arena on October 5, skating to 3–3 tie against the Pittsburgh Penguins. It was a tough season for the new-look squad, as they won just 17 games and lost 49, but the franchise was still alive and looked to have a good future.

*The Philadelphia Flyers made a great trade when they acquired Mark Howe (#2) to anchor their defense. In 1982–83, Howe scored 20 goals and 47 assists and earned a spot on the NHL's First All-Star Team. Howe was a Flyer for 10 seasons and was a First Team All-Star three times.*

McMullen was a New Jersey native who was bullish on his chances of success in East Rutherford, issuing an opening salvo by suggesting his team would be more aggressive than the well-established New York Rangers. But it would be quite a while before McMullen saw any success — the Devils would not get to the postseason until 1988. For geographical reasons, they were situated in the six-team Patrick Division (the others had just five), making it harder to pin down a playoff spot.

Other off-ice news included a change in suspensions for players striking officials. Referee Andy van Hellemond had been attacked by two players (Paul Holmgren and Terry O'Reilly) the previous year, and the NHL wanted to get tough. The league instituted a 20-game automatic suspension for any deliberate contact with the refs, and a three-game suspension for contact made incidentally while trying to get away from an official. The NHL still refused to consider overtime for regular season games, as the board of governors turned down the proposition by a margin of 11 to 10. In Toronto, play-by-play broadcaster Bill Hewitt, son of the legendary Foster Hewitt, announced his retirement at the age of 53. Hewitt was suffering from a blood disorder that forced him to miss the entire 1981–82 season. His final broadcast was of a Toronto-Montreal preseason game, and his performance indicated he was not well.

**Triumph and Tragedy in Boston**

For the first time since 1973–74, the Boston Bruins finished on top of the NHL with 110 points (edging out Philadelphia, Edmonton, and Chicago who all had over 100 points). The Bruins were led by great offensive performances from Barry Pederson, Rick Middleton, Keith Crowder, and Peter McNabb. Ray Bourque was the leader of the blueline brigade, recording 73 points (22 goals, 51 assists) with Mike O'Connell (53 points) and veteran Brad Park (36 points) helping out the backline. First-overall selection Gord Kluzak played in 70 games for the Bruins, recording 105 penalty minutes, and was a rising star on

*Boston goaltender Pete Peeters (#1) keeps a close eye on Mike Bossy (#22) of the New York Islanders, while defenseman Mike O'Connell (#20) tries to tie up the high-scoring forward. Peeters won the Vezina Trophy in 1982–83 when he led the NHL in wins and shutouts. Bossy scored 60 goals for the Islanders, while O'Connell scored 14 for the Bruins.*

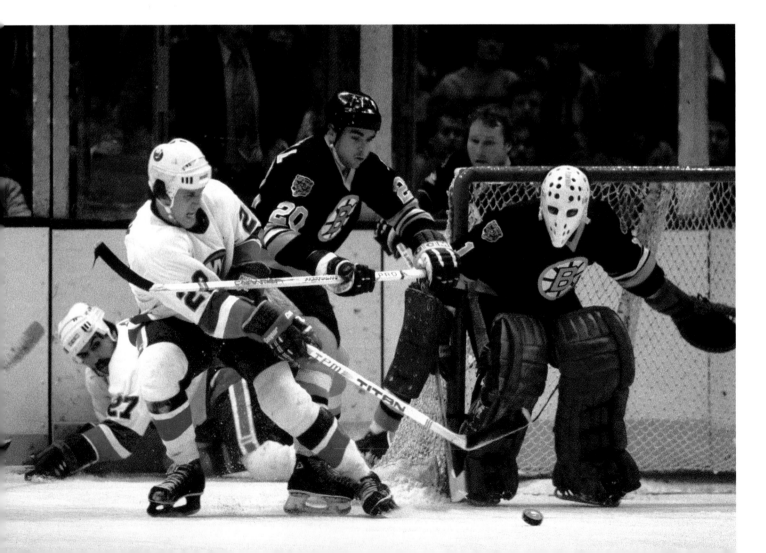

defense. Youngsters like Mike Krushelnyski (23 goals), Tom Fergus (28 goals), Craig MacTavish, and Luc Dufour all made contributions to the Bruins league-leading 50 wins. But the real surprise of the year was goaltender Pete Peeters, who would win the Vezina Trophy for a performance that included a league-best eight shutouts. The Bruins had given up a quality young defenseman (Brad McCrimmon) to Philadelphia to acquire Peeters in the off-season, and the goalie played in 62 games in '82–'83, winning 42 times, also tops in the league, with a 2.36 goals-against average. It would be Peeters' best year as a Bruin, and he would earn a place on the First All-Star Team (Bourque and Pederson would get spots on the second squad).

The Bruins' season was a great achievement considering the near tragedy of October 23, when 19-year-old Normand Leveille suffered a brain aneurysm during a game against the Vancouver Canucks. The native of Montreal had joined the Bruins after a standout career in Chicoutimi of the Quebec Major Junior Hockey League (QMJHL), with Boston selecting the left winger 14th overall in the 1981 entry draft. He recorded 33 points (including 14 goals) in 66 games in his rookie year, and had nine points in nine games to start the 1982–83 campaign before he was struck down. Leveille would partially recover and served as an inspiration to his team throughout the season and beyond. On December 4, the Bruins even won their first regular-season game at the Montreal Forum since the 1976–77 season! They made it to the final four in the playoffs, but then ran into the New York Islanders, who easily eliminated Boston on their way to another appearance in the finals.

*Calgary's Lanny McDonald (#9) scored a career-high 66 goals for the Flames during the 1982–83 season.*

### Hawks Soar

The Chicago Blackhawks had one of the best seasons in team history, with 104 points and 47 victories. They had eight more points than second-place Minnesota in the revamped Norris Division, and they did it primarily with an attack lead by center Denis Savard. The Blackhawks got incredibly lucky at the 1980 draft when the Canadiens decided to select Doug Wickenheiser first overall instead of hometown hero Savard. Winnipeg selected defenseman Dave Babych second, which left Savard for the Hawks. He started producing immediately, scoring 28 goals and 75 points as a rookie. He put up 119 points in 1981–82, and the 1982–83 season saw him record 121 points (35 goals, 86 assists) for the third highest total in the league, behind Wayne Gretzky and Peter Stastny. But Savard was not alone in the Blackhawks' 338-goal onslaught. Winger Al

*Marcel Dionne (#16) of Los Angeles scored his 500th career goal on December 14, 1982, during a 7–2 loss to the Washington Capitals. The superbly talented center recorded 107 points (56 goals, 51 assists) in 1982–83.*

Secord scored 54 times playing alongside Savard, while rookie-of-the-year Steve Larmer would record 90 points (43 goals, 47 assists). Hard-nosed center Darryl Sutter chipped in 31 goals, while Rich Preston (25 goals) and Tom Lysiak (23 goals) were also part of the vaunted attack. Three guys named Doug — Wilson (69 points), Crossman (53 points), and Brown (27 assists) — manned the blueline and helped set up a number of goals. The netminding duties were split between Tony Esposito (23 wins) and Murray Bannerman (24 wins), but neither was capable of taking the team all the way in the playoffs. Coach Orval Tessier won the Jack Adams Award for the job he did in reviving the once moribund club.

The Philadelphia Flyers had one of the best records in the regular season with 106 points (49–23–8) under coach Bob McCammon, who was now also the team's GM, replacing long-time boss Keith Allen.

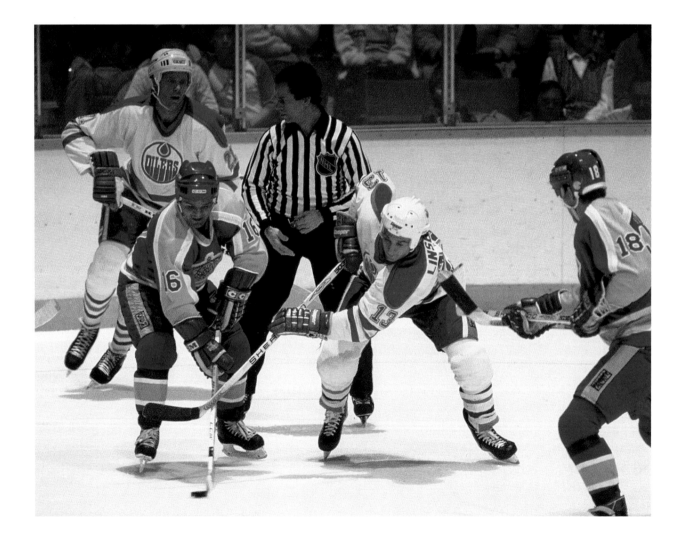

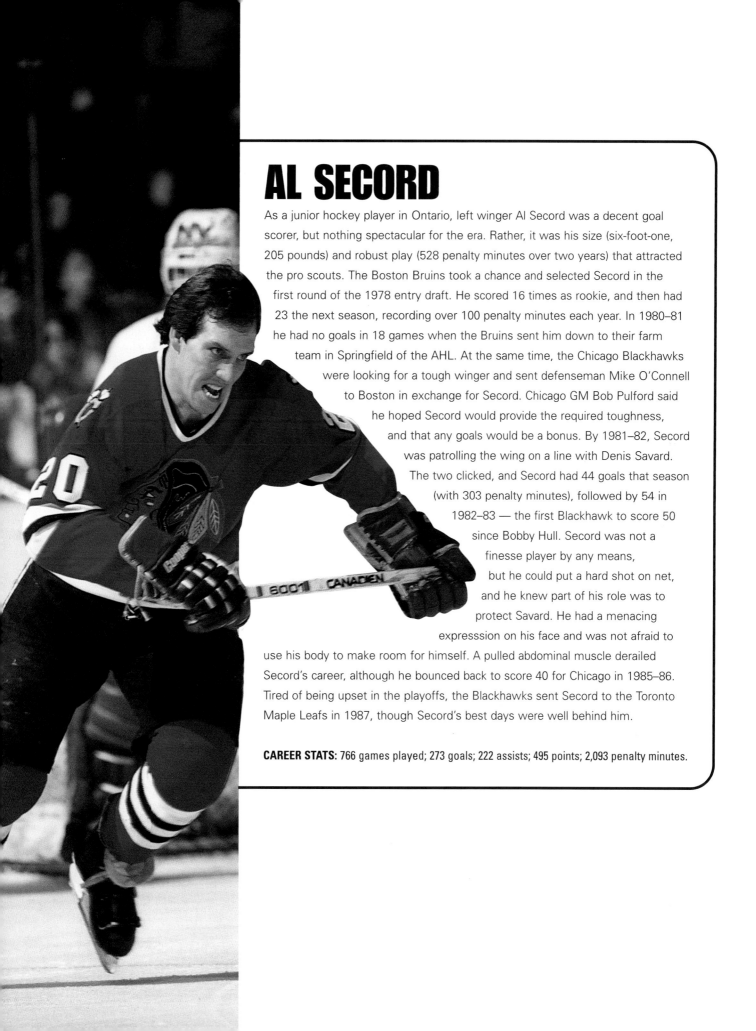

# AL SECORD

As a junior hockey player in Ontario, left winger Al Secord was a decent goal scorer, but nothing spectacular for the era. Rather, it was his size (six-foot-one, 205 pounds) and robust play (528 penalty minutes over two years) that attracted the pro scouts. The Boston Bruins took a chance and selected Secord in the first round of the 1978 entry draft. He scored 16 times as rookie, and then had 23 the next season, recording over 100 penalty minutes each year. In 1980–81 he had no goals in 18 games when the Bruins sent him down to their farm team in Springfield of the AHL. At the same time, the Chicago Blackhawks were looking for a tough winger and sent defenseman Mike O'Connell to Boston in exchange for Secord. Chicago GM Bob Pulford said he hoped Secord would provide the required toughness, and that any goals would be a bonus. By 1981–82, Secord was patrolling the wing on a line with Denis Savard. The two clicked, and Secord had 44 goals that season (with 303 penalty minutes), followed by 54 in 1982–83 — the first Blackhawk to score 50 since Bobby Hull. Secord was not a finesse player by any means, but he could put a hard shot on net, and he knew part of his role was to protect Savard. He had a menacing expresssion on his face and was not afraid to use his body to make room for himself. A pulled abdominal muscle derailed Secord's career, although he bounced back to score 40 for Chicago in 1985–86. Tired of being upset in the playoffs, the Blackhawks sent Secord to the Toronto Maple Leafs in 1987, though Secord's best days were well behind him.

**CAREER STATS:** 766 games played; 273 goals; 222 assists; 495 points; 2,093 penalty minutes.

*Montreal netminder Rick Wamsley (#1) tries to cover up against the Quebec Nordiques with defenseman Rick Green (#5) looking on. Wamsley won a career-high 27 games for the Habs in 1982–83, just one year after he had shared in the Jennings Trophy with Denis Heron in 1982. Green provided Montreal with 26 points and a strong presence on the blueline after his acquisition from Washington.*

Veterans Bobby Clarke (85 points), Darryl Sittler (43 goals) and Bill Barber (60 points) led the way, but the Flyers had a good sprinkling of youngsters in Brian Propp (40 goals), Ron Flockhart (60 points), Ray Allison (51 points), and Ilka Sinisalo (50 points). Howe was a tremendous addition to the defense (20 goals, 67 points) that also included talents like McCrimmon, Brad Marsh, and the physical Behn Wilson. The Flyers never really shed the Broad Street Bullies image they had cultivated in the seventies, and forwards Glen Cochrane (237 penalty minutes) and Holmgren (176) kept the spirit alive. The hard-nosed Clarke posted 115 penalty minutes of his own, taking the Selke Trophy as the NHL's best defensive forward (the last award of his playing career). But the Flyers lacked depth, and their goaltending was still suspect under Bob Froese and an emerging Pelle Lindbergh. The New York Rangers stunned them in the first round of the playoffs with a three-game sweep, and the Flyers knew they would need to make more changes before becoming serious contenders.

### The Inevitable Showdown

The New York Islanders got off to a poor start but by the time the regular season was over, the defending champs had racked up 96 points and were sixth overall — a perfect position to sneak up on the favorites in the postseason. The Islanders were now a veteran club that knew they would be judged by their performance in the playoffs, but that did not mean some of their players did not put up some impressive totals in the regular season. Mike Bossy scored 60, becoming the first player in NHL history to score 50 or more in his first three years, while linemate and best friend Bryan Trottier had 89 points (34 goals). Defenseman Denis Potvin had his usual stellar season with 66 points (54 assists) and Roland Melanson, who posted the NHL's best save percentage at .910, joined veteran Billy Smith in net. The pair combined to win the Jennings Trophy for fewest goals against (226) and Melanson was named to the Second All-Star Team. The Islanders had a respectable offense (308 goals) but their strength was a defensive group that included Potvin, Ken Morrow, Tomas Jonsson, Stefan Persson, Dave Langevin, Mike McEwen, and Gord Lane.

If the Islanders plodded along before the start of the playoffs, the Edmonton Oilers were in high gear for the entire season. The team scored a league-high 424 goals and won 47 games on the way to a

*Montreal's Ryan Walter (#11) looks to screen Islanders goalie Billy Smith. Walter had 29 goals and 75 points in his first year with the Canadiens after a controversial trade with the Washington Capitals. Smith shared the Jennings Trophy in 1982–83 with Roland Melanson, posting a 18–14–7 record in the regular season. He then won 13 playoff games to take his team to the Stanley Cup for the fourth time.*

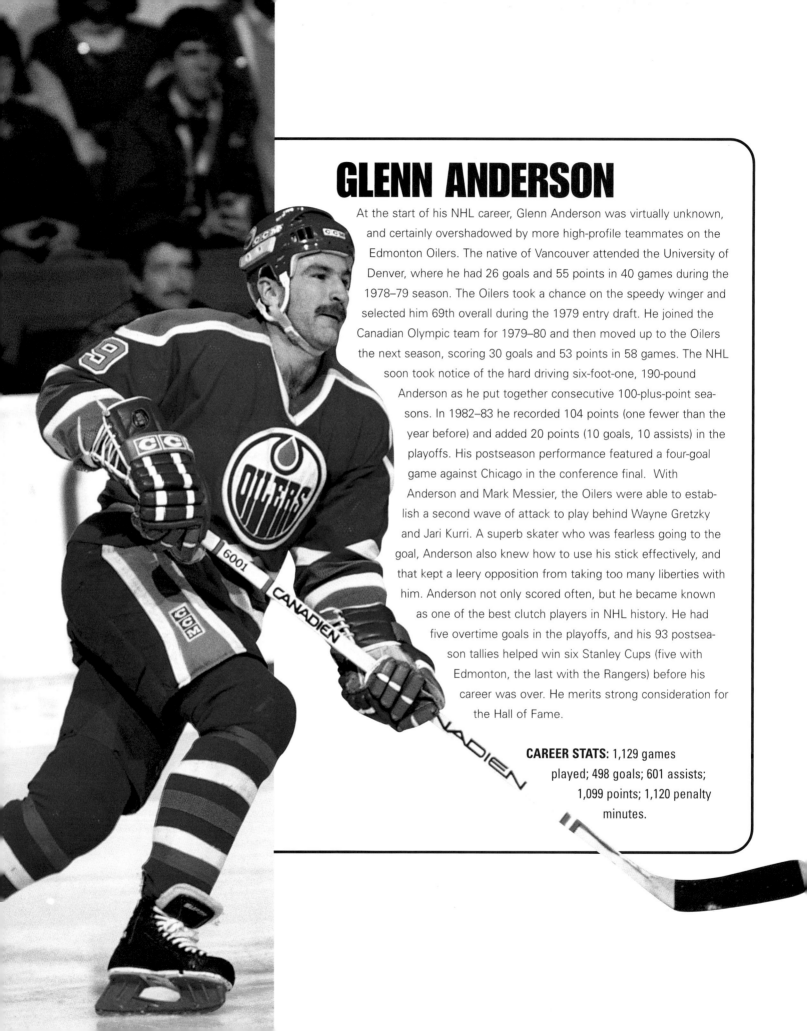

# GLENN ANDERSON

At the start of his NHL career, Glenn Anderson was virtually unknown, and certainly overshadowed by more high-profile teammates on the Edmonton Oilers. The native of Vancouver attended the University of Denver, where he had 26 goals and 55 points in 40 games during the 1978–79 season. The Oilers took a chance on the speedy winger and selected him 69th overall during the 1979 entry draft. He joined the Canadian Olympic team for 1979–80 and then moved up to the Oilers the next season, scoring 30 goals and 53 points in 58 games. The NHL soon took notice of the hard driving six-foot-one, 190-pound Anderson as he put together consecutive 100-plus-point seasons. In 1982–83 he recorded 104 points (one fewer than the year before) and added 20 points (10 goals, 10 assists) in the playoffs. His postseason performance featured a four-goal game against Chicago in the conference final. With Anderson and Mark Messier, the Oilers were able to establish a second wave of attack to play behind Wayne Gretzky and Jari Kurri. A superb skater who was fearless going to the goal, Anderson also knew how to use his stick effectively, and that kept a leery opposition from taking too many liberties with him. Anderson not only scored often, but he became known as one of the best clutch players in NHL history. He had five overtime goals in the playoffs, and his 93 postseason tallies helped win six Stanley Cups (five with Edmonton, the last with the Rangers) before his career was over. He merits strong consideration for the Hall of Fame.

**CAREER STATS:** 1,129 games played; 498 goals; 601 assists; 1,099 points; 1,120 penalty minutes.

*Paul Coffey (#7) of the Edmonton Oilers looks to skate away from Tom Lysiak of Chicago. The smooth-skating Coffey recorded 96 points (29 goals, 67 assists) in 1982–83 and then added 14 points in 16 playoff games, which helped the Oilers make the finals for the first time. Lysiak had 61 points (23 goals, 38 assists) in 61 games for the Blackhawks in '82–'83.*

106-point season. Gretzky led all scorers with 196 points (71 goals, 125 assists) and was joined in the top 10 by Mark Messier (48 goals, 106 points), Glenn Anderson (48 goals, 106 points), and Jari Kurri (45 goals, 104 points). Defenseman Paul Coffey added 96 points, while the newly acquired Ken Linseman registered 75. The Oilers paid little attention to defense and allowed a whopping 315 goals — Andy Moog played 50 games in net and sported a 3.54 goals-against average, while Grant Fuhr averaged 4.29 goals against in 32 games! It seemed the only way Edmonton would win was to score five or six goals a game — and they were quite capable of doing so. But the high-flying club was not yet ready to take the ultimate step.

### Filling the Nets

The emphasis during 1982–83 was still very much on skills and scoring. Most teams could ice at least two lines that could score regularly, and defensemen were encouraged to join the attack. Squads that did not have speed and passing skills were being left behind. Teams valued mobility and creativity on the attack, and the majority lacked quality checkers, defensive blueliners, and top-notch goaltenders. The top scoring teams were Edmonton, Montreal (350), Quebec (343), and Chicago (338), while Hartford (403), Pittsburgh (394), Los Angeles

(365), and Detroit (344) allowed the most goals. Gretzky led the charge with 71 goals, but Calgary's Lanny McDonald was not far behind with 66, and Bossy had 60. Michel Goulet, Marcel Dionne, Al Secord, and Rick Vaive all had 50 or more goals. Eleven players had 100 or more points in the race for the Art Ross Trophy, which Gretzky won for the third straight year. More European names crept into the upper echelon of the scoring statistics, with Peter Stastny, Kent Nilsson, Jari Kurri, Anton Stastny, and Tomas Gradin all in the top 25.

# The PLAYOFFS

As the Stanley Cup playoffs began it seemed that the favorites were going to romp through the opposition, but as usual in the eighties, things were not so predictable. The Montreal Canadiens had put up another good season (42–24–14) under coach Bob Berry, but their tradition of turning it on in the postseason was quickly becoming a thing of the past. In the first round, the Buffalo Sabres won three straight against the Habs, marking the third year in a row they were ousted in the opening series. The Sabres had turned in a decent regular season

*Denis Potvin (#5) is about to pound the puck into the St. Louis Blues net. Potvin was named to the First All-Star Team for the 1982–83 season when he scored 12 goals and totaled 66 points in 69 games. The dominating blueliner also had 20 points in 20 playoff games, helping the Islanders win their fourth consecutive Stanley Cup.*

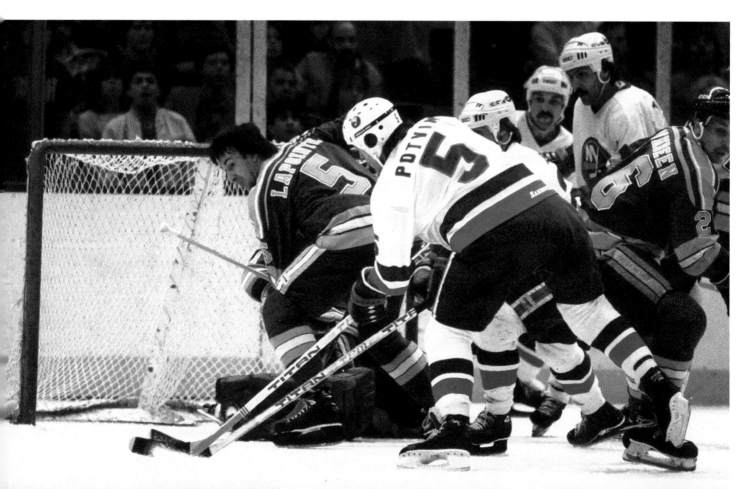

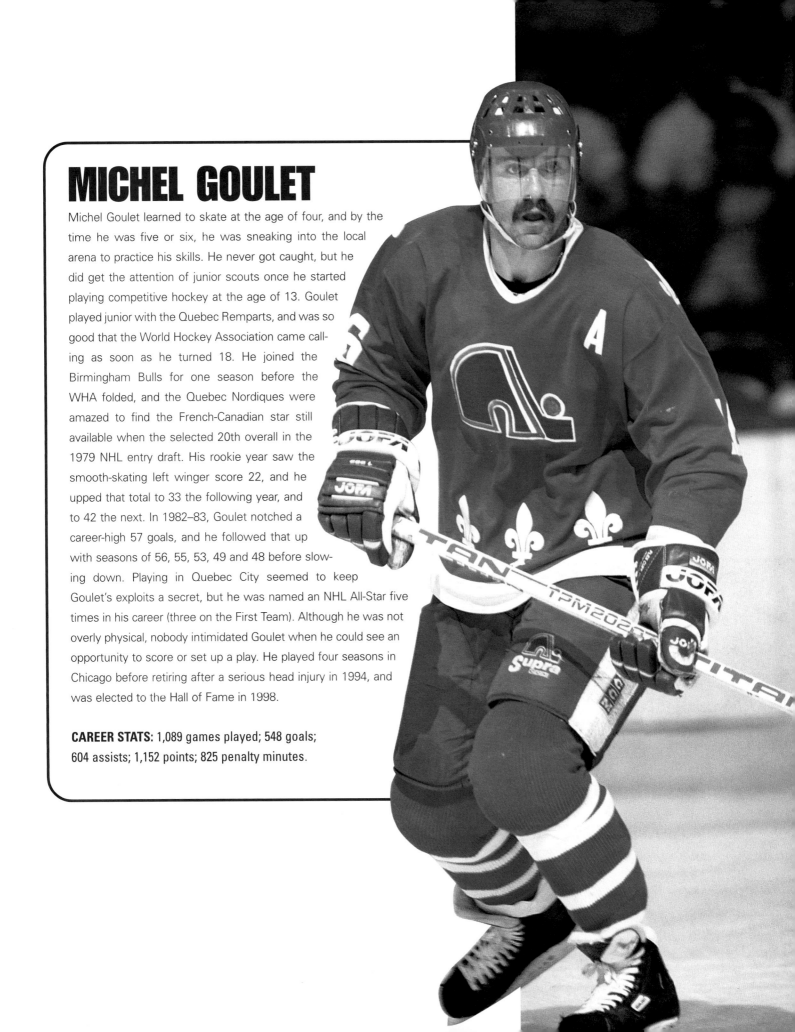

# MICHEL GOULET

Michel Goulet learned to skate at the age of four, and by the time he was five or six, he was sneaking into the local arena to practice his skills. He never got caught, but he did get the attention of junior scouts once he started playing competitive hockey at the age of 13. Goulet played junior with the Quebec Remparts, and was so good that the World Hockey Association came calling as soon as he turned 18. He joined the Birmingham Bulls for one season before the WHA folded, and the Quebec Nordiques were amazed to find the French-Canadian star still available when the selected 20th overall in the 1979 NHL entry draft. His rookie year saw the smooth-skating left winger score 22, and he upped that total to 33 the following year, and to 42 the next. In 1982–83, Goulet notched a career-high 57 goals, and he followed that up with seasons of 56, 55, 53, 49 and 48 before slowing down. Playing in Quebec City seemed to keep Goulet's exploits a secret, but he was named an NHL All-Star five times in his career (three on the First Team). Although he was not overly physical, nobody intimidated Goulet when he could see an opportunity to score or set up a play. He played four seasons in Chicago before retiring after a serious head injury in 1994, and was elected to the Hall of Fame in 1998.

**CAREER STATS:** 1,089 games played; 548 goals; 604 assists; 1,152 points; 825 penalty minutes.

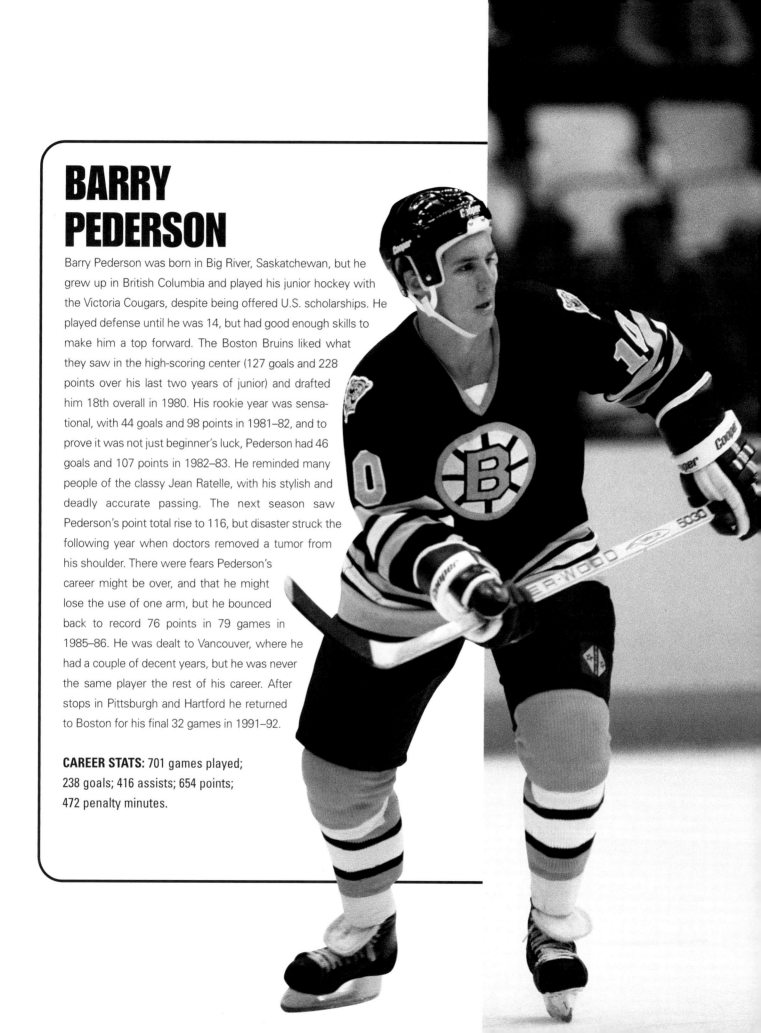

# BARRY PEDERSON

Barry Pederson was born in Big River, Saskatchewan, but he grew up in British Columbia and played his junior hockey with the Victoria Cougars, despite being offered U.S. scholarships. He played defense until he was 14, but had good enough skills to make him a top forward. The Boston Bruins liked what they saw in the high-scoring center (127 goals and 228 points over his last two years of junior) and drafted him 18th overall in 1980. His rookie year was sensational, with 44 goals and 98 points in 1981–82, and to prove it was not just beginner's luck, Pederson had 46 goals and 107 points in 1982–83. He reminded many people of the classy Jean Ratelle, with his stylish and deadly accurate passing. The next season saw Pederson's point total rise to 116, but disaster struck the following year when doctors removed a tumor from his shoulder. There were fears Pederson's career might be over, and that he might lose the use of one arm, but he bounced back to record 76 points in 79 games in 1985–86. He was dealt to Vancouver, where he had a couple of decent years, but he was never the same player the rest of his career. After stops in Pittsburgh and Hartford he returned to Boston for his final 32 games in 1991–92.

**CAREER STATS:** 701 games played; 238 goals; 416 assists; 654 points; 472 penalty minutes.

(89 points), and after their upset of the Habs they pushed the Bruins to seven games before losing the final contest in overtime on a goal by Brad Park. The other surprise in the first round came from the New York Rangers who, despite a mediocre season (35–35–10), upset Philadelphia in a sweep. The Rangers were making a habit of stinging the Flyers in the playoffs, but they were expelled in the next round by their cross-state rivals, the Islanders, in six games.

The Oilers were much better prepared for the playoffs in 1983, and went straight through to the final after easy wins over Winnipeg, Calgary, and Chicago. Only the Flames managed to win a game in those first three rounds, and the Oilers overwhelmed the Blackhawks by scoring 25 goals in four games during the conference final. The Islanders had a more difficult time taking out the Bruins in the other conference final, but a hat trick by Bossy in an 8–3 win in the fourth game put New York up for good. The Bruins won game five, but Bossy scored four goals in the last game to put an exclamation point on the series.

The hockey world looked forward to a great final between the Islanders dynasty and the young challengers of Edmonton, but it never materialized. The Islanders won the first two games in Edmonton by scores of 2–0 and 6–3. They returned home and won two more in convincing style, 5–1 and 4–2, to secure their fourth straight Stanley Cup. Islanders netminder Billy Smith took the Conn Smythe Trophy with 13 playoff wins and a 2.68 goals against average. The Oilers were severely criticized for their weak-kneed performance in the finals, and Gretzky (no goals, four assists in the series) was especially targeted by fans and media alike. The Islanders were simply a more experienced team, though they were on their last legs, while the Oilers were still youngsters with plenty to learn about what it takes to win the ultimate prize in hockey. After the final game, many Oilers commented that as they passed the Islanders dressing room they noticed a lot less whooping and hollering than one might expect from the champions. Instead, they saw a bruised and battered club quietly savoring the moment as they tended to their wounds. That lesson was not lost on the Oilers, and they would have to wait just one more year for a chance to redeem themselves.

*St. Louis captain Brian Sutter (#11) scored a career-high 46 goals in 1982–83 and had 76 points. Sutter played 12 years in the NHL, all as a member of the Blues. He finished with 303 goals and 636 points in 779 career games.*

# 1983–84

*Barrasso makes his debut, Capital gains in Washington, and the Oilers enjoy the Cup and Coffey*

**THE** 1983–84 season was a year of hopes and dreams for many of the 21 NHL franchises. For Montreal and Detroit the hopes were strongest at the beginning of the year, while the hapless Penguins and Devils dreamed of next season. The Canadiens began a new era under president Ronald Corey (he was hired in late 1982), who quickly sought to remake the Habs into a contender. He selected Serge Savard as the new director of hockey operations, and though it would take a while to get the Habs back on course, the Canadiens pulled off two playoff upsets in 1984 after a poor regular season. In another Original Six city, the Detroit Red Wings hired manager Jim Devellano, a onetime scouting guru for the New York Islanders. He vowed to rebuild the sad-sack Red Wings, and he was true to his word, taking center Steve Yzerman in the first round of the 1983 entry draft. If Detroit and Montreal were heading in the right direction under new management, Pittsburgh and New Jersey had their eyes on a young junior named Mario Lemieux who by all accounts would be the new savior.

### NHL Gets Younger

When 11 veteran players retired prior to the 1983–84 season, it left the NHL with an average age of 25.5 years. (The previous year, the league had 70 players who were 21 years old, 19 players were 20, and

---

*Edmonton netminder Andy Moog (#35) makes a save against the New York Islanders. Moog was in net when the Oilers won their first Stanley Cup on May 19, 1984, defeating the Islanders 5–2 in the fifth game of the finals.*

*Washington Capitals defense-man Scott Stevens (#3) tries to cover Ron Francis (#10) of the Hartford Whalers. Named to the NHL's All-Rookie Team in 1982–83 when he had 25 points, Stevens improved his performance in 1983–84 with 45 points (13 goals, 32 assists) while recording 201 penalty minutes. Francis scored 23 goals and added 60 assists in '83–'84.*

five who were just 18.) Yzerman led this young force with 87 points as a rookie, while Dave Poulin (Philadelphia), Sylvain Turgeon (Hartford), and Kelly Kisio (New York Rangers) all had 60 or more points. Other notable rookies who would have long careers were Doug Gilmour (St. Louis), Al MacInnis (Calgary), Pat Verbeek (New Jersey), and Cam Neely (Boston). The biggest surprise was netminder Tom Barrasso, who came right out of an American high school to play 42 games for the Buffalo Sabres and took home the Calder Trophy. His performance was so impressive he was also awarded the Vezina Trophy as the league's best goalie — going 26–12–3 with a 2.84 goals-against average as an 18-year-old. By contrast, the oldest player going into the season was 40-year-old goaltender Tony Esposito.

In Buffalo and Washington, a pair of 20-year-old defensemen named Phil Housley and Scott Stevens led their teams to a spell of good fortune. Scotty Bowman had reshaped the team since his takeover in 1979, helping the Sabres contend for a number of years, and in '83–'84 their youth had a chance to develop. Barrasso in goal and Housley (31 goals, 77 points) on defense were the most noticeable youngsters, but

Dave Andreychuk (38 goals, 80 points), Mike Foligno (32 goals), Gilles Hamel (21 goals), Lindy Ruff (45 points), Sean McKenna (20 goals), Mike Ramsey (31 points), and John Tucker (12 goals in 21 games) were the heart of the young team. Holdovers included the great Gilbert Perreault (who led the team in scoring with 90 points), Bill Hajt, Craig Ramsey, and the reclaimed Jerry Korab, but with the exception of Perreault their significance was diminishing rapidly. The '83–'84 campaign saw the team win 48 games and record 103 points, but a playoff loss in the first round derailed the Sabres again, ruining their otherwise good year.

In Washington, the Capitals put together their first 100-point season when they won 48 games and finished just one point behind the defending champion New York Islanders. Coach Bryan Murray was now in his third season, and he was getting through to forwards like Mike Gartner (40 goals), Bengt Gustafsson (32 goals, including five in one game against Vancouver), Dave Christian (81 points), Bobby Carpenter (28 goals), and Allan Howarth (24 goals). The team had good speed on the wings and was not afraid to go on the attack. They were also well fortified on defense: Stevens proved he was a steal at fifth overall in the 1982 draft, Rod Langway won his second Norris Trophy, and the newly acquired Larry Murphy added more offense

*Buffalo netminder Tom Barrasso (#30) took the NHL by storm in 1983–84 and was named the league's best rookie. He played in 42 games and posted a 26–12–3 record with two shutouts and a 2.84 goals-against average. His performance also earned the first-year goalie the Vezina Trophy.*

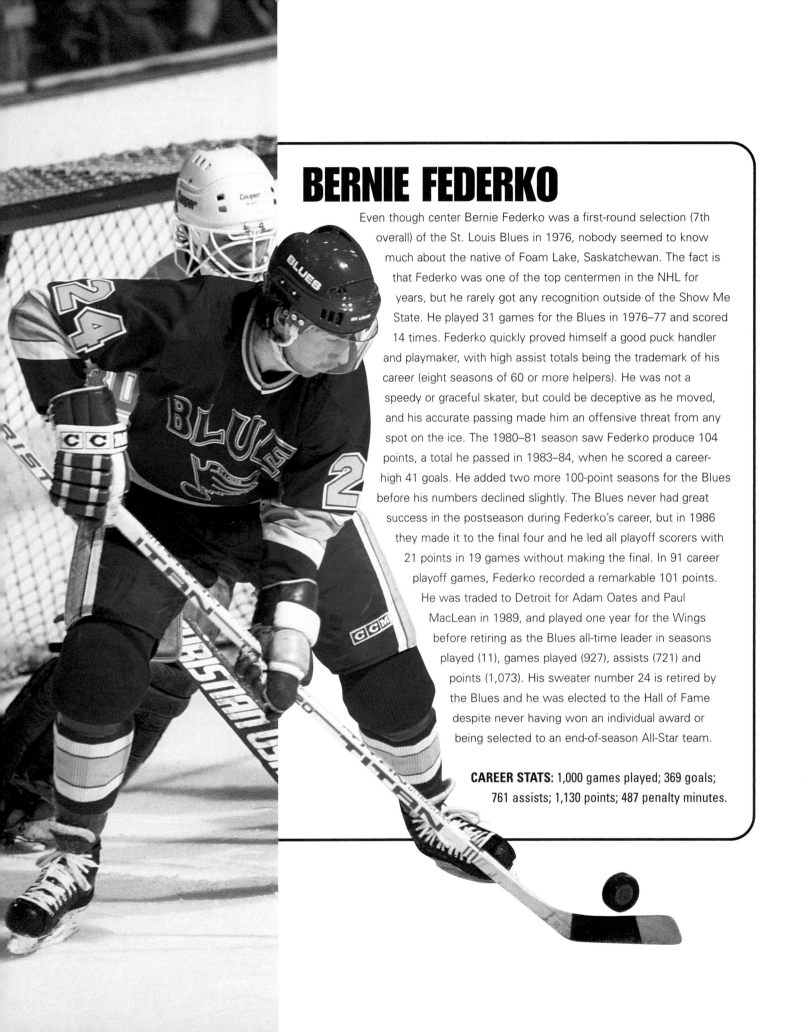

# BERNIE FEDERKO

Even though center Bernie Federko was a first-round selection (7th overall) of the St. Louis Blues in 1976, nobody seemed to know much about the native of Foam Lake, Saskatchewan. The fact is that Federko was one of the top centermen in the NHL for years, but he rarely got any recognition outside of the Show Me State. He played 31 games for the Blues in 1976–77 and scored 14 times. Federko quickly proved himself a good puck handler and playmaker, with high assist totals being the trademark of his career (eight seasons of 60 or more helpers). He was not a speedy or graceful skater, but could be deceptive as he moved, and his accurate passing made him an offensive threat from any spot on the ice. The 1980–81 season saw Federko produce 104 points, a total he passed in 1983–84, when he scored a career-high 41 goals. He added two more 100-point seasons for the Blues before his numbers declined slightly. The Blues never had great success in the postseason during Federko's career, but in 1986 they made it to the final four and he led all playoff scorers with 21 points in 19 games without making the final. In 91 career playoff games, Federko recorded a remarkable 101 points. He was traded to Detroit for Adam Oates and Paul MacLean in 1989, and played one year for the Wings before retiring as the Blues all-time leader in seasons played (11), games played (927), assists (721) and points (1,073). His sweater number 24 is retired by the Blues and he was elected to the Hall of Fame despite never having won an individual award or being selected to an end-of-season All-Star team.

**CAREER STATS:** 1,000 games played; 369 goals; 761 assists; 1,130 points; 487 penalty minutes.

from the blueline. The Capitals had lost their first seven games and had scored only 15 goals when they sent defenseman Brian Engblom and winger Ken Houston to the Los Angeles Kings for Murphy, who had recorded 62 points the previous year. Murphy helped to kick-start the Washington offense, and the team lost only 20 games the rest of the way. The goaltending tandem of Pat Riggin and Al Jensen were solid throughout the regular season and became the unlikely winners of the Jennings Trophy for allowing the fewest goals (226). The Capitals knocked off a good Philadelphia squad in the first round of the play-offs (in three straight no less), but were easily handled by the Islanders in the next round. The Capitals would have many good seasons during the eighties, but were usually a disappointment in the postseason.

## Oilers Prepare for the Playoffs

It was no great surprise the see Wayne Gretzky lead the Edmonton Oilers to a 119-point season and the best record overall in the NHL

*Buffalo Sabres defenseman Mike Ramsey (#5) works in front of the net guarded by Bob Sauve (#28). A native of Minnesota, Ramsey joined the Sabres after the 1980 Olympics and played more than 13 seasons in Buffalo. In 1983–84 he had nine goals and 31 points, while Sauve won 22 games.*

*Along with partner Al Jenson, goaltender Pat Riggin (#1) won the Jennings Trophy in 1983–84 when the Capitals allowed a league-best 226 goals against. Riggin was named to the Second All-Star Team and the two goalies shared the league lead in shutouts with four each. In 41 games, Riggin sported a 21–14–2 record.*

(57–18–5). But the team now understood that everything would ride on the playoffs — if they failed to get to the finals, their year would be declared a failure. Gretzky notched another 200-point season when he scored 87 goals and added 118 assists. Second in scoring was fellow Oiler Paul Coffey, who recorded 126 points (40 goals, 86 assists), marking the first time teammates finished one-two since Bobby Orr and Phil Esposito did it in 1974–75 for the Boston Bruins. Winger Jari Kurri scored 52 times and Glenn Anderson had 54 to give the Oilers three players with 50 or more goals. Mark Messier had a 101-point season to give the team four 100-point players, and others like Ken Linseman (67 points), Pat Hughes (27 goals including five in one game versus Calgary), Dave Hunter (22 goals), and Willy Lindstrom (22 goals) all contributed to an offense that racked up 446 goals. Even goaltender Grant Fuhr got in on the act with 14 assists, still an NHL record. The Oilers also gave up 314 goals, but they were still not worried about defense. They knew they were easily the best team in the Smythe Division, and that would pit them against the winner of the weak Norris Division in the semi-finals. By playing to their strength, the Oilers were virtually assured a spot in the finals.

Gretzky, now the team captain, was determined to lead the Oilers to the Stanley Cup and started the season by picking up at least one point in his first 51 games. During a December 18 meeting with Winnipeg, Gretzky had two goals and two assists to record his 100th point in only his 34th game of the season. The lowly Los Angeles Kings (27–41–12 on the season) stopped Gretzky's streak on January 28, when unknown goaltender Markus Mattson held the Oilers to just two goals in a 4–2 win. During his incredible streak, Gretzky accumulated 153 points, including 61 goals. It was not all a bed of roses for the Oilers, who were whipped 11–0 by the Hartford Whalers on February 12, but that lopsided defeat to a vastly inferior opponent gave Edmonton the slap in the face they needed to realize they would have to still work hard, despite all their talent.

## Mickey Mouse Club

After the Oilers shellacked the New Jersey Devils 13–4 on November 19, Gretzky ripped into the Devils' management by saying that they were a "Mickey Mouse" operation, and that teams like New Jersey were ruining hockey. Gretzky was taken aback by the furor over his harsh comments and apologized, saying his real intention was to argue that the weaker NHL teams needed help. Nonetheless, it was an accurate assessment by Gretzky, and soon afterwards Billy MacMillan was gone as the Devils' general manager and coach. He was replaced behind the bench by Tom McVie, who seemed to specialize in working for awful hockey teams, having been with Washington and Winnipeg previously. McVie fared no better with the Devils, posting a 15–38–7 record in 60 games, but they managed to finish three points ahead of the Pittsburgh Penguins in the overall standings. The Penguins were the worst team in the NHL, with just 38 points, and some accused them of trying to finish last so they could select Lemieux first overall in the entry draft. No evidence was ever uncovered, but this  turtle derby between the Devils and Penguins — followed by another in 1990–91, when it looked like the Quebec Nordiques were doing all they could to finish in the basement so they might select Eric Lindros — would eventually force the NHL to change its draft rules.

*Edmonton's Pat Hughes (#16) netted five goals against the Calgary Flames on February 3, 1984, during a 10–5 Oilers victory. Hughes scored three goals against Don Edwards and two on Reggie Lemelin. He finished with a career-high 27 goals and 55 points for the season.*

## Drive for Five

If the defending champion New York Islanders needed any motivation to stay on top, they started the season determined to match Montreal's record of five straight Stanley Cups (1956 to 1960). "Drive for Five" became the rallying cry on Long Island, and the team produced another fine season, with 104 points to top the Patrick Division. Their 50 wins was second only to Edmonton, and their point total tied them for second overall with the Boston Bruins, who won 49 games. Mike Bossy continued his excellence with 51 goals and 118 points, while Bryan Trottier had 111 points. Denis Potvin (85 points) and John Tonelli (67 points) were solid veteran contributors, but a few new faces also helped out, includ-

*Pat Flatley (#8) and Pat LaFontaine (#16) of the New York Islanders crowd the Edmonton crease during the Stanley Cup finals. Both forwards joined the squad late in the season and helped the team reach the finals for the fifth straight year. Flatley had 15 points in 21 playoff games, while LaFontaine had nine points in 16 postseason games.*

ing Greg Gilbert (31 goals in just his second year) and rookies Pat LaFontaine (U.S.) and Pat Flatley (Canada), who joined the team after the 1984 Olympics. LaFontaine played in just 15 regular-season games, but he scored 13 times, while Flatley had nine points in 16 contests, and both youngsters made a strong impression in the playoffs. The Islanders were confident they could go all the way again, but they had strong challenges from the New York Rangers and Montreal Canadiens before they hooked up with the Oilers again in the finals.

### Notable Achievements

Michel Goulet of the Nordiques scored 56 times in '83–'84, and Rick Vaive of Toronto made it a hat trick when he scored 52 times to give him three straight seasons of 50 or more. Vaive commented that he thought the critics would now have to admit that his 50-goal seasons were no flukes. The Leafs were still terrible (45 losses), but there was no doubt the flashy winger was a bona fide star. New players to enter the 50-goal circle were Tim Kerr of Philadelphia with 54, and Mike Bullard, who notched 51 for the last-place Penguins.

When Rich Sutter scored for Philadelphia on October 23, 1983, he became the sixth Sutter brother to score a goal in the NHL. Rich joined his twin brother Ron on the Flyers after a multi-player deal with Pittsburgh. Meanwhile, their oldest brother, Brian, was playing in St. Louis, where he began his career in 1976–77, while Darryl was captain of the Chicago Blackhawks, and Brent and Duane were with

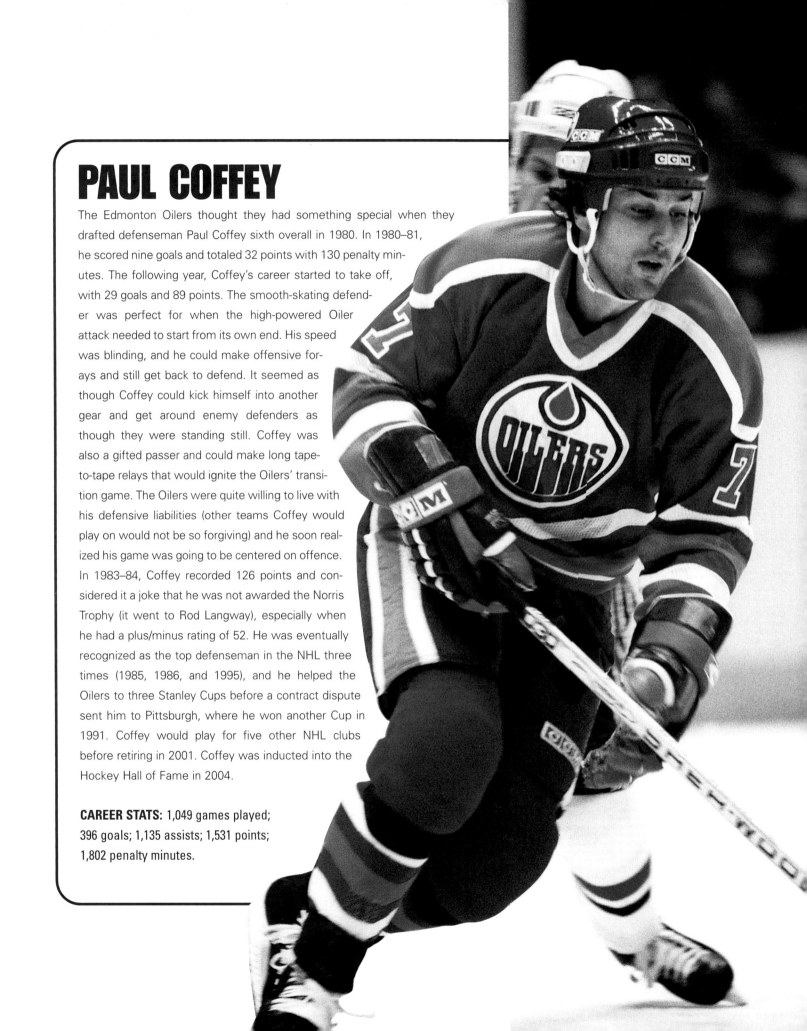

# PAUL COFFEY

The Edmonton Oilers thought they had something special when they drafted defenseman Paul Coffey sixth overall in 1980. In 1980–81, he scored nine goals and totaled 32 points with 130 penalty minutes. The following year, Coffey's career started to take off, with 29 goals and 89 points. The smooth-skating defender was perfect for when the high-powered Oiler attack needed to start from its own end. His speed was blinding, and he could make offensive forays and still get back to defend. It seemed as though Coffey could kick himself into another gear and get around enemy defenders as though they were standing still. Coffey was also a gifted passer and could make long tape-to-tape relays that would ignite the Oilers' transition game. The Oilers were quite willing to live with his defensive liabilities (other teams Coffey would play on would not be so forgiving) and he soon realized his game was going to be centered on offence. In 1983–84, Coffey recorded 126 points and considered it a joke that he was not awarded the Norris Trophy (it went to Rod Langway), especially when he had a plus/minus rating of 52. He was eventually recognized as the top defenseman in the NHL three times (1985, 1986, and 1995), and he helped the Oilers to three Stanley Cups before a contract dispute sent him to Pittsburgh, where he won another Cup in 1991. Coffey would play for five other NHL clubs before retiring in 2001. Coffey was inducted into the Hockey Hall of Fame in 2004.

**CAREER STATS:** 1,049 games played; 396 goals; 1,135 assists; 1,531 points; 1,802 penalty minutes.

# TIM KERR

Although Tim Kerr had the size most NHL scouts drool over (six-foot-three, 230 pounds), he developed a reputation in junior hockey as an unmotivated big guy. But Philadelphia scout Eric Colville saw potential in Kerr and convinced the team to pay a $10,000 signing bonus to get the forward's name on a contract (as a native of Windsor, Ontario, he had considered going to nearby Detroit to join the Red Wings). Kerr was expecting to play in the minors in 1980–81, but he made the big team when Ken Linseman broke his leg at training camp. He scored 22 times as a rookie and started to show soft hands. He was never a prototypically mean and nasty Flyer despite his size, but he was willing to absorb the punishment that went with hanging around the net. He also developed a history of injuries starting in 1982–83, when he hurt his knee, but he worked hard to rehabilitate and returned to score 54 goals in 1983–84. Kerr was a load to deal with in the slot, and his quick wrists made sure his shots were on net as soon as the puck hit his stick. He recorded four straight years of 50 or more goals (58 was his highest total) and added one 48-goal season before injuries hampered his career, which ended after brief stints with the New York Rangers and Hartford Whalers.

**CAREER STATS:** 655 games played; 370 goals; 304 assists; 674 points; 596 penalty minutes.

the champion New York Islanders. Most of the Viking, Alberta, clan would have long careers and two, Brian and Darryl, were naturals to become NHL coaches. In 2003–04 they were both still pacing behind the bench.

In Calgary, the Flames moved into their new arena, the Olympic Saddledome, and it was sold out every game. The Flames were now in a much better position to fight the Battle of Alberta with the Oilers, and they would use their new financial resources to build a team that would soon be a serious Stanley Cup contender.

## Dark Moments

Tom Lysiak of the Blackhawks was suspended for 20 games for upending linesman Ron Foyt during a game at the Chicago Stadium, the first time such a suspension was imposed. And that wasn't the only negative news in the hockey world — one-time NHL bad boy Steve Durbano said publicly that 20 to 25 percent of all NHL players used drugs, ranging from marijuana to cocaine and speed. (Durbano was in prison at the time, completing a seven-year sentence for drug smuggling.) Former NHLer Vaclav Nedomansky sued NHLPA executive director Alan Eagleson for more than $1 million over the buyout provisions in his contract. The claims of breach of contract and negligence were dismissed against Eagleson, but it would be the start of many court proceedings for the previously unassailable union leader.

*New York Islanders defenseman Ken Morrow (#6) scored the biggest goal of his career during the 1984 playoffs when his overtime marker eliminated the New York Rangers in the fifth and deciding game of their first-round series. Morrow played his entire career (550 games) with the Islanders and scored 17 regular season goals, but had 11 in the playoffs.*

# The PLAYOFFS

The story of the 1984 playoffs was the sudden resurgence of the Montreal Canadiens. After suffering through one of their worst seasons in recent memory (35–40–5) and dumping coach Bob Berry in the process, nobody expected anything from the team in the postseason. But new mentor Jacques Lemaire had turned the team around in late February, and they opened the first round with an upset of the Boston Bruins in three straight games. The Adams Division final pitted the

*The Quebec Nordiques and the Montreal Canadiens staged a vicious and ugly playoff series in 1984, highlighted by a brawl-filled game six. Montreal won the Adams Division final, with the last contest won on Forum ice by a score of 5–3.*

Habs against their provincial rival, the Quebec Nordiques, and featured one of the bloodiest brawls in playoff history. At the end of the second period of game six at the Forum, both benches cleared — brothers Mark and Dale Hunter exchanged blows, Mario Tremblay broke Peter Stastny's nose, and Montreal's Jean Hamel suffered a serious eye injury in a scrap with Louis Sleigher. Ten players were ejected, but they were not informed during the intermission, and when the teams returned to the ice for the third period they went right back at it. The Canadiens kept their composure, and rookie goaltender Steve Penney kept the Nords off balance and took the series with a 5–3 win. It would not be the last installment of the Battle of Quebec.

Penney kept up his heroics (he had been outstanding against the high-scoring Bruins) for two more games against the New York Islanders, but the veteran club eventually overpowered Montreal to take the semi-final in six games. The Islanders got a scare in the first round again, when the Rangers took them to overtime in the fifth and deciding game — a goal from Ken Morrow saved them from an early elimination. After ending

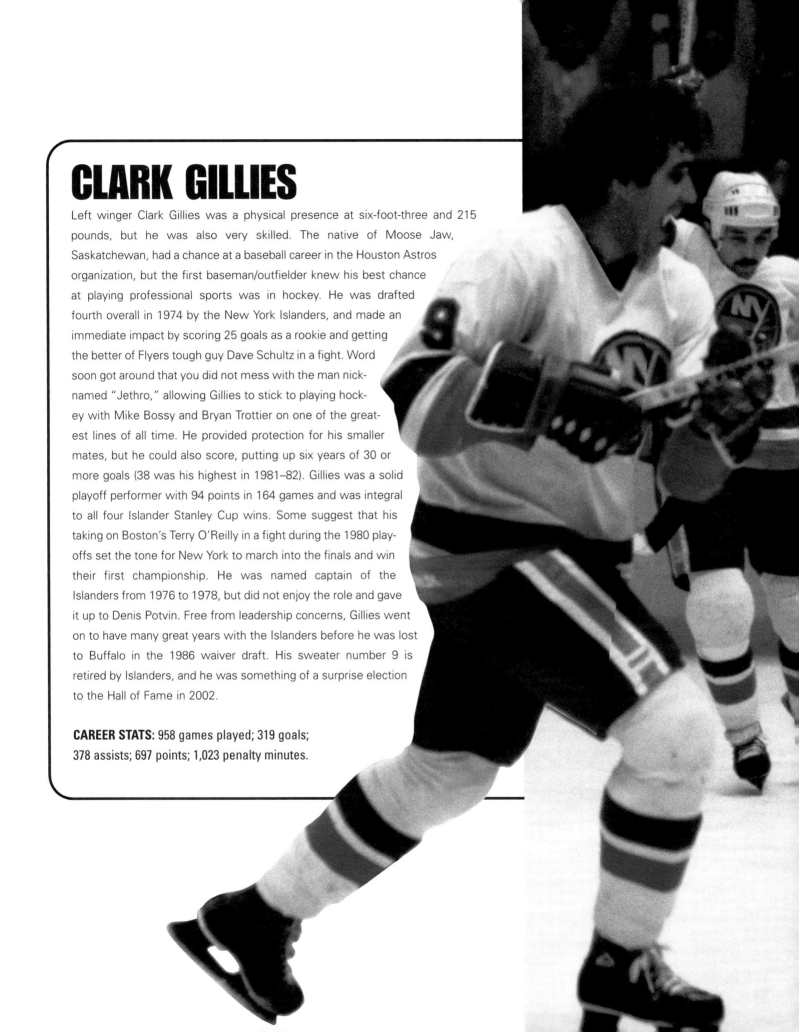

# CLARK GILLIES

Left winger Clark Gillies was a physical presence at six-foot-three and 215 pounds, but he was also very skilled. The native of Moose Jaw, Saskatchewan, had a chance at a baseball career in the Houston Astros organization, but the first baseman/outfielder knew his best chance at playing professional sports was in hockey. He was drafted fourth overall in 1974 by the New York Islanders, and made an immediate impact by scoring 25 goals as a rookie and getting the better of Flyers tough guy Dave Schultz in a fight. Word soon got around that you did not mess with the man nicknamed "Jethro," allowing Gillies to stick to playing hockey with Mike Bossy and Bryan Trottier on one of the greatest lines of all time. He provided protection for his smaller mates, but he could also score, putting up six years of 30 or more goals (38 was his highest in 1981–82). Gillies was a solid playoff performer with 94 points in 164 games and was integral to all four Islander Stanley Cup wins. Some suggest that his taking on Boston's Terry O'Reilly in a fight during the 1980 playoffs set the tone for New York to march into the finals and win their first championship. He was named captain of the Islanders from 1976 to 1978, but did not enjoy the role and gave it up to Denis Potvin. Free from leadership concerns, Gillies went on to have many great years with the Islanders before he was lost to Buffalo in the 1986 waiver draft. His sweater number 9 is retired by Islanders, and he was something of a surprise election to the Hall of Fame in 2002.

**CAREER STATS:** 958 games played; 319 goals; 378 assists; 697 points; 1,023 penalty minutes.

# JARI KURRI

Edmonton superscout Barry Fraser had watched Finnish right winger Jari Kurri for two years (since he was 17 years old) before the Oilers drafted the six-foot-one, 195 pounder. The persuasive bird dog convinced Oilers GM Glen Sather that Kurri could play for the NHL right away, and Sather selected him 69th overall in 1980 and never regretted it. When he first arrived in North America, the Helsinki-born Kurri had a little difficulty learning English, but he watched television shows like *Happy Days* and quickly became fluent in the new language. Kurri was also comfortable skating alongside Wayne Gretzky, who played a European style of game, and they became the most dangerous pair in the NHL for eight consecutive years during the eighties. They understood each other perfectly, Kurri realizing that playing with Gretzky required him to be ready for a pass at any point, and they could switch from defense to offense in the blink of an eye. Kurri kept his stick on the ice, and when the puck arrived his quick release meant the puck was in the back of the net before the goalie could react. He scored 45 goals in 1982–83, then followed up with seasons of 54, 71, and a league-leading 68 in 1985–86. For all his goals, Kurri was a valuable defensive player, and he could steal the puck from opponents with remarkable ease. The Gretzky-Kurri tandem was broken up in 1988, but reunited in Los Angeles, where the pair got the Kings into the finals for the first time in their history in 1993. He was elected to the Hall of Fame in 2001.

**CAREER STATS:** 1,251 games played; 601 goals; 797 assists; 1,398 points; 545 penalty minutes.

Montreal's dream of going all the way, New York was going to meet a younger and more rested club in the finals, which for the first time would alternate home and away games in a 2–3–2 format.

Edmonton's only challenge in the postseason was a seven-game series against the Flames, after which they rolled into the finals with a four-game sweep of Minnesota. The Oilers took the first game 1–0 on a Grant Fuhr shutout in Long Island, but Clark Gillies scored three the next game in a 6–1 win for the Isles. The next three games were at the Northlands Coliseum, and the Oilers pounded out two consecutive 7–2 wins before mercifully ending the slaughter with a 5–2 win in the fifth game. A pair of third-period goals by LaFontaine gave the Islanders a bit of life, but Gretzky (35 points in the playoffs), Kurri (28 points), and Messier (26 points, and winner of the Conn Smythe Trophy) were determined to take the Cup on home ice. New York fought gamely but they were overmatched at this point, and their dynasty came to an end. It had been a glorious run for the Islanders, but now it was the era of Gretzky and the Oilers.

*Edmonton captain Wayne Gretzky holds every hockey player's dream, the Stanley Cup, after his Oilers defeated the New York Islanders in five games during the 1984 finals. Gretzky had four goals and three assists in the finals.*

# 1984–85

The Jets fly with Hawerchuk, even Mario can't help the Penguins, and the Oilers make it two in a row

IN the summer of 1984, hockey talk centered around the NHL entry draft. The Pittsburgh Penguins, as everyone expected, took center Mario Lemieux, a 282-point player in his last year with Laval in the QMJHL. For the first time, the draft was televised and Lemieux made headlines by refusing to go down to the Penguins table after his name was announced. It was not a wise public relations move on the player's part, and it made a struggling franchise look even worse. As skilled and talented as Lemieux was, his initial *faux pas* was the beginning of a rough relationship with the media. Lemieux's public image took a beating for many years, but his magnificence would eventually win over hockey fans everywhere, and he would one day lead his team to the promised land, although that was well into the future.

The Montreal Canadiens also made some noise on draft day by bringing out Czech defenseman Petr Svoboda and selecting him fifth overall. The Habs had gone to some lengths to get Svoboda to defect from his homeland, and then had him make a dramatic entrance before the television cameras. Svoboda would not prove to be worth all the effort, but other first-round draft picks that year would have eventful careers, including Kirk Muller, Ed Olczyk, Al Iafrate, Shayne Corson, and Gary Roberts.

The third Canada Cup was played in September 1984, and Team Canada was looking for a chance to avenge the disaster of the previous

---

*Mario Lemieux (#66) made his debut for the Pittsburgh Penguins on October 11, 1984, against the Boston Bruins and scored a goal on his very first shot, beating Pete Peeters. This photo was taken during that game, which the Penguins lost 4–3.*

tourney in 1981. The Canadians were fractious group made up of many New York Islanders and Edmonton Oilers players, under the guidance of coach Glen Sather. The team was very ordinary during the first round of the tournament, finishing fourth, though making the playoff round due to a change in format. But they caught fire in the semi-final game against the Soviet Union. Defenseman Paul Coffey broke up a play during overtime and then charged up the ice to help set up the winning goal by Mike Bossy for Canada. The club then rolled over Sweden in a best-of-three final to take the Canada Cup back, but it was the extra-time winner against the Soviets that conjured up memories of great international hockey games of the past.

### Flying High Again

After a number of good regular seasons followed by early playoff failures, the Philadelphia Flyers decided it was time to bring in new management. Bobby Clarke retired, renamed himself Bob, and was promptly named the team's GM. Clarke had been apprenticing while still a player, so it was not a steep climb to upper management for the Philadelphia icon. In a surprise move, he hired unknown Mike Keenan as his head coach. Keenan had great success with Rochester in the American Hockey League, coaching the team to the championship, and prior to that he had coached at the University of Toronto, who had also won a title under his tutelage. A tough, demanding and at times abrasive coach, Keenan was a perfect fit for a team that had added many new players to its roster. Peter Zezel, Derrick Smith, Murray Craven, Dave Poulin, Rick Tocchet, and the Sutter twins (Rich and Ron) were all young and eager to please their new mentor. The newcomers mixed per-

*Philadelphia forward Brian Propp had a 97-point season (43 goals, 54 assists) in 1984–85, helping the Flyers record a league-best 113 points. It was the second of three straight years that saw Propp record more than 90 points. Propp scored 425 goals and added 579 assists "in 1,016 career games.*

fectly with veterans Mark Howe, Brian Propp, Ilkka Sinisalo, Brad McCrimmon, and Brad Marsh to form a powerful club that racked up a league-high 113 points in the regular season (53–20–7). Under Keenan, the team played an aggressive but highly disciplined style of game that could score (348 goals) and play defense as well (241 goals against). Keenan would go on to coach several teams in the NHL, but his first year in the City of Brotherly Love was his best until he led the New York Rangers to 112 points and the Stanley Cup nine seasons later.

Another of Clarke's interesting moves was his sudden trading of Darryl Sittler to the Detroit Red Wings. Sittler had been told he was going to be named team captain, but on the day the announcement was supposed to be made, he was instead told he was going to Detroit for Craven and Joe Patterson. A stunned Sittler said he would retire instead (he did go to the Red Wings after a few days), but that would not sway Clarke. It was the first of many times that the Flyer manager would show a cruel side in dealing with players — as he often had on the ice.

Anchoring the team was goaltender Pelle Lindbergh, a third-round draft choice in 1979, who was playing in just his third full season. He led the league with 40 wins and posted a 3.02 goals-against average in 65 games during '84–'85, winning the Vezina Trophy and earning a spot on the NHL's First All-Star Team. It looked like the Flyers' goaltending was as good as in the Stanley Cup days, when Bernie Parent was minding the Philadelphia net.

As good as the Flyers were, they had company near the top of the Patrick Division with the Washington Capitals securing 101 points (46–25–9) of their own. The Capitals had spent years quietly acquiring talented players, and the 1984–85 campaign proved they were going in the right direction. The Capitals offense centered around two exciting players in Mike Gartner (50 goals, 102 points) and American-born center Bobby Carpenter (53 goals, 95 points). The strength of

*Flyers goaltender Pelle Lindbergh (#31) won the Vezina Trophy in 1984–85 when he won 40 games and posted a 3.02 goals-against average. The First Team All-Star then won 12 games in the playoffs as the Flyers returned to the finals for the first time since 1980.*

*Washington's Bobby Carpenter (#10) keeps close to Mike Bossy (#22) of the New York Islanders. Carpenter scored 53 goals and 95 points for the Capitals in 1984–85, while Bossy had 58 markers for the Islanders while totaling 117 points.*

the Washington team was a commitment to defense, which was unusual in this era, but forwards like Doug Jarvis, Gaetan Duchesne, Craig Laughlin, Allan Howarth, and Bobby Gould could check the opposition to a standstill and pop in the occasional goal. A stout defense had Washington allowing 240 goals, just three fewer than league-leading Buffalo. Goalies Bob Mason, Pat Riggin, and Al Jensen could not take the Capitals deep in to the playoffs, but at least coach Bryan Murray, assisted by brother Terry, had the team competitive every night.

# BOBBY CARPENTER

As a native of Beverly, Massachusetts, BOBBY CARPENTER was hoping to be drafted by Hartford at the 1981 entry draft. He was all set to go to the Whalers when the Washington Capitals made a deal with Colorado and secured the third pick overall, taking Carpenter. The Caps had their eye on Carpenter since the youngster led his high-school team to the state title, and had watched him excel at the World Junior tournament. The six-foot, 200-pound center considered attending Providence College, but a $620,000 contract over three years convinced Carpenter to give professional hockey a try. He joined the Capitals for the 1981–82 season, scored 32 goals and 67 points as a rookie, and then produced similar totals for the next two seasons. They were good numbers, but much more was expected from the player who had appeared on the cover of *Sports Illustrated* with the tag line "The Can't Miss Kid." Then in 1984–85, Carpenter scored 53 goals and had 95 points in what was considered a breakthrough season. He was the first American player to pass the 50-goal mark, and his offensive flair made him a star attraction. His big year got him a lucrative new contract, but he was never the same player again. Two years later he was moved to the New York Rangers, then to Los Angeles and Boston. He returned to Washington for one season (1992–93) before finding himself in New Jersey, where was skilled enough to reinvent himself as a defensive specialist. He won a Stanley Cup with the Devils and has stayed in the organization in various coaching capacities.

**CAREER STATS:** 1,178 games played; 320 goals; 408 assists; 728 points; 919 penalty minutes.

*One of the few Maple Leafs to have a decent year in 1984–85, John Anderson (#10) scored 32 goals and added 31 assists. Anderson had put together four straight seasons of 30 or more goals, yet the Leafs traded him to Quebec in the summer of 1985.*

## Mario's Magnificent Debut

With so much expected of the rookie superstar, all eyes were on Mario Lemieux when he stepped on the ice against the Bruins in Boston on October 11, 1984. He did not disappoint, with a goal on his very first shot, on his very first shift. He would go on to score 43 goals and 100 points — only the third first-year player to reach that milestone — and take the Calder Trophy. The Penguins were still a wretched hockey team, winning only 24 games and securing a mere 53 points. It would take Pittsburgh six seasons to even make the playoffs, despite having the second-best player in the league. Some of the better Penguins on the '84–'85 squad were Warren Young (who scored 40 goals as Lemieux's left winger), Doug Shedden, Mike Bullard, and John Chabot. Clearly the Penguins had a massive rebuilding job to do but it would take quite a bit of time — and three general managers — to get the team into contention.

The only team worse than the Penguins were the Toronto Maple Leafs, now coached by Dan Maloney. The Leafs finished dead last in the NHL with a ghastly record of 20–52–8, for a grand total of 48 points. The Leafs had only one line of any caliber — Rick Vaive, John Anderson, and Bill Derlago — and their defense was one of the worst in hockey, allowing 358 goals against (Vancouver allowed a league-high 401). The Toronto club had a lot of raw young talent, but it was nowhere close to being competitive at the NHL level. Gary Nylund (a minus 37 on the season), Allan Bester, Ken Wregget, Russ Courtnall, and Iafrate all should have been in the minors, or back in junior, but Leafs general manager Gerry McNamara was determined to become known as one who developed young players, even though he was risking their future in the process. The only good thing for the Maple Leafs was that would be able to select first overall (a year too late to take Lemieux) in the 1985 entry draft, which would be held in Toronto.

In April 1985, the entire hockey world mourned the loss of broadcasting pioneer Foster Hewitt, who died at the age of 82. The obituaries called him most famous person in Canada, and during his career there can be no doubt Hewitt was the most recognizable name in hockey.

The Vancouver Canucks hired junior-hockey coach Bill Laforge to take over the team, but he got off to a horrific start at 4–14–2 and was gone by November 20. General manager Harry Neale was forced to take over as coach once again, realizing that the inexperienced Laforge was in over his head. Laforge was known for having tough hockey teams in junior, but if Neale hoped the coach could transform the Canucks into a similar operation, that notion failed miserably. (Laforge would not get another opportunity in the NHL.) Other coaching casualties during the season included Minnesota's Bill Mahoney, who was replaced by Glen Sonmor, and Orval Tessier in Chicago. The coach of the year in 1983, Tessier was run out of town and replaced by GM Bob Pulford, who was, and still is, forever replacing someone in the Blackhawks organization. Tessier had led the Blackhawks to some playoff success, but he blew up at his team after a bad loss to Edmonton in the '83 postseason, saying he wished he could arrange for the Mayo Clinic to provide heart transplants! He had been living on borrowed time ever since.

Vancouver finished last in the Smythe Division with only 59 points, but the coaching changes gave Minnesota (62 points) and Chicago (83 points) some life and a playoff berth. Rangers general manager Craig Patrick took over from Herb Brooks, and Boston replaced Gerry Cheevers with general manager Harry Sinden taking over, but these moves proved futile.

## Canadian Teams in Contention

Even though the Leafs and Canucks were faring poorly, other Canadian teams were strong contenders in 1984–85. The Montreal Canadiens picked up 94 points (41–27–12) playing an entire season under Jacques Lemaire. The new coach made it clear that firewagon hockey was a thing of the past in Montreal, and Mats Naslund was the team's leading scorer with just 79 points (42 goals, 37 assists). Mario Tremblay had 31

*Guy Lafleur (#10) retired from the Montreal Canadiens after he could not get untracked under new coach Jacques Lemaire early in the 1984–85 season. Lafleur was only 33 at the time, but had just five points in 19 games and was discouraged with his icetime. He scored 518 goals with the Canadiens during his career.*

# DALE HAWERCHUK

When Dale Hawerchuk was playing his first year of organized hockey as a child, he did not score a goal until the final game of the season. It might have been the only time he did not challenge for the league lead in points. Hawerchuk was a highly sought-after young player who hoped to play in Oshawa, Ontario, like his idol Bobby Orr had years earlier. But a scout from the Cornwall Royals of the OHL knew that Hawerchuk was a special talent. He would lead the Royals to consecutive Memorial Cups (a difficult feat to accomplish even once in Canadian junior hockey) and would be the first-overall pick of the Winnipeg Jets in 1981. He was a true franchise player, and quickly established himself with a 103-point season in 1981–82 to win the Calder Trophy. Hundred-point seasons soon became common-place for Hawerchuk while he played in Winnipeg — he passed the century mark five years in a row beginning in 1983–84. Not a big man at five-foot-11 and 190 pounds, Hawerchuk was a durable player — he missed a total of seven games during his nine seasons as a Jet — and was not afraid to put himself into dangerous spots if it meant scoring a goal. His anticipation allowed him to see the play developing well ahead of the opposition, and his leadership skills were recognized when he was made team captain before the 1984–85 season. Putting the C on his jersey seemed to inspire Hawerchuk, and he had 130 points (53 goals, 77 assists) that year. But the Jets could never surround their star with enough talent to take them far in the playoffs, and he eventually asked for a trade from the city where he once seemed firmly settled. He was dealt to Buffalo in 1990, where he played five seasons. He scored his 500th goal with St. Louis in 1996, ensuring himself a place in the Hall of Fame.

**CAREER STATS:** 1,188 games played; 518 goals; 891 assists; 1,409 points; 730 penalty minutes.

goals, but no other Hab had anywhere close to 30 markers. Lost in the conversion was 33-year-old Guy Lafleur, who could no longer see himself playing in a stifling system that emphasized defense. Early in the season, Lafleur decided to retire — the Canadiens would not, indeed *could not* trade him — despite being a top-caliber skater who could still play the game. Teammate Bob Gainey felt it was all mental with Lafleur — the flashy winger had not devoted himself to the game as he once had, and would again in three years. Lafleur was the second great loss to the Canadiens that year — prior to the season, the legendary broadcaster Danny Gallivan also announced his retirement.

The Quebec Nordiques finished only three points behind the Canadiens in the Adams Division, and the Stastny bothers led the team in scoring — Peter had 100 points and Anton supplied another 80. Michel Goulet contributed his usual 55 goals, while Dale Hunter had 72 points. A Nordiques-Canadiens battle was brewing for the postseason and it would be a classic, decided in overtime of the seventh game by a goal from Peter Stastny.

*Winnipeg's Thomas Steen (#25) had a good year in 1984–85 when he scored 30 goals and 84 points. Steen played his entire career in Winnipeg and scored 264 goals and 817 points in 950 games for the Jets between 1981 and 1995.*

The Winnipeg Jets had their best year in franchise history with 96 points (43–27–10), finishing second to Edmonton in the hotly contested Smythe Division. The Jets were led by young superstar Dale Hawerchuk, who was third in league scoring with 130 points (53 goals, 77 assists). Paul MacLean racked up 101 points playing alongside Hawerchuk, while Tomas Steen, Laurie Boschman, and Brian Mullen all had 70 or more. Right behind the Jets were the Calgary Flames, who accumulated 94 points (41–27–12) with Kent Nilsson leading the attack with 37 goals and 62 assists.

The best Canadian club was still the Edmonton Oilers, who had a 109-point season (49–20–11). Wayne Gretzky showed no signs of letting up, with a record 135 assists to go along with 73 goals. His 208-point total was 73 better than his nearest rival, which happened to be teammate Jari Kurri with 71 goals and 64 assists. Gretzky also

*Calgary defenseman Paul Reinhart (#23) was one of the best defensemen in the NHL in 1984–85 when he scored 23 times and had 69 points. Originally a first-round pick of the Atlanta Flames in 1979, Reinhart notched 559 points in 648 games before his career was shortened due to injuries.*

recorded his 1,000th point during the season when picked up an assist on December 19, 1984, in a game against the Los Angeles Kings. The mark came in Gretzky's 424th contest, making him the fastest to achieve the milestone — almost 300 games faster than Lafleur, who held the previous mark of 1,000 points in 720 games. Paul Coffey added 121 points from the blueline, while newly acquired Mike Krushelnyski (picked up in a trade with Boston for Ken Linesman) had 43 goals and 88 points for the streaking Oilers. The team got off to a great start by going 15 games without a loss (12–0–3) to begin the season, and they never looked back. No team could challenge the Oilers in the Campbell Conference playoffs, and they had only to be ready to face the champion of the Wales Conference in the finals.

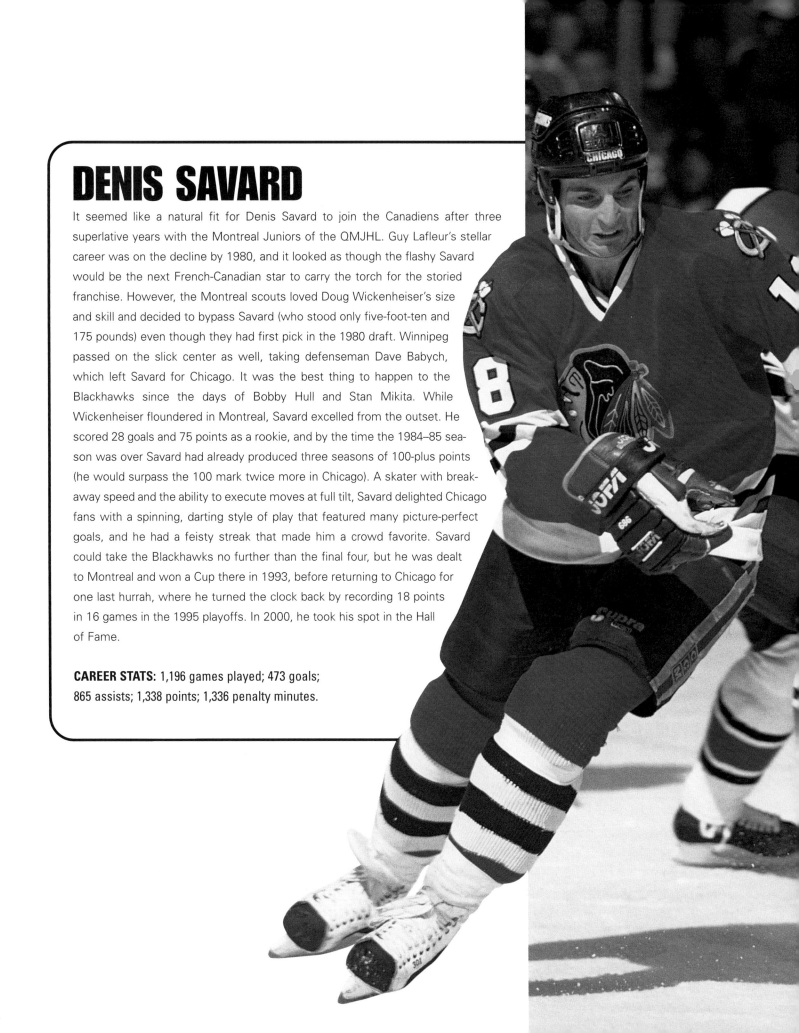

# DENIS SAVARD

It seemed like a natural fit for Denis Savard to join the Canadiens after three superlative years with the Montreal Juniors of the QMJHL. Guy Lafleur's stellar career was on the decline by 1980, and it looked as though the flashy Savard would be the next French-Canadian star to carry the torch for the storied franchise. However, the Montreal scouts loved Doug Wickenheiser's size and skill and decided to bypass Savard (who stood only five-foot-ten and 175 pounds) even though they had first pick in the 1980 draft. Winnipeg passed on the slick center as well, taking defenseman Dave Babych, which left Savard for Chicago. It was the best thing to happen to the Blackhawks since the days of Bobby Hull and Stan Mikita. While Wickenheiser floundered in Montreal, Savard excelled from the outset. He scored 28 goals and 75 points as a rookie, and by the time the 1984–85 season was over Savard had already produced three seasons of 100-plus points (he would surpass the 100 mark twice more in Chicago). A skater with breakaway speed and the ability to execute moves at full tilt, Savard delighted Chicago fans with a spinning, darting style of play that featured many picture-perfect goals, and he had a feisty streak that made him a crowd favorite. Savard could take the Blackhawks no further than the final four, but he was dealt to Montreal and won a Cup there in 1993, before returning to Chicago for one last hurrah, where he turned the clock back by recording 18 points in 16 games in the 1995 playoffs. In 2000, he took his spot in the Hall of Fame.

**CAREER STATS:** 1,196 games played; 473 goals; 865 assists; 1,338 points; 1,336 penalty minutes.

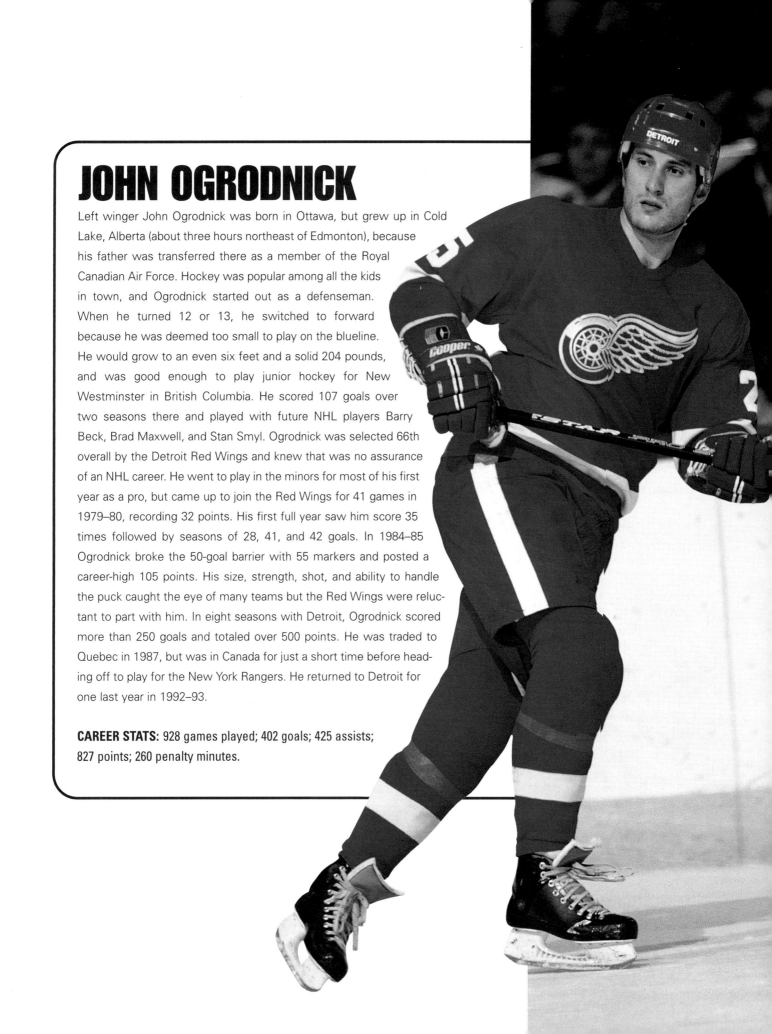

# JOHN OGRODNICK

Left winger John Ogrodnick was born in Ottawa, but grew up in Cold Lake, Alberta (about three hours northeast of Edmonton), because his father was transferred there as a member of the Royal Canadian Air Force. Hockey was popular among all the kids in town, and Ogrodnick started out as a defenseman. When he turned 12 or 13, he switched to forward because he was deemed too small to play on the blueline. He would grow to an even six feet and a solid 204 pounds, and was good enough to play junior hockey for New Westminster in British Columbia. He scored 107 goals over two seasons there and played with future NHL players Barry Beck, Brad Maxwell, and Stan Smyl. Ogrodnick was selected 66th overall by the Detroit Red Wings and knew that was no assurance of an NHL career. He went to play in the minors for most of his first year as a pro, but came up to join the Red Wings for 41 games in 1979–80, recording 32 points. His first full year saw him score 35 times followed by seasons of 28, 41, and 42 goals. In 1984–85 Ogrodnick broke the 50-goal barrier with 55 markers and posted a career-high 105 points. His size, strength, shot, and ability to handle the puck caught the eye of many teams but the Red Wings were reluctant to part with him. In eight seasons with Detroit, Ogrodnick scored more than 250 goals and totaled over 500 points. He was traded to Quebec in 1987, but was in Canada for just a short time before heading off to play for the New York Rangers. He returned to Detroit for one last year in 1992–93.

**CAREER STATS:** 928 games played; 402 goals; 425 assists; 827 points; 260 penalty minutes.

### Highlights and Lowlights

Gretzky was not the only player to record his 1,000th point in the '84–'85 season. The Islanders' Bryan Trottier accomplished the feat on January 29, when New York tied Minnesota 4–4. Trottier's point (a goal) came in his 726th game, giving him the third fastest mark to that point in NHL history. Buffalo coach Scotty Bowman became the NHL's all-time leader in victories on December 19, when the Sabres defeated the Chicago Blackhawks 6–3, marking his 691st win.

Top players Mark Messier (10 games), Brian Propp (four games), and goaltender Billy Smith (six games) were suspended for serious stick infractions or vicious hits. Noted tough guy Paul Holmgren, now with Minnesota, got a 10-game suspension for a stick assault on fellow goon Torrie Robertson of the Hartford Whalers. The sentences handed down by NHL vice-president Brian O'Neill were strong, but seemed to have little effect on deterring the players.

*Tony McKegney began the 1984–85 season with the Quebec Nordiques before he was dealt to the Minnesota North Stars. The Montreal native was selected 32nd over-all in 1978 by Buffalo, where he enjoyed five good seasons with the Sabres, twice scoring more than 35 goals. He had a 24-goal season with the Nordiques in 1983–84 and finished his career with 320 goals and 319 assists.*

# The PLAYOFFS

For one of the few times in recent NHL history, the best two teams over the regular season met for the Stanley Cup. The defending champion Edmonton Oilers and upstart Philadelphia Flyers romped to the final with little opposition. Edmonton easily handled the Los Angeles Kings and the Winnipeg Jets in the first two rounds, and then hammered the Chicago Blackhawks in six games to reach the final. Against Chicago, the Oilers won by scores of 11–2, 7–3, 10–5 and 8–2, and the Blackhawks deserve credit for somehow winning two games. The Flyers easily knocked off the New York Rangers in the first round, then handled the Islanders in five. The Nordiques gave Philadelphia a little harder time (Quebec had knocked off the Habs in seven games during the second round) but the Flyers took the series in six to get back to the finals for the first time since 1980.

As much as fans looked forward to seeing the top two teams com-

*Edmonton's Mike Krushelnyski (#26) battles Philadelphia's Peter Zezel in the face-off circle. Krushelnyski had a great season for the Oilers in 1984–85 with 43 goals and 88 points. In the playoffs he added 13 points in 18 games, winning the first of three Stanley Cups in his career.*

pete, it was really no contest after the first game. The Flyers took the opener at home 4–1, but lost the next game 3–1 to even the series. The next three contests were held in Edmonton, and the Oilers took their second straight Cup with 4–3, 5–3, and 8–3 wins. The last game of the series got nasty at the end, as the Flyers realized their dream of upsetting the champions was about to be shattered. Plenty of roughing, high-sticking, and fighting went on late into the third period. Oilers coach Glen Sather was furious at Keenan, but the Flyers were going to go down scratching and clawing — not a very classy ending to the championship series. Gretzky, with 47 points (still an NHL record), took the Conn Smythe Trophy as the best player in playoffs, but a number of Oilers could have won the award. Coffey had 37, and Kurri, Messier, and Glenn Anderson all had 25 or more playoff points. The Edmonton club simply overwhelmed the opposition and it looked like they would not be stopped for years to come.

# GRANT FUHR

For many years after the implementation of the universal entry draft, teams rarely selected a goaltender in the first round. One exception was Grant Fuhr, who was taken eighth overall by the Edmonton Oilers in 1981, a move that was considered high-risk at the time. But the Oilers knew they needed a quality netminder who would be comfortable on a team geared to speed and attack. With his acrobatic style, quick reflexes, and easygoing manner, Fuhr was perfect for the job of guarding the Oilers net. He did give up a lot of goals, but his trademark was not giving up the backbreaker, the goal that would shift momentum to the other team. A bad goal would not bother him, and he was well aware that his teammates could get him enough goals to win most games. He was often left to defend against odd-man rushes, but he seemed to relish the opportunity to make the big stop at the right moment. In 1983–84 Fuhr won 30 of 45 appearances, although he was not in net the night the Oilers won their first Cup, and followed that up with 26 wins in 1984–85. That year he put in a strong performance in the finals against the Flyers, stopping two penalty shots on the way to the Oilers winning a second Stanley Cup. Fuhr soon locked up his position as the Oilers' number-one goalie, and this would lead to the departure of partner Andy Moog for Boston in 1988. Fuhr was on a total of five Cup-winning teams as an Oiler before he was traded to Toronto in 1991. He also played four strong seasons in St. Louis (including a record 76 consecutive games for the Blues in 1995–96) before announcing his retirement in 2000. He was inducted into the Hall of Fame in 2003.

**CAREER STATS:** 868 games played; 403 wins; 295 losses; 114 ties; 25 shutouts; 3.38 goals-against average.

# 1985–86

Clark, Suter, and Roy lead a bumper crop of rookies, tragedy strikes Philadelphia, and the Cup returns to Montreal

**ONE** of the main features of the 1985–86 season was the excellent crop of rookies that joined the NHL. Two of them stood out, but many newcomers would make their mark before the season and playoffs were over. Calgary Flames defenseman Gary Suter won the Calder Trophy with a 68-point performance, including 50 assists, but Wendel Clark may have made the most impact of any first-year player during the regular season. Drafted first overall by the Maple Leafs in 1985, Clark took the city of Toronto by storm with an abrasive, bashing style that included 34 goals, the most of any rookie. Maple Leaf Gardens came alive every time the left winger took to the ice with his lightning-quick wrist shot and his propensity for dropping the gloves and pounding an opponent. Another Toronto rookie, Steve Thomas, popped in 20 goals and had 57 points in 65 games. As a team, the Leafs were not much better than the previous year, but they did make the playoffs, and then pulled off an upset.

In Calgary, Suter was not the only good rookie on the team. Center Joel Otto scored 25 times and became a physical presence for the rising Flames. Mike Vernon was in his first year as netminder, and his career would have a great impact on the club. Other top rookies in the NHL included Kjell Dahlin of Montreal (71 points, the most points of any first-year player), Per-Erik Eklund of Philadelphia (66 points), Mike Ridley of the Rangers (65 points), Petr Klima of Detroit (32

*For the first time since 1967, two Canadian teams made it to the Stanley Cup finals. The Montreal Canadiens would defeat the Calgary Flames in five games.*

105

goals), and Dean Evason of Hartford (48 points in 55 games). Joining Vernon as newcomers in goal were Darren Jensen of Philadelphia, Jon Casey of Minnesota, Wendel Young of Vancouver, and Patrick Roy of the Canadiens. Roy played in 47 regular season games, posting a 23–18–3 record, but saved his greatest performance for the playoffs.

### Oilers Try to Make it Three

The Edmonton Oilers were the favorites to win their third straight Stanley Cup, and went out and recorded a league-high 56 wins and 119 points, earning them the first President's Trophy, a new award given to the team with the most points during the regular season. (A $100,000 bonus accompanied the trophy, to be spilt among all the players.) Gretzky took the Art Ross Trophy for the sixth consecutive season, setting new records with 215 points and an incredible 163 assists — more than anyone else's point total (Mario Lemieux had 141 points to finish second). Teammate Paul Coffey made history on April 2, when he scored his 46th and 47th goals of the season to establish a new mark for defensemen. He just missed another when his 138 points left him one short of Bobby Orr's record for blueliners. Coffey's best night came on March 14, when he had two goals and six assists in a 12–3 shellacking of the Detroit Red Wings. The eight points equaled the feat of Flyers defenseman Tom Bladon in 1977. Coffey then went on establish a another record for defenders with a point in 28 consecutive games. Jari Kurri (131) and Glenn Anderson (102) both topped the century mark in points, while the newest Edmonton players, Craig MacTavish (23 goals) and Mark Napier (24 goals), added another dimension to the slick-skating, high-powered club (426 goals scored). It appeared the Oilers would be a lock to romp back to the Stanley Cup finals, but their season did not end on a happy note.

The biggest challenge to the Oilers would come from within their own division, as the Flames were ready to mount a serious effort to oust Edmonton from their lofty perch. Years of adding and subtracting players was finally paying off for general manager Cliff Fletcher as Calgary produced an 89-point regular season, including 40 wins. Al MacInnis was an emerging talent on the blueline with 68 points in '85–'86, and was aided greatly by the addition of Suter. The defensive corps

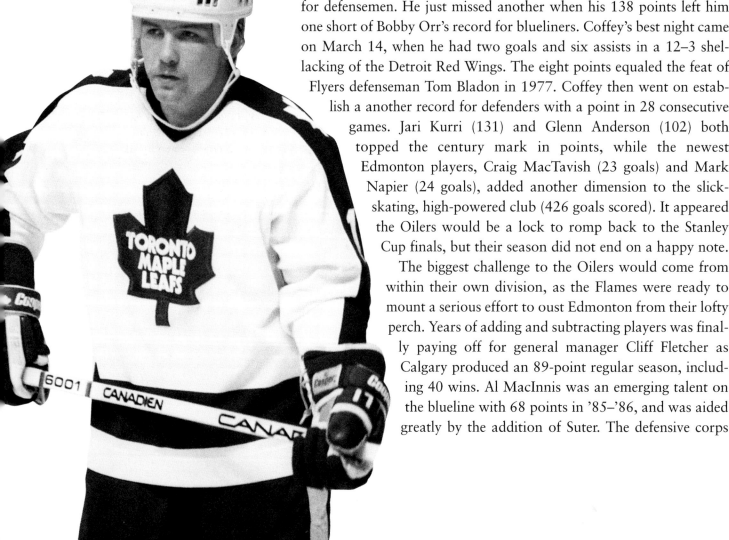

*Toronto rookie Wendel Clark (#17) made quite an impression on the NHL with a 34 goals and 227 penalty minutes.*

also had offensive-minded Paul Reinhart and free agent Jamie Macoun. Up front, the Flames still relied on Hakan Loob (31 goals) and Lanny McDonald, who was not scoring as much now, with only 28 on the year. But others emerged in Dan Quinn (30 goals), Jim Peplinski (24), Carey Wilson (29) and Steve Bozek (21), to give the Flames a powerful 354-goal attack. Fletcher saw a couple of opportunities to add talent, and did not hesitate to acquire Joe Mullen from St. Louis and John Tonelli from the New York Islanders during the regular season. Mullen gave Calgary a legitimate sniper (44 goals) and Tonelli gave them leadership and a winning presence in the dressing room. Fletcher was also not afraid of picking up big contracts — both Mullen and Tonelli had just signed new deals with their previous teams. Nobody in Calgary seemed to mind, especially when the Flames made it to the finals for the first time in their history.

*Edmonton's Glenn Anderson (#9) battles with Mark Howe (#2) of Philadelphia while Mark Messier (#11) looks for a rebound from goalie Bob Froese. Anderson had 54 goals and 102 points in 1985–86, while Froese led all NHL goalies with 31 wins and earned a spot on the Second All-Star Team.*

### Free Spending in Detroit
The Calgary Flames were not the only team willing to spend money to advance in the standings. Owner Mike Ilitch wanted to desperately get the Red Wings back to their former glory, and went after free agents

# MIKE FOLIGNO

Mike Foligno was born in Sudbury, Ontario, but his family moved to Italy when he was two, and he lived there for the next five years. Naturally, he took up soccer during that time, but when his family returned to Canada, his father took him to a junior hockey game and Foligno was hooked on the excitement, the crowd, and the toughness of the game. His family lived near an outdoor rink in Sudbury, and he was able to refine his skills that way. Foligno was lucky enough to play junior hockey in his hometown, with the Wolves of the OHA, and in 1978–79 he scored 65 goals in 68 games and a league-leading 150 points. That led Detroit to select him third overall in 1979, and as a rookie with the Red Wings, Foligno scored 36 goals and 71 points, displaying a quick, hard shot and a strong drive to succeed. The chiseled six-foot-two, 195-pound right winger also had a powerful skating stride and showed a willingness to get tough when required. After a 28-goal season the following year, Scotty Bowman stole Foligno in one of the Buffalo GM's best moves. Detroit got Danny Gare, Jim Schoenfeld, and Derek Smith, all of whom had seen better days, while Foligno would go on to have eight seasons of 20-plus goals for the Sabres. His best year was 1985–86, when he collected a career-high 41 goals and 80 points. He was dealt to Toronto in 1991 and played well for the Maple Leafs when given an opportunity. After a badly broken leg that year, he returned to give the Leafs a spark in their 1993 playoff run, scoring a key overtime goal against his original team, the Red Wings.

**CAREER STATS:** 1,018 games played; 355 goals; 372 assists; 727 points; 2,049 penalty minutes.

with gusto. Detroit signed Warren Young and a group of U.S. college players including Adam Oates, Tim Friday, and Ray Staszak. But from this group only Oates would emerge as a legitimate NHL star, and he would not blossom until he was traded to St. Louis. The team helped Klima to defect from Czechoslovakia, and he would be a good addition when he was focused and ready to play (which was not as often as it should have been during his days in Detroit), and youngsters Adam Graves, Bob Probert, Gerard Gallant, and Joe Kocur gave the Red Wings a mixture of toughness and scoring. None of the moves had any effect, though, and the team finished dead last with just 40 points (17–57–6), prompting changes in the front office after the season was over. Former star defenseman Brad Park was hired as coach during the season, replacing Harry Neale, but even he had no answers. Many were glad to see Detroit flounder after they paid so much to free agents, since they were the first team to try to buy a winner in this controversial manner. The hockey community has always frowned upon simply throwing cash at a problem, but Ilitch realized it was the fastest way to rebuild a team. The Red Wings would just need to spend their money more wisely in the future.

### Flyers Star Goalie Killed

The Philadelphia Flyers were expected to be Stanley Cup contenders, picking up where they finished the season before, when they made a trip to the finals. But that all changed in early November when goaltender Pelle Lindbergh, driving his Porsche, hit a wall and died from his injuries. Flyers general manager Bob Clarke said he had spoken to Lindbergh about driving his car too fast, but acknowledged that young men who think they're indestructible do not heed the advice of people in authority. Many of his shocked teammates said this was the first time they had to deal with the death of someone close to them. But amazingly the Flyers recovered to win 53 games and record 110 points. Brian Propp had 97 points, and Tim Kerr scored 58 goals to power the Flyers attack, while defenseman Mark Howe scored 24 goals. Ilkka Sinsalo scored 39 times, and captain Dave Poulin — an articulate spokesman during the grieving period after Lindbergh's death — scored 27 goals and 69 points to give the team good depth. But the Flyers could not replace Lindbergh in net, although veteran Bob Froese had a good season and was backed up by Darren Jensen and Glenn "Chico" Resch, who was picked up in a late-season deal.

*Twin brothers Rich (#15) and Ron (#14) Sutter check Barry Pederson of the Bruins, with help from teammate Lindsay Carson. The Sutters played together in Philadelphia for the 1985–86 season after the Flyers made a deal with Pittsburgh to acquire Rich in 1983. They combined for 32 goals, 99 points, and 358 penalty minutes in '85–'86.*

Close on the heels of the Flyers in the Patrick Division were the Washington Capitals, who recorded 50 wins and 107 points. The Caps also had a good rookie in defenseman Kevin Hatcher (19 points in 79 games), and now boasted a backline that included Scott Stevens (53 points), Larry Murphy (65 points), and Rod Langway. Despite having four quality defenders, a luxury nobody dreams of in today's hockey, the Capitals were never able to take advantage of their good fortune. It certainly proved that the eighties were all about offense, and that without a star goalie, something the Caps never had, a team could not hope to win in the playoffs.

## Trades and Milestones

The biggest deal of the season saw the Flames get Mullen, Terry Johnson, and Rik Wilson from St. Louis, while the Blues acquired Gino Cavallini, Charlie Bourgeois, and Eddy Beers in return. The trade helped both teams immensely, and they would meet in the conference final, a series that would be decided in seven hard-fought games. Calgary also got tired of Kent Nilsson and sent him to Minnesota for a couple of high draft picks. The Adams Division–leading Quebec Nordiques traded captain Mario Marois to Winnipeg for Robert Picard, but it didn't help at playoff time when they lost to Hartford in the first round. The Jets moved defenseman Dave Babych to the Whalers in a surprising deal that backfired: the Jets got forward Ray Neufeld, who spent just three years

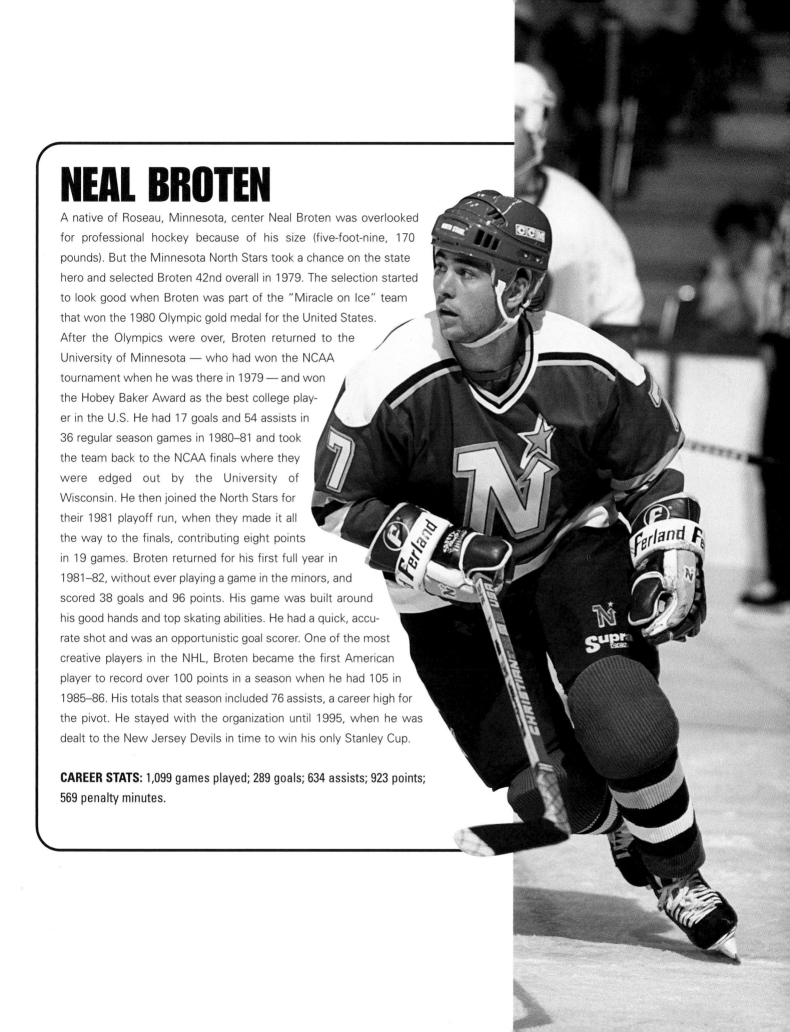

# NEAL BROTEN

A native of Roseau, Minnesota, center Neal Broten was overlooked for professional hockey because of his size (five-foot-nine, 170 pounds). But the Minnesota North Stars took a chance on the state hero and selected Broten 42nd overall in 1979. The selection started to look good when Broten was part of the "Miracle on Ice" team that won the 1980 Olympic gold medal for the United States. After the Olympics were over, Broten returned to the University of Minnesota — who had won the NCAA tournament when he was there in 1979 — and won the Hobey Baker Award as the best college player in the U.S. He had 17 goals and 54 assists in 36 regular season games in 1980–81 and took the team back to the NCAA finals where they were edged out by the University of Wisconsin. He then joined the North Stars for their 1981 playoff run, when they made it all the way to the finals, contributing eight points in 19 games. Broten returned for his first full year in 1981–82, without ever playing a game in the minors, and scored 38 goals and 96 points. His game was built around his good hands and top skating abilities. He had a quick, accurate shot and was an opportunistic goal scorer. One of the most creative players in the NHL, Broten became the first American player to record over 100 points in a season when he had 105 in 1985–86. His totals that season included 76 assists, a career high for the pivot. He stayed with the organization until 1995, when he was dealt to the New Jersey Devils in time to win his only Stanley Cup.

**CAREER STATS:** 1,099 games played; 289 goals; 634 assists; 923 points; 569 penalty minutes.

# MATS NASLUND

Mats Naslund was first noticed as a hockey player when he was just seven years old, when his photo appeared in a local paper in his native Sweden. He played competitive hockey in his hometown of Timra, eventually moving on to the Swedish first division, where he caught the eye of NHL scouts. Ron Caron was scouting for the Montreal Canadiens at the time, and the small left winger (five-foot-seven, 160 pounds) reminded him of former Hab greats like Yvan Cournoyer and Henri Richard. In 1978, Naslund finished tied with Wayne Gretzky for the most points at the World Junior championships. The Canadiens selected him 37th overall the next year, but Naslund played in Sweden for the next three seasons before deciding to try his luck in North America. He joined the Habs for the 1982–83 season and quickly established himself as an offensive force with 26 goals and 71 points. Naslund was motivated to do well in the NHL, because he was concerned about how Swedes would be viewed by the league. While he was not a physical player, he was tough enough to score 29 goals in his second year, and then 42 the next season. In 1985–86 he had a career-high 43 goals and 110 points, and then helped the Habs to their surprise Stanley Cup win with 19 points in 20 playoff games. His biggest goal came in the finals against Calgary, when he scored the go-ahead goal in the third game of the series, which the Habs won 5–3. Over the next four seasons, Naslund scored 25, 24, 33, and 21 goals and helped the Habs back to the finals in 1989. In 1990, he left to play hockey in Europe, and after winning a gold medal with Sweden at the 1994 Olympics, he signed as free agent with Boston. He played his final 34 games in the NHL with the Bruins, but Naslund will always be remembered as the Habs' main offensive weapon during the eighties.

**CAREER STATS:** 651 games played; 251 goals; 383 assists; 634 points; 111 penalty minutes.

in Winnipeg, while Babych went on to play in the NHL until 1999. (Jets GM John Ferguson and coach Barry Long reportedly disagreed on the trade.) The Jets were not a force in the Smythe Division (only 59 points), but the Whalers added John Anderson in a late-season deal, giving them more firepower. Perhaps the most interesting swap of the season was the trading of two goaltenders. The Washington Capitals picked up Pete Peeters from the Boston Bruins in exchange for Pat Riggin. Peeters had a pretty good year for the Capitals (19–11–3), and he stayed in Washington for four seasons with little playoff success, while Riggin was a Bruin for just a couple of years.

Some key veteran players reached milestones in 1985–86. On Long Island, sniper Mike Bossy recorded his 1,000th career point and his ninth straight season of 50 or more goals, finishing with 61. Teammate Denis Potvin passed Bobby Orr to become the NHL's all-time leader for defenseman when he recorded his 916th point, as well as the top-scoring blueliner when he got career goal number 271. Gilbert Perreault scored his 500th career goal with Buffalo — although the Sabres missed the playoffs, despite 80 points — and Marcel Dionne became the NHL's second all-

*Montreal rookie Claude Lemieux (#32) celebrates a goal against Mike Vernon of the Calgary Flames. Lemieux scored just once in 10 regular-season games in '85–'86, but then tallied 10 goals in the playoffs including two over-time winners. Vernon posted a 9–9–3 record during the season, and then won 12 games in the postseason to help his team to the finals.*

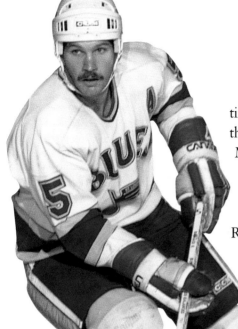

time point leader, passing Phil Esposito. In Chicago, Denis Savard passed the 600-career-point mark and linemate Al Secord scored his 200th goal. Montreal defenseman Larry Robinson recorded his 700th career point and played in his 1,000th game as a Hab.

### Montreal Goes with Youth

Robinson was one of the few veteran Montreal players in 1985–86, as a youth movement was in full swing. Claude Lemieux, Stephane Richer, Chris Chelios, Mike McPhee, Brian Skrudland, John Kordic, and Guy Carbonneau made this an exciting team, but the most intriguing newcomer to the Habs was goaltender Patrick Roy, who came out of nowhere to lead the team into the playoffs. Not much was expected of the team in the postseason after the club had gone 40–33–7. New coach Jean Perron (Jacques Lemaire no longer wanted to coach in Montreal) had some difficulties during the season, but he was confident that Roy was the best goalie in the organization. Making Roy the number-one goalie would prove to be the key move of the year.

*The St. Louis Blues gave two first round draft choices to New Jersey for defenseman Rob Ramage. The first-overall pick of 1979 was a valuable addition to the Blues and he had 66 points in 1985–86. Ramage was the only star on the St. Louis blueline, but the team came within one game of the finals.*

Heading into the playoffs, the St. Louis Blues were slightly above the .500 mark (37–34–9), good for third place in the Norris Division, but not considered much of a threat in the postseason. However, coach Jacques Demers got the absolute most out of forwards Doug Gilmour, Bernie Federko, Greg Paslawski and Mark Hunter, as well a group of virtually unknown defensemen. The Blues had one star on the blueline in Rob Ramage, who had been acquired for two number-one draft choices in 1982, and veteran goalies in Greg Millen and Rick Wamsley, plus some grinding forwards willing to mix it up. They would fight and scratch for all their wins, and it was no different in the playoffs when they would never say die.

# The PLAYOFFS

The 1986 playoffs featured the most surprising upsets in years. It started in the first round when Hartford ousted the Quebec Nordiques in three straight games, while the Flyers were knocked off in five games by the upstart Rangers. The Blueshirts had finished 32 points

# JOHN VANBIESBROUCK

An all-star performer in junior hockey with the Sault Ste. Marie Greyhounds, goaltender John Vanbiesbrouck was selected 72nd overall by the New York Rangers in the 1981 entry draft. He played two more seasons in the Soo before he was sent to Tulsa of the Central Hockey League, where he was named top goalie in 1983–84 with a 20–13–2 record and a 3.46 goals-against average. His minor-league performance got him a promotion and he played in 42 games for the Rangers in 1984–85, winning just 12 while losing 24. But Vanbiesbrouck played well in the 1985 World Championships in Czechoslovakia, and it seemed to renew his confidence. He went 31–21–5 during 1985–86, with three shutouts and a 3.32 goals-against average, good enough to earn him the Vezina Trophy. In the 1986 playoffs, Vanbiesbrouck won eight games and got the Rangers into the third round, where they lost to Montreal. A small goalie at five-foot-eight and 176 pounds, Vanbiesbrouck used the butterfly style and was good at cutting down the angles. He had a terrific glove hand and a knack for playing well in the big games. The Rangers let him go when Mike Richter came along, and he went on to play well for Florida, becoming the 15th goalie to record 300 career victories and getting the Panthers into the 1996 finals in his last great NHL moment. He also played for the Flyers, Islanders, and Devils before his career was over.

**CAREER STATS:** 882 games played; 374 wins; 346 losses; 119 ties; 40 shutouts; 2.98 goals against average.

*Montreal rookie Brian Skrudland (#39) scored nine goals in 66 regular-season games in 1985–86 and added two more in the playoffs. His most important goal came in the second game of the finals, when he scored after just nine seconds of overtime to set an NHL record and give the Habs a 3–2 win over the Calgary Flames.*

behind their division rivals, but the goaltending of John Vanbiesbrouck was the difference in the playoffs. Toronto, under coach Dan Maloney, trailed first-place Chicago by 29 points during the season, but it took the Leafs only three games to wipe out the Blackhawks with 5–3, 6–4, and 7–2 victories. St. Louis edged Minnesota in five games, with Gilmour getting five assists in the 6–5 deciding victory. Edmonton, Montreal, Calgary, and Washington were all favorites who survived the first round.

Hartford and Montreal staged a spirited seven-game battle in the second round. With Mike Liut in goal, the Whalers were just about the equal of the Habs, but a goal by Claude Lemieux gave Montreal a 2–1 overtime win at the Forum, advancing the Habs to the conference final. The Rangers continued their stellar postseason with a six-game series win over the Capitals. The New York club under coach Ted Sator was a mediocre team at best, but they were able to score key goals at the right time and got some great work from veteran Pierre Larouche (17 points in 16 games). The Leafs came close to upsetting the Blues in seven games, but St. Louis pulled out a 2–1 win at home to take the series. The turning point was the fifth game, when the young Leafs jumped out to a 3–0 lead, only to lose 4–3 in overtime.

Where the Whalers and Leafs failed, the Calgary Flames pulled off the upset of the playoffs by edging Edmonton in seven games. The gritty series between the Alberta rivals was ultimately decided by the flukiest of goals. Five minutes into the third period of game seven, with score tied 2–2, rookie defenseman Steve Smith tried to make a pass out of his own end, and the puck bounced off Grant Fuhr's leg into the Edmonton net. It was a crushing moment for Smith, but he would bounce back.

*Montreal netminder Patrick Roy (#33) played his first full season in the NHL in 1985–86, posting a 23–18–3 record. He was outstanding in the playoffs, going 15–5 and taking the Habs past the Calgary Flames to capture the Stanley Cup and the Conn Smythe Trophy.*

# TROY MURRAY

A native of Calgary, center Troy Murray played U.S. college hockey at North Dakota for a coach who stressed defense. Murray learned his lessons well, and he helped the Fighting Sioux win the NCAA tournament in 1982. Playing a two-way game was ideal for the six-foot-one, 195-pound Murray, who was not a hot prospect in his draft year, despite his all-star status in college hockey. The Chicago Blackhawks selected Murray 51st overall in 1980 and he joined the team for the 1982–83 season. He played in only 54 games that year, scoring eight goals and eight assists. Chicago management was not quite sure what they had in Murray, but he kept improving his offensive numbers each season. He scored 15 goals in his second year, and followed that up with 26 in 1984–85. A strong skater, Murray could pressure the opposition into mistakes, and then capitalize in the offensive zone. He also took pride in his defensive play, oftening going up against the opposing team's best center. In the 1985 playoffs, Murray was credited with stopping Wayne Gretzky long enough to give the Blackhawks a chance to win two games from the mighty Oilers (Murray also had 19 points in 15 playoff games). His best season came in 1985–86, when he scored a career-best 45 goals and 99 points while winning the Selke Trophy as best defensive forward. Although he played many more seasons, Murray was never as good as he was that year, though he did win a Stanley Cup with the Colorado Avalanche in 1996.

**CAREER STATS:** 915 games played; 230 goals; 354 assists; 584 points; 875 penalty minutes.

*Montreal captain Bob Gainey (#23) accepts the Stanley Cup, the fifth time he won the coveted trophy in his career. Gainey scored 20 times during the 1985–86 season and added five goals and ten points in the playoffs.*

Montreal met the Rangers in the next round, and after taking the first two games at home, the Habs needed the superlative work of Roy to survive 4–3 in overtime. In the extra session, Roy robbed the Rangers time and again — it may be one of the best goaltending performances in overtime history. Lemieux came through with the winner once again, and Montreal went on to take the series in five games. The Flames, meanwhile, eked past the pesky St. Louis team in seven games with a 2–1 victory on home ice. The Blues had looked all but done in the sixth game, but they staged a furious rally in the third period to send the game to overtime and won 6–5 on a goal by Doug Wickenheiser. They ran out of miracles in the last game, but they had tired out Calgary for the finals.

The Flames won the first game of the finals 5–2, but the resilient Habs won game two 3–2 in overtime, on a goal by Brian Skrudland just nine seconds into the extra session. That goal seemed to crush the Flames and rejuvenate the Canadiens, who took the next two games at home, 5–3 and 1–0. The final game was played in Calgary and it took a great save by Roy on Flames defenseman Jamie Macoun to preserve a 4–3 Montreal win for their 23rd championship. Just like Ken Dryden had done for the Habs in 1971, Roy had risen from the ranks of the unknown to capture the Stanley Cup and the Conn Smythe Trophy in his first playoff appearance.

# 1986–87

The Red Wings make a turnaround, Hextall shines between the pipes, and the Oilers redeem themselves with another championship

THE 1986–87 season was loaded with change and redemption. Changes started early in the off-season when the Detroit Red Wings lured coach Jacques Demers away from the St. Louis Blues, who thought they had their man under wraps. The Blues argued Demers had a binding verbal contract, while the Red Wings saw the lack of a formally registered deal on file with the NHL as a chance to approach Demers with a $1.1 million offer over five years. Demers jumped at the new opportunity, and even though the Blues strenuously objected (they later received some compensation), he was behind the Detroit bench to start the new season. With the selection of Joe Murphy as the first pick overall at the entry draft, the Red Wings thought they had made two key moves to secure their future.

Jacques Martin was named as Demers' replacement in St. Louis, and Dan Maloney jumped to the Winnipeg Jets when the Maple Leafs refused to give him the contract he wanted. John Brophy was named as Maloney's successor in Toronto, and while the long-time minor league player was an interesting and colorful choice, the Leafs would barely scrape into the playoffs. In New York, Terry Simpson took over as coach of the Islanders, replacing the legendary Al Arbour, who was moved into the front office.

The New York Rangers made another key management move by hiring Phil Esposito right out the broadcast booth to become their GM. As

*Philadelphia's Mark Howe (#2) tries to cover Wayne Gretzky (#99) during the 1987 Stanley Cup finals. The series pitted the two best teams during the regular season and it went the full seven games before the Oilers took their third championship.*

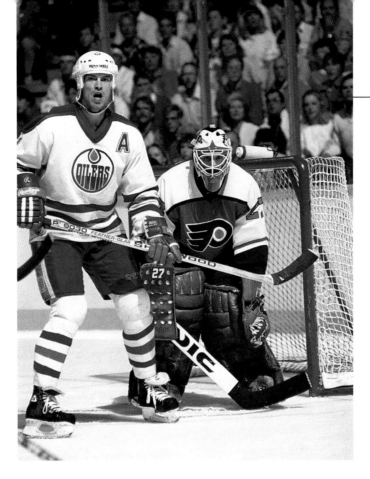

*Edmonton's Mark Messier (#11) takes up position in front of Philadelphia netminder Ron Hextall (#27). Messier recorded 107 points (37 goals, 70 assists) during the 1986–87 season to finish fourth in the scoring race. Hextall led all goalies with 37 victories and a .902 save percentage.*

the eighth general manager in the team's 60-year history, Esposito promised to be more aggressive than his predecessor, Craig Patrick. It would be the beginning of tumultuous times for the Rangers, as bodies started coming and going at an alarming rate. There appeared to be no plan in place, except that change was going to be a constant during the Esposito era, which lasted until 1989. But all the moves — most of which were downright confusing — were of no consequence to Ranger fortunes in the standings or in the playoffs.

Bruce McNall was now part owner of the Los Angeles Kings, with his purchase of up to 25 percent of the team (the Kings were valued between $10 and $15 million at the time). McNall came on board just as the NHL had signed a new collective agreement with the players for the next five years. Both sides were supposedly happy with the new deal, which included a lump-sum payment of $250,000 at the age of 55 for any player who appeared in at least 400 NHL games. As well, compensation for the signing of free agents was restricted to draft choices and not active players, and 18-year-olds could only be selected in the first three rounds of the entry draft.

### Oilers and Flyers Look to Rebound

The Edmonton Oilers and the Philadelphia Flyers were both looking for redemption during the 1986–87 season. Edmonton was still shocked over the turn of events in the previous year's playoffs, and came out determined to regain the Stanley Cup. They won a league-high 50 games to take the President's Trophy with 106 points. Once again Wayne Gretzky led the way with 183 points (62 goals, 121 assists) to win another Art Ross Trophy. Linemate Jari Kurri finished second in the scoring race with 108 points, while teammate Mark Messier had 107. Finland native Esa Tikkanen was now a regular contributor to the Oilers with 34 goals, and the team added Kent Nilsson from Minnesota for the stretch drive. With Messier making sure Nilsson knew what was expected of him, the slick Swede would make a solid contribution in the playoffs. The Oilers also got a break when

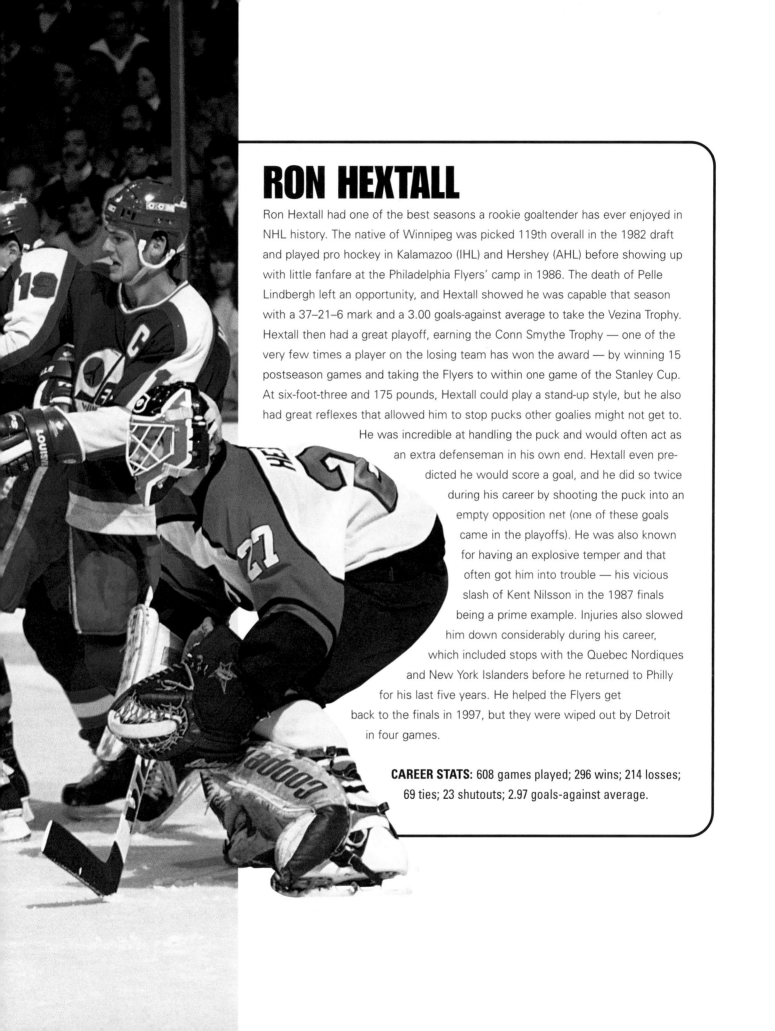

# RON HEXTALL

Ron Hextall had one of the best seasons a rookie goaltender has ever enjoyed in NHL history. The native of Winnipeg was picked 119th overall in the 1982 draft and played pro hockey in Kalamazoo (IHL) and Hershey (AHL) before showing up with little fanfare at the Philadelphia Flyers' camp in 1986. The death of Pelle Lindbergh left an opportunity, and Hextall showed he was capable that season with a 37–21–6 mark and a 3.00 goals-against average to take the Vezina Trophy. Hextall then had a great playoff, earning the Conn Smythe Trophy — one of the very few times a player on the losing team has won the award — by winning 15 postseason games and taking the Flyers to within one game of the Stanley Cup. At six-foot-three and 175 pounds, Hextall could play a stand-up style, but he also had great reflexes that allowed him to stop pucks other goalies might not get to. He was incredible at handling the puck and would often act as an extra defenseman in his own end. Hextall even predicted he would score a goal, and he did so twice during his career by shooting the puck into an empty opposition net (one of these goals came in the playoffs). He was also known for having an explosive temper and that often got him into trouble — his vicious slash of Kent Nilsson in the 1987 finals being a prime example. Injuries also slowed him down considerably during his career, which included stops with the Quebec Nordiques and New York Islanders before he returned to Philly for his last five years. He helped the Flyers get back to the finals in 1997, but they were wiped out by Detroit in four games.

**CAREER STATS:** 608 games played; 296 wins; 214 losses; 69 ties; 23 shutouts; 2.97 goals-against average.

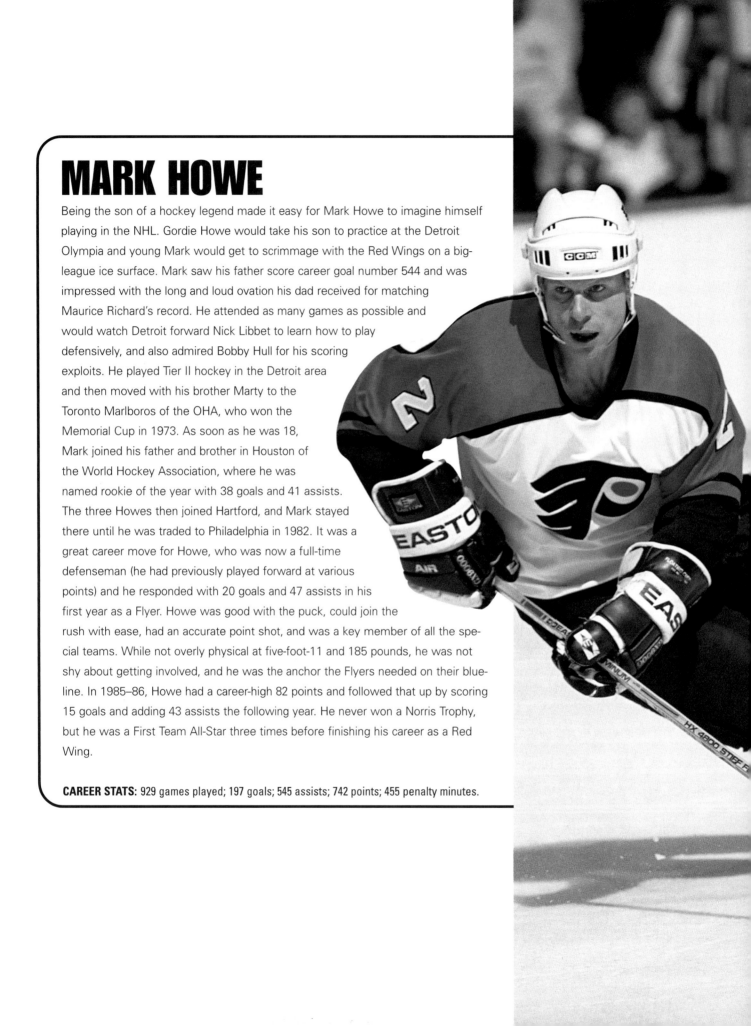

# MARK HOWE

Being the son of a hockey legend made it easy for Mark Howe to imagine himself playing in the NHL. Gordie Howe would take his son to practice at the Detroit Olympia and young Mark would get to scrimmage with the Red Wings on a big-league ice surface. Mark saw his father score career goal number 544 and was impressed with the long and loud ovation his dad received for matching Maurice Richard's record. He attended as many games as possible and would watch Detroit forward Nick Libbet to learn how to play defensively, and also admired Bobby Hull for his scoring exploits. He played Tier II hockey in the Detroit area and then moved with his brother Marty to the Toronto Marlboros of the OHA, who won the Memorial Cup in 1973. As soon as he was 18, Mark joined his father and brother in Houston of the World Hockey Association, where he was named rookie of the year with 38 goals and 41 assists. The three Howes then joined Hartford, and Mark stayed there until he was traded to Philadelphia in 1982. It was a great career move for Howe, who was now a full-time defenseman (he had previously played forward at various points) and he responded with 20 goals and 47 assists in his first year as a Flyer. Howe was good with the puck, could join the rush with ease, had an accurate point shot, and was a key member of all the special teams. While not overly physical at five-foot-11 and 185 pounds, he was not shy about getting involved, and he was the anchor the Flyers needed on their blue-line. In 1985–86, Howe had a career-high 82 points and followed that up by scoring 15 goals and adding 43 assists the following year. He never won a Norris Trophy, but he was a First Team All-Star three times before finishing his career as a Red Wing.

**CAREER STATS:** 929 games played; 197 goals; 545 assists; 742 points; 455 penalty minutes.

defenseman Randy Gregg returned to play after indicating he was going to pursue a career in medicine. Edmonton was now better able to play defense with maturing blueliners like Kevin Lowe, Craig Muni, Charley Huddy, and Steve Smith, and they allowed only 284 goals during the season. Paul Coffey recorded 67 points in 59 games to give Edmonton some offence from the backline, but his days in Edmonton were numbered as he fought with management about a new contract.

Philadelphia overcame the loss of Pelle Lindbergh in net by installing Ron Hextall as the their new number-one goalie. A virtual unknown, Hextall took the league by storm and wound up winning 37 games while taking the rookie-of-the-year award and the Vezina Trophy. The Flyers rode Hextall's hot goaltending to a 100-point season (46–26–8), and their young players showed they had gained valuable experience over the last two seasons. Tim Kerr was superb up front with 58 goals

*Oilers defenseman Kevin Lowe (#4) takes out Walt Poddubny of the Rangers at the Edmonton net. Lowe scored eight goals and added 29 assists in 1986–87 and was a blueline stalwart as the Oilers reclaimed the Stanley Cup. Poddubny scored 40 goals for New York after he was acquired from Toronto in a deal for Mike Allison.*

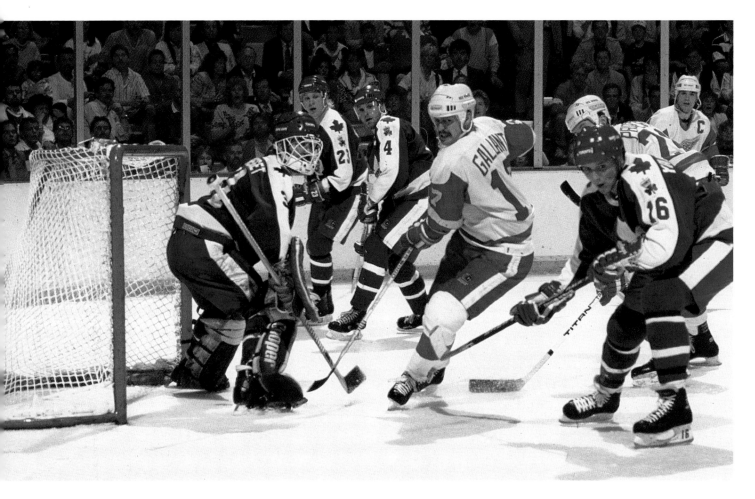

*The Detroit Red Wings drafted left winger Gerard Gallant 107th overall in 1981 and he scored 38 goals in 1986–87. An abrasive player who could also score, Gallant had four straight seasons of 30 or more goals for Detroit.*

and 95 points, while Peter Zezel (33 goals), Brian Propp (31 goals), Dave Poulin (25 goals), and Mark Howe (43 assists) provided more offense. Only the Montreal Canadiens (241) allowed fewer goals than the Flyers (245) during the regular season.

## Hot Wings

If the Oilers and Flyers were on their way back to the top, the Red Wings were just hoping to get out of the cellar, but they were able to do much more than anyone expected. Under the guidance of Demers, the Wings won 34 games and recorded 78 points, good for second place — albeit in a weak Norris Division, where .500 was considered a big year. Demers quickly realized the only significant offense was going to come from Steve Yzerman, so he played the young center as much as possible and got a 90-point season, including 59 assists, from his newly named captain. Gerard Gallant was a pleasant surprise for Detroit when he netted 38 goals, while

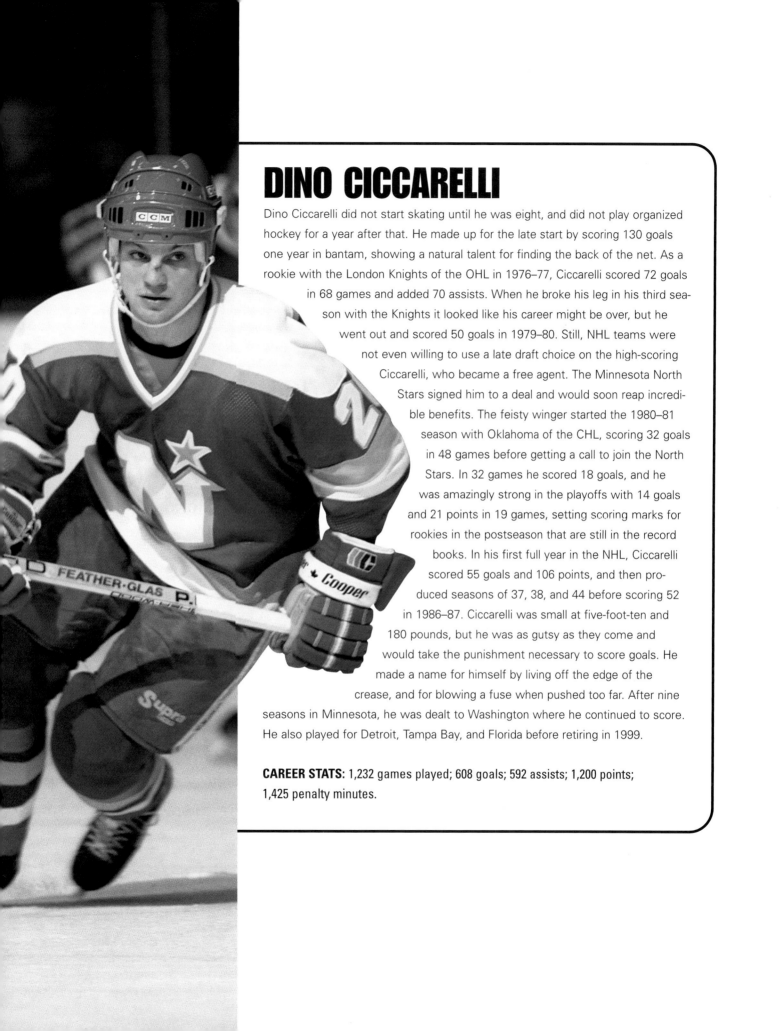

# DINO CICCARELLI

Dino Ciccarelli did not start skating until he was eight, and did not play organized hockey for a year after that. He made up for the late start by scoring 130 goals one year in bantam, showing a natural talent for finding the back of the net. As a rookie with the London Knights of the OHL in 1976–77, Ciccarelli scored 72 goals in 68 games and added 70 assists. When he broke his leg in his third season with the Knights it looked like his career might be over, but he went out and scored 50 goals in 1979–80. Still, NHL teams were not even willing to use a late draft choice on the high-scoring Ciccarelli, who became a free agent. The Minnesota North Stars signed him to a deal and would soon reap incredible benefits. The feisty winger started the 1980–81 season with Oklahoma of the CHL, scoring 32 goals in 48 games before getting a call to join the North Stars. In 32 games he scored 18 goals, and he was amazingly strong in the playoffs with 14 goals and 21 points in 19 games, setting scoring marks for rookies in the postseason that are still in the record books. In his first full year in the NHL, Ciccarelli scored 55 goals and 106 points, and then produced seasons of 37, 38, and 44 before scoring 52 in 1986–87. Ciccarelli was small at five-foot-ten and 180 pounds, but he was as gutsy as they come and would take the punishment necessary to score goals. He made a name for himself by living off the edge of the crease, and for blowing a fuse when pushed too far. After nine seasons in Minnesota, he was dealt to Washington where he continued to score. He also played for Detroit, Tampa Bay, and Florida before retiring in 1999.

**CAREER STATS:** 1,232 games played; 608 goals; 592 assists; 1,200 points; 1,425 penalty minutes.

*Doug Jarvis (#27) began his NHL career with Montreal in 1975 and also played for Washington before joining the Hartford Whalers in 1985. In 1986–87 he set the record for most consecutive games played when he suited up for his 915th straight contest. He would finish his career with 964 games played.*

Petr Klima had 30 markers in his second season. Youngsters Adam Graves (15 goals) and Shawn Burr (22 goals) also made significant contributions to the attack, but Demers stressed the use of good veterans on defense just as he had in St. Louis. Unheralded blueliners like Lee Norwood, Harold Snepsts, Gilbert Delorme, Dave Lewis, and Mike O'Connell all found new life, and they reduced the team's goals against by 141 over the previous season. The Wings also had plenty of toughness with Dave Barr and Tim Higgins willing to work the corners, while Bob Probert and Joey Kocur were more than capable when it came to fisticuffs. Some of the best battles the Red Wings had came against the Maple Leafs, which saw the rival coaches sniping at each other as a prelude to the confrontation on the ice. A playoff meeting between the two would prove to be one of the best in the eighties.

Montreal's surprise Cup win the previous spring led to high expectation in the hockey-mad city, and the team produced a 41–29–10 record for 92 points, just one behind first-place Hartford. The Habs strong defense was the key to their team, which scored just 277 goals with only Mats Naslund (a team-high 80 points) and Bobby Smith (75 points) providing anything resembling a consistent attack. Brian

Hayward and Patrick Roy provided solid goaltending, but Montreal's offensive players did not give the team the firepower it needed to have a real chance of holding on to the Stanley Cup. Claude Lemieux (27 goals), Guy Carbonneau (18 goals), and Stephane Richer (20 goals) were still trying to find consistency in their game. Hartford was able to turn the confidence gained in its '86 playoff performance into a 43-win, 93-point season to finish on top of the Adams Division. Led by Ron Francis (93 points) and Kevin Dineen (79 points), the Whalers had eight players score 20 or more goals, including 23 from Sylvain Turgeon, the second overall pick in 1983, who had a career-best 45 the year before. The Hartford club was speedy and aggressive enough to cause trouble for most teams, but had only two good defenders in Dave Babych and Joel Quenneville, while others like Dana Murzyn and Ulf Samuelsson were still too green to be significant at this point.

**Penguins, Sabres, and Nordiques Flounder**
The Pittsburgh Penguins won their first seven games of the season, but would only have 30 wins by the end of the year. Their 72 points left them four out of a playoff spot. Mario Lemieux had a knee injury that reduced his playing time to 63 games, but he still managed a remarkable 54 goals and 53 assists, good for third place in the scoring race. The Penguins were trying to build a team around Lemieux, and it was proving to be a slow process, although second-year player Craig Simpson showed promise with 26 goals. In Buffalo, Scotty Bowman was dismissed as coach and general manager and replaced by Gerry Meehan when the club looked bad in the early going. Ted Sator, fired by the New York Rangers, was brought in to coach the team in December, but the Sabres still finished with only 64 points, tied with New Jersey for the worst mark in the NHL. It would be the only time in Bowman's illustrious career that he was ever fired. The Devils were accumulating many young players with high draft choices, but these prospects were not yet ready to win at the NHL level. However, Kirk Muller, John MacLean, and Pat Verbeek would form a solid nucleus of forwards to be reckoned with in the near future, and Bruce Driver and Ken Daneyko were promising defensemen. The Quebec Nordiques had one of their worst regular seasons in the eighties when they posted a 31–39–10 record, which gained them the final playoff spot in the Adams Division only because the Sabres were so bad. Michel Goulet was still outstanding, with 49 goals and 96 points, but

Peter Stastny was down to 77 points during the season, a low number for him. Vancouver (66 points) and Minnesota (70 points) also missed the playoffs, although the North Stars were actually tied with the Maple Leafs in points, but won two fewer games.

## High Numbers and Good Rookies

Marcel Dionne recorded his 1,600th career point with the Los Angeles Kings on October 9 in a 4–3 win over the St. Louis Blues. He was just the second player in NHL history to achieve the milestone, but that did not stop the Kings from dealing him to the New York Rangers five months later. New York sent Bobby Carpenter, recently acquired from the Washington Capitals, and Tom Laidlaw to the Kings in return for Dionne, the team's first and only superstar to that point in their history. It is interesting to note that the Rangers had sent three players to the Capitals to land Carpenter, including Kelly Miller and Mike Ridley, in the hopes of getting a young star to build around, but then suddenly switched to an aging veteran to lead them.

*Not much was expected of Luc Robitaille considering he was drafted 171st overall in 1984 by Los Angeles, but he surprised everyone with 45 goals and 84 points as a rookie in 1986–87.*

Doug Jarvis of the Hartford Whalers set the new iron-man record by appearing in his 915th consecutive game on December 26, breaking the mark held by Garry Unger. (Ironically, it would be Jarvis's last full season in the NHL, and he would not reach 1,000 career contests.) Denis Potvin of the New York Islanders became the NHL's all-time leader in assists by defensemen with his 684th helper on October 16 in a 7–4 win over the Washington Capitals. Late in the season, Potvin became the first defenseman to record 1,000 points. No season would be complete without a couple of significant achievements by Gretzky, and he came through with his 500th goal and his 1,500th point.

Good rookies were the order of the day in 1986–87, led by Luc Robitaille and Jimmy Carson of the Los Angeles Kings. Robitaille scored 45 times while Carson counted 37 goals and the dynamic duo was looked upon as the future of the Kings. Robitaille was hardly projected to be a star— he was selected 171st overall in 1984 — but he quickly showed that his Quebec junior league scoring was no fluke. Steve Duchesne was another good rookie for the Kings, scoring 13 goals

and 38 points on defense. Another former Quebec junior star was Vincent Damphousse, selected sixth overall in 1986, and he scored 21 goals for the Maple Leafs, while defenseman Brian Benning had 49 points for the Blues. Christian Ruutu was one of the few bright lights in the Sabres dismal season when he scored 22 goals in his first year.

## Parity Arrives

The huge discrepancies in talent, always noticeable since the NHL's great expansion of 1967, were becoming much less prevalent, and for the first time in many years, a number of teams emerged as potential contenders for the Stanley Cup. Only three of the 21 teams in the league finished with less than 70 points, while only two finished with 100 or more. None of the clubs in the Norris Division could even hit the break-even point, but the five teams had many entertaining and rough battles throughout the year. The NHL was becoming more defensive (no team came close to scoring 400 goals this season) and better goaltending was one of the main reasons for the decline in scoring, although this was nowhere near the problem it became in the late nineties and beyond. As the talent gap closed, games got more intense, and there was a fair amount of brawling in the NHL during 1986–87. Montreal and Vancouver had a bench-clearing fight on November 2, while the Flyers were back to their old ways by battling with the Islanders and the Devils. The hostility within divisions would carry over and make for some very testy series in the playoffs.

*Just when it looked like the Maple Leafs were on their way up, Toronto won only 32 games in 1986–87 and made the playoffs on the last weekend on the season. Rugged Wendel Clark (#17) was a bright light with his team-leading 37 goals and 271 penalty minutes.*

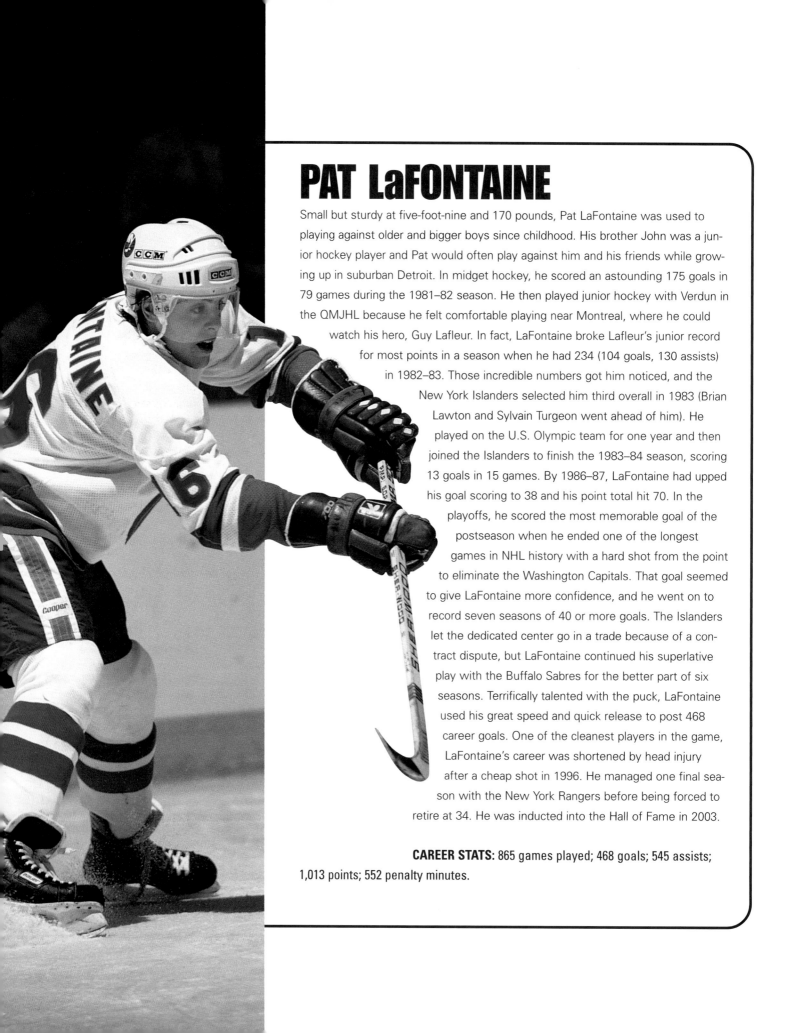

# PAT LaFONTAINE

Small but sturdy at five-foot-nine and 170 pounds, Pat LaFontaine was used to playing against older and bigger boys since childhood. His brother John was a junior hockey player and Pat would often play against him and his friends while growing up in suburban Detroit. In midget hockey, he scored an astounding 175 goals in 79 games during the 1981–82 season. He then played junior hockey with Verdun in the QMJHL because he felt comfortable playing near Montreal, where he could watch his hero, Guy Lafleur. In fact, LaFontaine broke Lafleur's junior record for most points in a season when he had 234 (104 goals, 130 assists) in 1982–83. Those incredible numbers got him noticed, and the New York Islanders selected him third overall in 1983 (Brian Lawton and Sylvain Turgeon went ahead of him). He played on the U.S. Olympic team for one year and then joined the Islanders to finish the 1983–84 season, scoring 13 goals in 15 games. By 1986–87, LaFontaine had upped his goal scoring to 38 and his point total hit 70. In the playoffs, he scored the most memorable goal of the postseason when he ended one of the longest games in NHL history with a hard shot from the point to eliminate the Washington Capitals. That goal seemed to give LaFontaine more confidence, and he went on to record seven seasons of 40 or more goals. The Islanders let the dedicated center go in a trade because of a contract dispute, but LaFontaine continued his superlative play with the Buffalo Sabres for the better part of six seasons. Terrifically talented with the puck, LaFontaine used his great speed and quick release to post 468 career goals. One of the cleanest players in the game, LaFontaine's career was shortened by head injury after a cheap shot in 1996. He managed one final season with the New York Rangers before being forced to retire at 34. He was inducted into the Hall of Fame in 2003.

**CAREER STATS:** 865 games played; 468 goals; 545 assists; 1,013 points; 552 penalty minutes.

Flyers goaltender Ron Hextall chops down Edmonton forward Kent Nilsson with a vicious slash. Hextall won the Conn Smythe Trophy for his stellar performance in the finals, but this was not a shining moment. Nilsson had 19 points in 21 playoff games for Edmonton.

# The PLAYOFFS

The first round of the playoffs produced its usual share of upsets, starting with the Maple Leafs taking out the favored St. Louis Blues in six games. The Leafs got great goaltending from Ken Wregget and an overtime winner from defenseman Rick Lanz to steal the series. Toronto center Dan Daoust did a marvelous job of checking Doug Gilmour (a 105-point man in the season), causing the Blues pivot to explode with rage as the series came to a close. The Quebec Nordiques turned the tables on the Hartford Whalers and pulled off a six-game upset of their own, and Winnipeg managed another when they beat Calgary in six games, ending the Flames hopes of getting back to the finals. The best conclusion to a first-round series came when the New York Islanders won the seventh game against the Washington Capitals in the fourth overtime period. After a rather dull regulation time that ended 2–2, the two teams put on a great show for 68 minutes and 47 seconds before Pat LaFontaine scored the winner for the Isles. Goalies Kelly Hrudey (New York) and Bob Mason (Washington) were both remarkable in the extra session. Detroit, Montreal, Edmonton, and Philadelphia also advanced rather easily to the next round.

The second round saw three of four series go the distance. Toronto

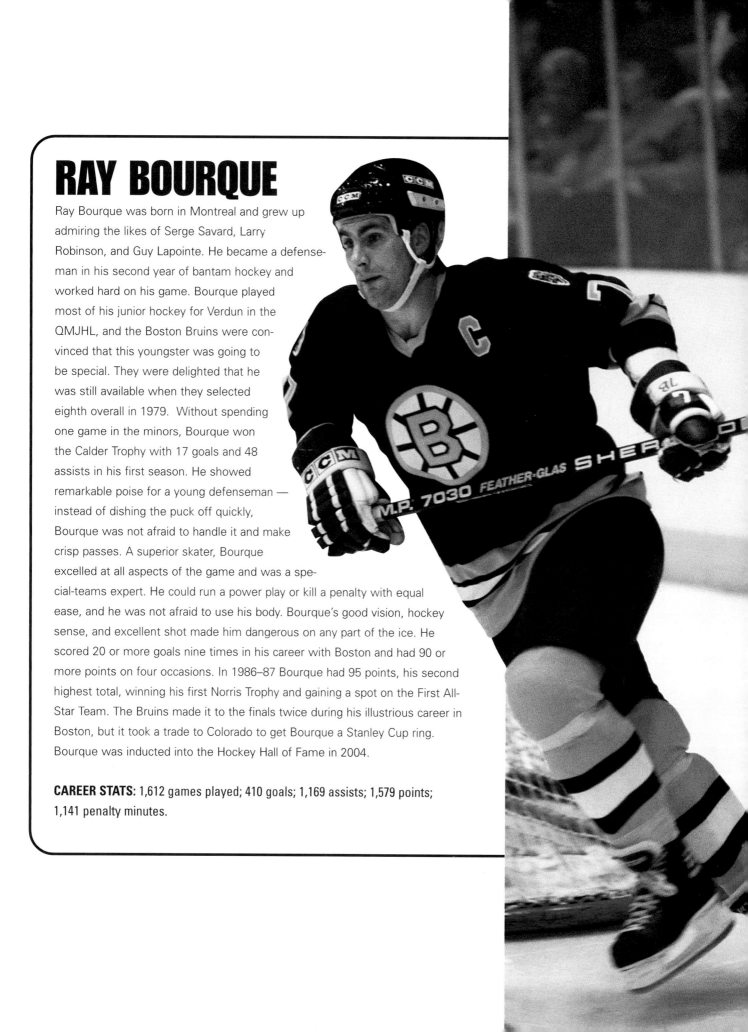

# RAY BOURQUE

Ray Bourque was born in Montreal and grew up admiring the likes of Serge Savard, Larry Robinson, and Guy Lapointe. He became a defenseman in his second year of bantam hockey and worked hard on his game. Bourque played most of his junior hockey for Verdun in the QMJHL, and the Boston Bruins were convinced that this youngster was going to be special. They were delighted that he was still available when they selected eighth overall in 1979. Without spending one game in the minors, Bourque won the Calder Trophy with 17 goals and 48 assists in his first season. He showed remarkable poise for a young defenseman — instead of dishing the puck off quickly, Bourque was not afraid to handle it and make crisp passes. A superior skater, Bourque excelled at all aspects of the game and was a special-teams expert. He could run a power play or kill a penalty with equal ease, and he was not afraid to use his body. Bourque's good vision, hockey sense, and excellent shot made him dangerous on any part of the ice. He scored 20 or more goals nine times in his career with Boston and had 90 or more points on four occasions. In 1986–87 Bourque had 95 points, his second highest total, winning his first Norris Trophy and gaining a spot on the First All-Star Team. The Bruins made it to the finals twice during his illustrious career in Boston, but it took a trade to Colorado to get Bourque a Stanley Cup ring. Bourque was inducted into the Hockey Hall of Fame in 2004.

**CAREER STATS:** 1,612 games played; 410 goals; 1,169 assists; 1,579 points; 1,141 penalty minutes.

built a 3–1 lead in games, but allowed Detroit to win the very physical series with a convincing 3–0 victory on home ice during the seventh game. The Canadiens and Nordiques staged another round of the Battle of Quebec, with Montreal winning the seventh game in the Forum by a 5–3 count. The Islanders fought hard to get back into their series with the Flyers, but Philadelphia wrapped it up with a 5–1 win at home. The Oilers, meanwhile, made short work of the Winnipeg Jets, wiping them out in four straight.

Montreal lost to the Flyers in a six-game semi-final to end their brief reign as champs. The last game featured a fight during the pregame warm-ups, started by Claude Lemieux of the Canadiens and Ed Hospodar of the Flyers. Players on both teams came charging out of their dressing rooms to join the battle, which was later shown on television before the game. The brawl was a black mark for hockey, and it did nothing to fire up the

*Edmonton defenseman Steve Smith holds the Stanley Cup aloft after the Oilers regained the coveted trophy after the 1987 playoffs. It was a sweet moment for Smith, who was blamed for the Oilers' loss in the 1986 playoffs to Calgary.*

Canadiens, who were defeated 4–3 on home ice to end the series. Detroit surprised the Oilers in the first game with a 3–1 victory, but that would be the only win for the Red Wings in the semi-final, as Edmonton won it in five.

Edmonton jumped out to a 3–1 series lead in the finals, but the Flyers would not quit. They won the fifth game in Edmonton to deny the Oilers a home-ice celebration, and then won the sixth game at home 3–2 to force a seventh game back in Edmonton. Propp scored an early goal for the Flyers, but the Oilers persisted and scored the next three to take the game 3–1. The Flyers had played in a record 26 postseason games, but fell just short of their target. When Gretzky took the Cup, the first teammate he passed it to was Steve Smith, considered the playoff goat just one year before. It was Smith who had the ultimate redemption in the 1986–87 season as he held the shiny Cup over his head in triumph.

# 1987-88

*Lemieux unseats Gretzky as scoring champ, the Flames are smoking in the Smythe, but Stanley stays in Edmonton*

**ANOTHER** Canada Cup tournament preceded the 1987–88 NHL season, and it was one of the best international hockey gatherings ever held. It marked the first time Wayne Gretzky and Mario Lemieux played together, and old rivals Canada and the Soviet Union met in the best-of-three final, each game ending up 6–5. In the deciding match, after Canada rallied back from a 3–0 deficit, Gretzky fed a perfect pass to Lemieux for the winning goal with less than a minute and a half left. It was a coming of age for the Penguins star, who learned what it took to win from watching and playing with the great Gretzky. Lemieux's natural talents were unquestioned, but his desire to excel was something everyone seemed to have reservations about until the '87 Canada Cup. Lemieux had 18 points in the tournament, second to Gretzky's 21, and would use his performance as a springboard into the NHL season. Lemieux won his first Art Ross Trophy with 70 goals and 98 assists for 168 points, beating Gretzky by 19. It was the first time in nine seasons that Gretzky would walk away without the scoring title.

To go along with the changing of the guard in scoring, a number of new coaches began patrolling behind NHL benches, including Bob Murdoch in Chicago, Bob McCammon in Vancouver, and Pierre Creamer in Pittsburgh. Phil Esposito went so far as to trade his first-round draft choice to Quebec to secure Michel Bergeron to lead the

---

*Mario Lemieux (#66) and Wayne Gretzky (#99) were a deadly duo during the 1987 Canada Cup tournament. Lemieux would go on to win his first Art Ross Trophy in 1987–88 with 168 points, while Gretzky finished second in NHL scoring with 149.*

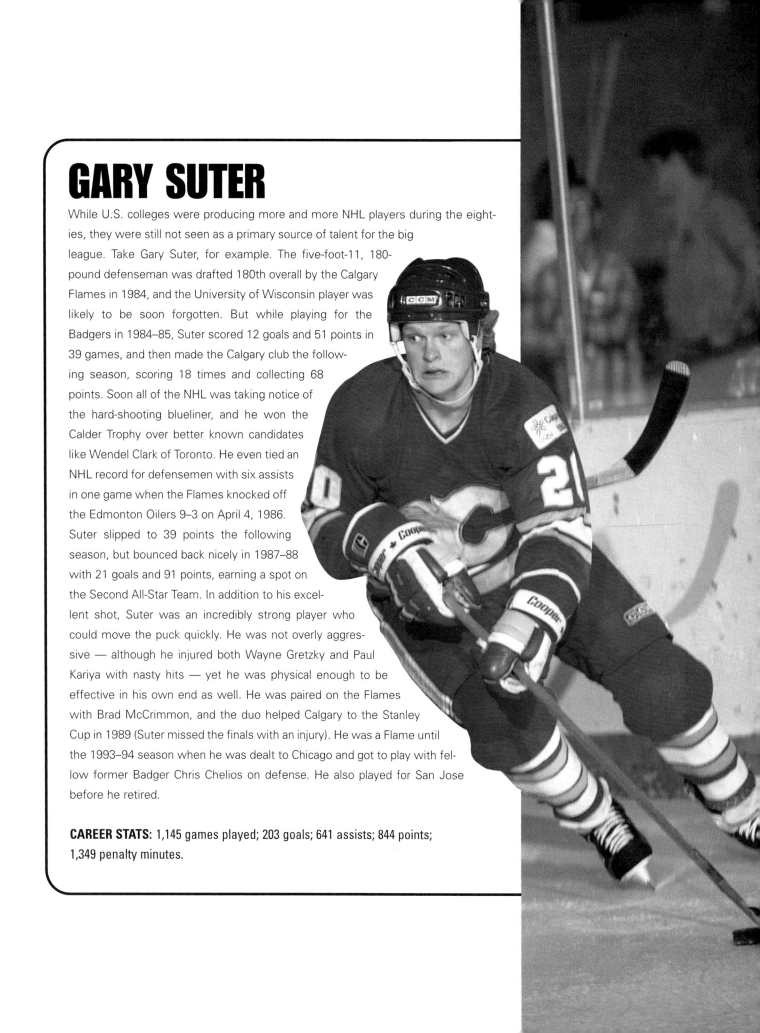

# GARY SUTER

While U.S. colleges were producing more and more NHL players during the eight-ies, they were still not seen as a primary source of talent for the big league. Take Gary Suter, for example. The five-foot-11, 180-pound defenseman was drafted 180th overall by the Calgary Flames in 1984, and the University of Wisconsin player was likely to be soon forgotten. But while playing for the Badgers in 1984–85, Suter scored 12 goals and 51 points in 39 games, and then made the Calgary club the follow-ing season, scoring 18 times and collecting 68 points. Soon all of the NHL was taking notice of the hard-shooting blueliner, and he won the Calder Trophy over better known candidates like Wendel Clark of Toronto. He even tied an NHL record for defensemen with six assists in one game when the Flames knocked off the Edmonton Oilers 9–3 on April 4, 1986. Suter slipped to 39 points the following season, but bounced back nicely in 1987–88 with 21 goals and 91 points, earning a spot on the Second All-Star Team. In addition to his excel-lent shot, Suter was an incredibly strong player who could move the puck quickly. He was not overly aggres-sive — although he injured both Wayne Gretzky and Paul Kariya with nasty hits — yet he was physical enough to be effective in his own end as well. He was paired on the Flames with Brad McCrimmon, and the duo helped Calgary to the Stanley Cup in 1989 (Suter missed the finals with an injury). He was a Flame until the 1993–94 season when he was dealt to Chicago and got to play with fel-low former Badger Chris Chelios on defense. He also played for San Jose before he retired.

**CAREER STATS:** 1,145 games played; 203 goals; 641 assists; 844 points; 1,349 penalty minutes.

New York Rangers. (Andre Savard replaced Bergeron in Quebec and lasted just 24 games.) A couple of Americans secured key positions as well, with Herb Brooks getting back into the NHL as head coach of the Minnesota North Stars, and an unknown named Lou Lamoriello, 44, was hired by the New Jersey Devils as team president. Lamoriello was soon the general manager of the Devils, and the former athletic director of Providence College would have a profound effect in New Jersey for years to come.

**Big Deals**
There was plenty of player movement prior to the season, not the least of which was Toronto trading Rick Vaive, Steve Thomas, and Bob McGill to Chicago for Al Secord and Ed Olczyk. The Leafs got the worst of the transaction, as Secord's career was fading, but they did manage to get good production out of Olczyk for a few seasons (Vaive got 43 goals in his only full year as a Blackhawk). The Quebec Nordiques not only changed coaches, they also dealt Dale Hunter to Washington for goalie Clint Malarchuk and a first-round draft choice, which they used to select Joe Sakic 15th overall in 1987.

Perhaps the best moves were made by the Calgary Flames, who added defenseman Brad McCrimmon from Philadelphia for a couple of draft choices, and then hired Terry Crisp as head coach. Both men would have a significant impact on the Flames' fortunes, though not necessarily in 1987–88. Late in the year, Calgary sent Brett Hull and Steve Bozek to St. Louis for defenseman Rob Ramage and Rick Wamsley in a deal that was supposed to put them over the top, but it did not work out that way. Boston acquired goalie Andy Moog from Edmonton in exchange for netminder Bill Ranford and winger Geoff Courtnall. The biggest trade of the season, however, occurred on November 24, 1987, when the Oilers sent disgruntled defenseman Paul Coffey along with Dave Hunter and Wayne Van Dorp to Pittsburgh for Craig Simpson, Chris Joseph, Dave Hannan, and Moe Mantha. It was believed the deal would spell the end of the Oilers, but Simpson had a terrific year, scoring 56 goals, while the team became more responsible defensively.

*Calgary's Hakan Loob (#12) had a great season in 1987–88 when he scored 50 goals and 106 points. The smallish right winger played for the Flames between 1983 and 1989, scoring 193 goals and 429 points in 450 games. He returned to play in Europe after the 1988–89 season.*

*In just his second season, Los Angeles center Jimmy Carson (#17) scored 55 goals and added 52 assists in 1987–88. The young pivot would find himself involved in the greatest trade in hockey history in the summer of 1988.*

As usual the Oilers were led by Gretzky (149 points), Mark Messier (111 points), Jari Kurri (96 points), and Glenn Anderson (88 points), but Calgary was challenging with the likes of Hakan Loob (50 goals), Mike Bullard (48 goals), Gary Suter (91 points), Joe Mullen (40 goals), Al MacInnis (25 goals), and rookie Joe Nieuwendyk, who scored 51 times to the surprise of just about everyone. The Flames collected 105 points, the best mark in the NHL, edging Edmonton by six points. It appeared that the best two teams in the league were both in the Smythe Division — but only one would make it out.

### Canadiens, Red Wings, and Bruins Strong

The only other team to record more than 100 points during the '87–'88 season was the Montreal Canadiens, who went 45–22–13 for a total of 103. Center Bobby Smith led the way with 93 points, while Stephane Richer appeared to put his problems in Montreal behind him with a 50-goal season. Mats Naslund turned in another good year with 83 points, while Claude Lemieux scored 31 goals. Defenseman Chris Chelios produced an outstanding season with 61 points while giving Montreal a strong presence on the blueline. Mostly, though, the Habs relied on Patrick Roy and Brian Hayward to give them top netminding, and the team gave up the fewest goals in the league (238).

Another serious contender was the Detroit Red Wings, who posted 93 points, based on a 41–28–11 record. Captain Steve Yzerman recorded 102 points, including 50 goals, in just 64 games before a knee injury ended his season prematurely. Yzerman received an incredible amount of icetime under coach Jacques Demers, and he responded well to the challenge. Winger Bob Probert thrived playing alongside the captain, as did Gerard Gallant (34 goals). Petr Klima scored 37 goals, while the much traveled Brent Ashton scored 29. But Detroit was not strong in goal — Glen Hanlon and Greg Stefan were the best available — and lacked a star on defense, although they were easily the best team in a poor Norris Division.

Another Original Six club, the Boston Bruins, also had a fine season

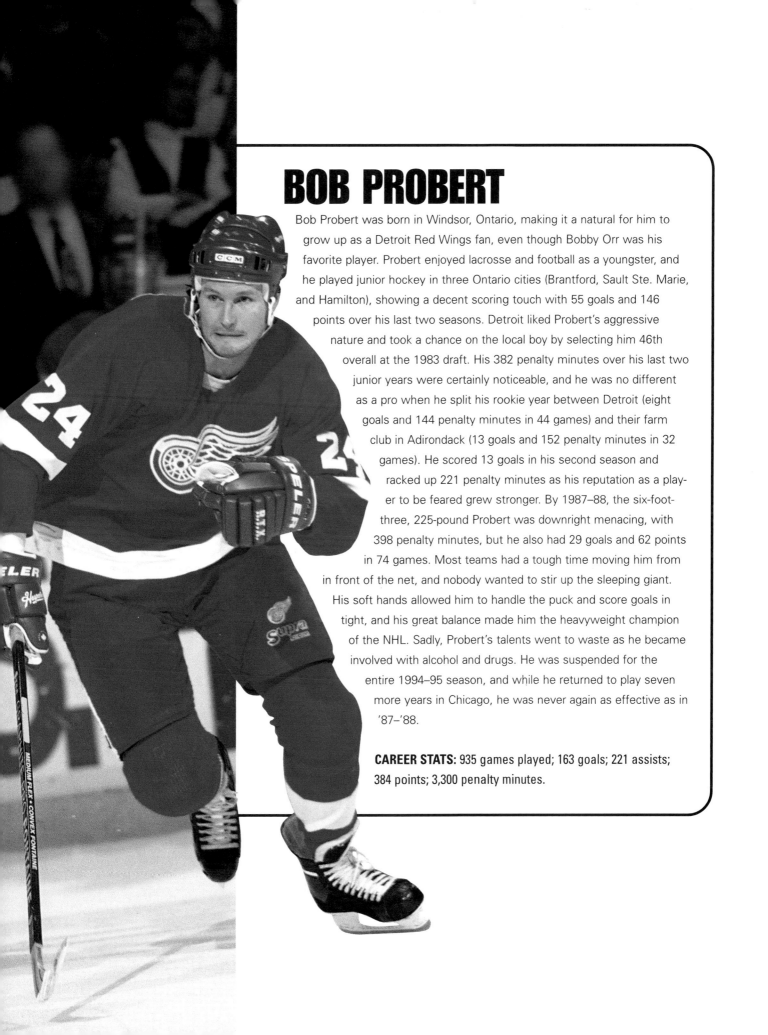

# BOB PROBERT

Bob Probert was born in Windsor, Ontario, making it a natural for him to grow up as a Detroit Red Wings fan, even though Bobby Orr was his favorite player. Probert enjoyed lacrosse and football as a youngster, and he played junior hockey in three Ontario cities (Brantford, Sault Ste. Marie, and Hamilton), showing a decent scoring touch with 55 goals and 146 points over his last two seasons. Detroit liked Probert's aggressive nature and took a chance on the local boy by selecting him 46th overall at the 1983 draft. His 382 penalty minutes over his last two junior years were certainly noticeable, and he was no different as a pro when he split his rookie year between Detroit (eight goals and 144 penalty minutes in 44 games) and their farm club in Adirondack (13 goals and 152 penalty minutes in 32 games). He scored 13 goals in his second season and racked up 221 penalty minutes as his reputation as a player to be feared grew stronger. By 1987–88, the six-foot-three, 225-pound Probert was downright menacing, with 398 penalty minutes, but he also had 29 goals and 62 points in 74 games. Most teams had a tough time moving him from in front of the net, and nobody wanted to stir up the sleeping giant. His soft hands allowed him to handle the puck and score goals in tight, and his great balance made him the heavyweight champion of the NHL. Sadly, Probert's talents went to waste as he became involved with alcohol and drugs. He was suspended for the entire 1994–95 season, and while he returned to play seven more years in Chicago, he was never again as effective as in '87–'88.

**CAREER STATS:** 935 games played; 163 goals; 221 assists; 384 points; 3,300 penalty minutes.

under their new coach, the former grinding winger Terry O'Reilly. The Bruins tallied 44 wins and 94 points, and their attack was led by Norris Trophy winner Ray Bourque (17 goals, 81 points). The star blueliner also showed his class when the team decided to retire Phil Esposito's number, then being worn by Bourque. During the ceremony, he took off the sweater with the seven on the back and gave it to Esposito, and then revealed his new numeral would be 77. Winger Cam Neely scored 42 goals, making the deal with Vancouver for him look like an absolute steal for the Bruins, while Ken Linseman (74 points), Steve Kasper (70 points), Randy Burridge (27 goals), and rookie Bob Sweeney (22 goals) also contributed to the Boston cause. Rejean Lemelin held the fort in goal until Moog arrived in the trade with Edmonton. The Bruins' emphasis on team play would hold them in good stead for the playoffs.

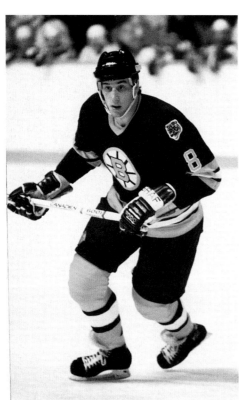

*Cam Neely (#8) scored 42 goals in 1987–88 for the Bruins, who ended up going to the Stanley Cup finals. Neely had 17 points in 19 playoff games and would go onto to record three seasons of 50 or more goals for Boston before an injury forced him to retire prematurely.*

### Devils Get Hot

The New Jersey Devils became the story of the year when they made the playoffs on the last night of the regular season. Needing a win, the Devils defeated Chicago 4–3 in overtime on a goal by John MacLean to sneak into the post-season. Fifty games into the season, Lamoriello had fired coach Doug Carpenter and replaced him with former NHL defenseman Jim Schoenfeld, who had coached in Buffalo the previous season. Under Schoenfeld, the Devils went 17–12–1 and were further boosted by the play of rookie netminder Sean Burke, who joined the club after the 1988 Olympics. Burke posted a 10–1 record and gave his team new confidence. Kirk Muller led the Devils with 94 points, followed closely by Aaron Broten with 83. Pat Verbeek scored a team-leading 46 goals and MacLean fired in 23, while Bruce Driver contributed 15 goals and 55 points from the blueline. One of the Devils' most promising rookies was right winger Brendan Shanahan, selected second overall in 1987, who scored seven times, his first coming on a wicked 40-foot wrist shot that fooled Rangers netminder John Vanbiesbrouck. The 18-year-old was so thrilled that he kissed teammate Claude Loiselle on the cheek to celebrate! By getting into the playoffs with a late-season drive and a big win on the last night, the Devils went into the postseason on a roll and that often leads to a great run when it matters most.

The Devils made the playoffs with 82 points, edging out the New York Rangers (who also had 82 points, but two fewer victories) and the rebuilding Penguins, who finished with 81 points despite Lemieux's great season and Coffey's arrival on the backline, where he had 67 points in 46 games. Creamer did not prove to be a great coach and was replaced at the end of the season, but he had little to work with — after Lemieux, his top forwards were Dan Quinn (79 points), Randy Cunneyworth (74 points), and rookie Rob Brown (24 goals). Missing the postseason caused the Penguins to bring in former Chicago star netminder Tony Esposito as general manager, replacing Ed Johnston. The Penguins hoped Esposito would do a better job than his brother was doing with the Rangers. New York certainly had a

*New Jersey netminder Sean Burke (#1) tries to stop Washington forward Dave Christian (#27). Burke joined the Devils after the 1988 Olympics and helped them win two playoff series. Christian scored 37 goals for the Capitals in 1987–88.*

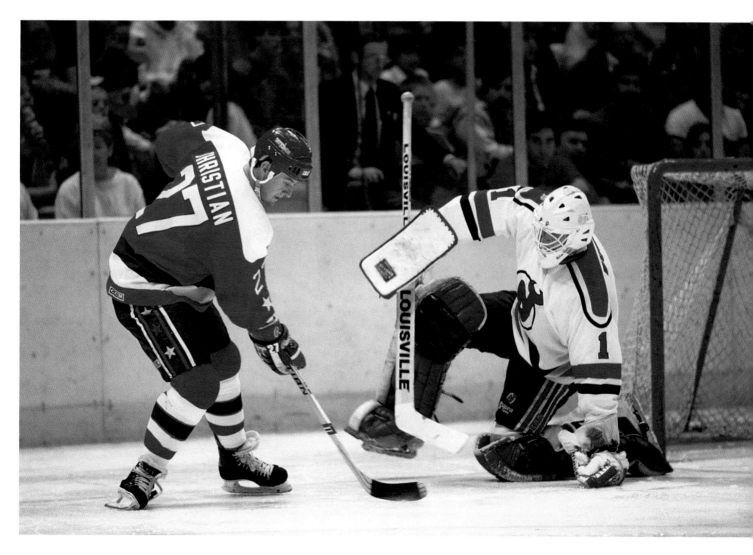

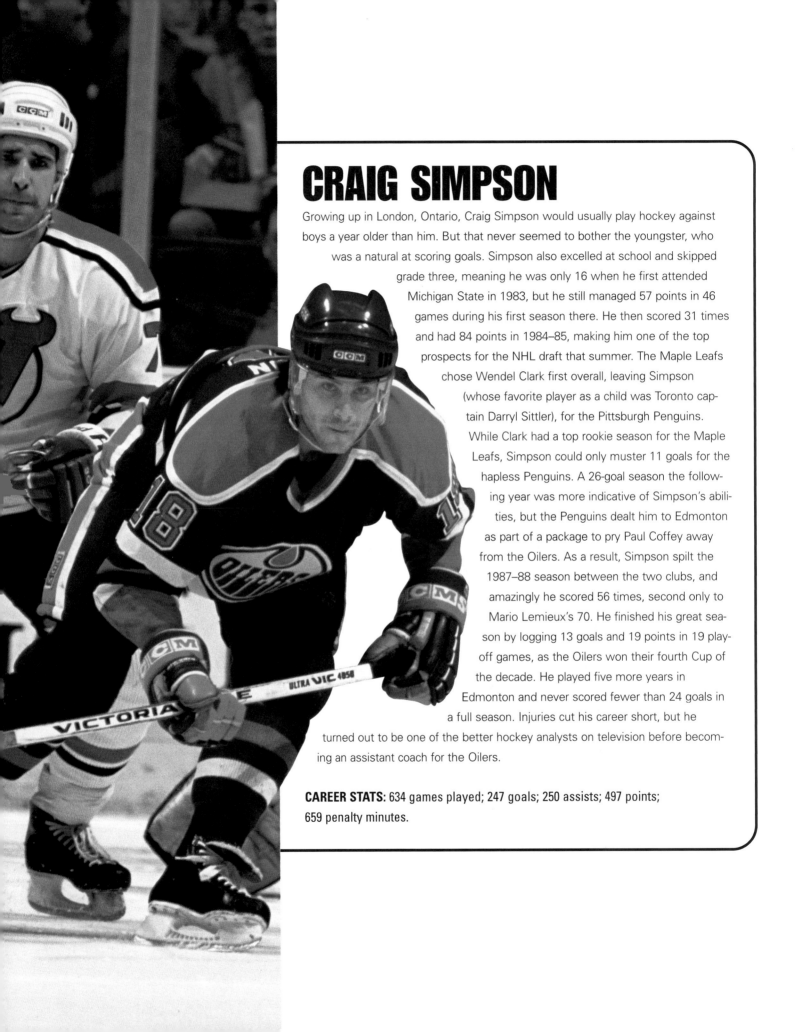

# CRAIG SIMPSON

Growing up in London, Ontario, Craig Simpson would usually play hockey against boys a year older than him. But that never seemed to bother the youngster, who was a natural at scoring goals. Simpson also excelled at school and skipped grade three, meaning he was only 16 when he first attended Michigan State in 1983, but he still managed 57 points in 46 games during his first season there. He then scored 31 times and had 84 points in 1984–85, making him one of the top prospects for the NHL draft that summer. The Maple Leafs chose Wendel Clark first overall, leaving Simpson (whose favorite player as a child was Toronto captain Darryl Sittler), for the Pittsburgh Penguins. While Clark had a top rookie season for the Maple Leafs, Simpson could only muster 11 goals for the hapless Penguins. A 26-goal season the following year was more indicative of Simpson's abilities, but the Penguins dealt him to Edmonton as part of a package to pry Paul Coffey away from the Oilers. As a result, Simpson spilt the 1987–88 season between the two clubs, and amazingly he scored 56 times, second only to Mario Lemieux's 70. He finished his great season by logging 13 goals and 19 points in 19 playoff games, as the Oilers won their fourth Cup of the decade. He played five more years in Edmonton and never scored fewer than 24 goals in a full season. Injuries cut his career short, but he turned out to be one of the better hockey analysts on television before becoming an assistant coach for the Oilers.

**CAREER STATS:** 634 games played; 247 goals; 250 assists; 497 points; 659 penalty minutes.

decent attack, led by Walt Poddubny (a team-high 86 points), Kelly Kisio (78 points), and Tomas Sandstrom (68 points in 69 games). In addition, Brian Mullen, John Ogrodnick (picked up in a deal with the Nordiques when he objected to living in Quebec City) and rookie Ulf Dahlen all scored more than 20 goals. Marcel Dionne had his last good year in the NHL when he had 31 goals and 65 points in 67 games, but it was still not enough to get the team into the postseason, even with the addition of Bergeron behind the bench. Esposito's player changes were proving fruitless, and he would be given just one more year as general manager.

*Tony Tanti (#9) joined the Vancouver Canucks after a 1983 deal with Chicago and the right winger recorded 45, 39, 39, and 41 goals in his first four years on the West Coast. He scored 40 in 1987–88 and ended his career with 287 goals and 560 points in 697 games.*

### Maple Leafs, Canucks, and North Stars Struggle

After looking like they were making significant progress (largely because they kept drafting so high year after year), the Maple Leafs took another step backwards during the '87–'88 season. They finished with a pitiful record of 21–49–10 and a grand total of 52 points, but still made the playoffs. Leafs coach John Brophy was at odds with GM Gerry McNamara, and eventually owner Harold Ballard chose to keep the coach and release his manager. The Leafs needed a win in their last game to make the playoffs, and they came back from a 3–0 deficit against Detroit to win 5–3 and secure the final berth in the Norris Division. The win got the Leafs three home playoff dates (they lost in six games to Detroit), but missing the postseason would have given them a chance to draft one of the two top junior prospects, Mike Modano or Trevor Linden, a much better scenario in the long run. The only Leafs to have a decent year were the newly acquired Olczyk, who somehow managed to pot 42 goals, and Gary Leeman, who scored 30. Wendel Clark lived through the first of many injury-filled seasons with a back problem that proved to be chronic, and he played in only 28 games.

The North Stars were even worse, with a 19–48–13 record, and they lost their final game of the year to ensure first pick at the 1988 draft,

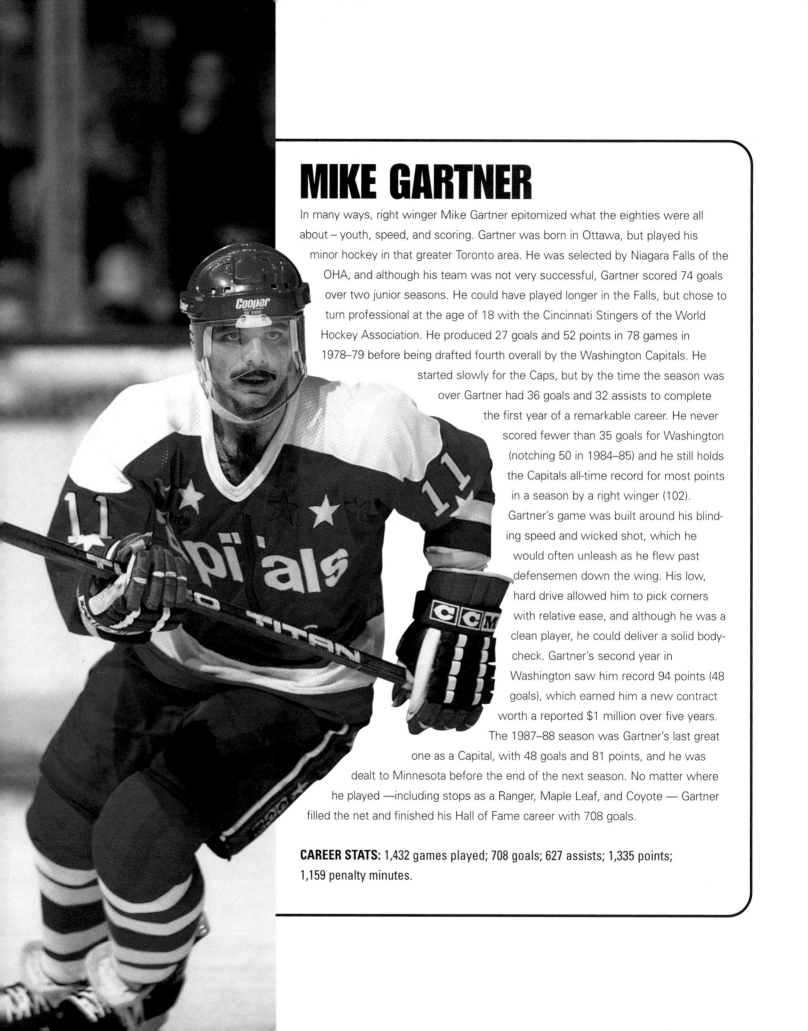

# MIKE GARTNER

In many ways, right winger Mike Gartner epitomized what the eighties were all about – youth, speed, and scoring. Gartner was born in Ottawa, but played his minor hockey in that greater Toronto area. He was selected by Niagara Falls of the OHA, and although his team was not very successful, Gartner scored 74 goals over two junior seasons. He could have played longer in the Falls, but chose to turn professional at the age of 18 with the Cincinnati Stingers of the World Hockey Association. He produced 27 goals and 52 points in 78 games in 1978–79 before being drafted fourth overall by the Washington Capitals. He started slowly for the Caps, but by the time the season was over Gartner had 36 goals and 32 assists to complete the first year of a remarkable career. He never scored fewer than 35 goals for Washington (notching 50 in 1984–85) and he still holds the Capitals all-time record for most points in a season by a right winger (102). Gartner's game was built around his blinding speed and wicked shot, which he would often unleash as he flew past defensemen down the wing. His low, hard drive allowed him to pick corners with relative ease, and although he was a clean player, he could deliver a solid body-check. Gartner's second year in Washington saw him record 94 points (48 goals), which earned him a new contract worth a reported $1 million over five years. The 1987–88 season was Gartner's last great one as a Capital, with 48 goals and 81 points, and he was dealt to Minnesota before the end of the next season. No matter where he played —including stops as a Ranger, Maple Leaf, and Coyote — Gartner filled the net and finished his Hall of Fame career with 708 goals.

**CAREER STATS:** 1,432 games played; 708 goals; 627 assists; 1,335 points; 1,159 penalty minutes.

where they would take Modano. Dino Ciccarelli (41 goals) and Brian Bellows (40 goals) provided some punch up front, but there was little behind them to excite fans in Minnesota. The highly regarded Brooks walked away after the season when he realized he was not being considered for the general manager's post, which was about to be vacated by Lou Nanne, and Pierre Page took over in 1988.

Vancouver actually had more points than the Leafs (59), but got to select second overall because they did not make the playoffs in the Smythe Division. The Canucks certainly needed the help provided through the draft, since only Tony Tanti (40 goals) and Greg Adams (36 goals) provided any offense. Selecting Linden was the first major move general manager Pat Quinn would make in reshaping the Canucks over the next few seasons.

*New Jersey forward Patrik Sundstrom (#17) recorded just 51 points in the 1987–88 regular season but had an eight-point night (three goals, five assists) against the Washington Capitals on April 22, 1988, setting a new NHL playoff mark that would be equaled by Mario Lemieux one year later.*

### Magic Moments

Flyers goaltender Ron Hextall became the first goalie in NHL history to score a goal by shooting a puck into the opposing net when he fired a long shot into the empty Boston goal on December 8, 1987. Dionne recorded his 700th goal and 1,000th assist during the season, while Borje Salming of the Maple Leafs became the first European-born player to appear in 1,000 career games. Denis Potvin became the first defenseman to score 300 career goals, and Gretzky recorded his 1,050th assist to pass Gordie Howe all-time mark of 1,049. The Edmonton wonder kid established the mark in just nine years, while Howe established his mark over 26 NHL seasons during a very different era.

# The PLAYOFFS

The first round of the playoffs did not produce any shockers, but there were some notable moments. The New Jersey Devils rolled to a six-

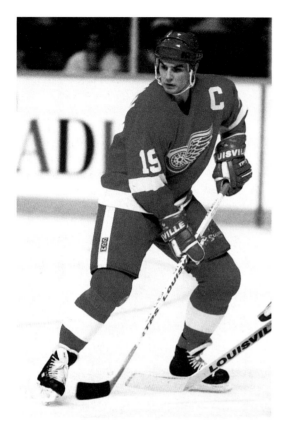

*Detroit captain Steve Yzerman (#19) scored 50 goals and added 52 assists in 1987-88. It was the first of six consecutive seasons that would see Yzerman record over 100 points.*

game series win over the New York Islanders in a mild upset, and the Washington Capitals came back from a 3–1 deficit in games against Philadelphia to win the seventh match 5–4 in overtime on a goal by Dale Hunter. Blowing the series would prompt the Flyers to dismiss coach Mike Keenan at the end of the year. The Leafs were humiliated 8–0 in their fourth game against Detroit, and the normally placid Toronto fans unleashed a storm of debris onto the ice in the third period — included a once-revered Leafs sweater, now reduced to a symbol of frustration. Toronto bounced back on an Ed Olczyk hat trick to win the next contest 6–5 in overtime, but Detroit wrapped up the series with a 5–3 win in game six.

In the second round, Boston was anxious to take a playoff series from Montreal, something they had not done in 45 years, and the Bruins won four straight after losing the opener, to take the series in five. The loss would cost Jean Perron his coaching job in Montreal before the start of the next season. New Jersey got an eight-point performance from Patrik Sundstrom in one contest (a 10–4 victory) against the Capitals, but it took the Devils seven games to win the series. Detroit easily beat St. Louis in five, but the real surprise came when the Oilers knocked off the Flames in four straight games. Gretzky may have scored the biggest goal of the series when his howitzer beat Mike Vernon in overtime of the second game in Calgary. Two home losses seemed to shake the Flames, and they lost the next two in Edmonton by scores of 4–2 and 6–4 to exit the play-offs meekly.

The Oilers went on to play the Red Wings in the conference final and took the series in five games, even though Yzerman made a quick recovery from his knee injury to join his team for the third round. The other conference final, pitting the upstart Devils against the Bruins, was filled with bitterness and controversy. The teams split the first two games in Boston but when the Bruins won the third game 6–1 in New Jersey, Devils coach Jim Schoenfeld was livid about the refereeing. He confronted Don Koharski at the officials' exit at the end of the game and earned a one-game suspension with an insulting remark about that referee's ample weight. When the

Devils fought the suspension, the officials scheduled to work the next game refused to take to the ice if Schoenfeld was behind the bench. With the building filled with fans, the NHL was forced to recruit unqualified minor officials to referee the contest, won by the Devils 3–1. NHL president John Ziegler was nowhere to be found, and chairman of the board Bill Wirtz was making the decisions. Schoenfeld finally served the suspension during game five (a 7–1 Bruins victory) but New Jersey was able to force a seventh game. Their incredible story came to an end with a 6–3 Boston win, pitting the Bruins against Edmonton in the finals.

*New Jersey's Kirk Muller (#9) battles with Boston's Steve Kasper (#11) for control of the puck. Muller scored 37 goals in 1987–88 and totaled a career-best 94 points. He added 12 points in the play-offs and helped the Devils get within one game of the finals. Kasper had his best season in '87–'88 when he scored 26 goals and added 44 assists.*

# STEVE LARMER

As good as Steve Larmer was for the Chicago Blackhawks, he was always seen as the *other* choice the team made in 1980. The most celebrated pick that year was Denis Savard (third overall) and Larmer was almost an afterthought when he was taken 120th. Perhaps size was an issue, since Larmer was just five-foot-10 and 185 pounds, but the scouts should have measured his heart instead. Larmer grew up in Peterborough, Ontario, and would finish his junior career with Niagara Falls, where he scored 100 goals over his last two seasons. He was assigned to Chicago's AHL farm team in New Brunswick, and Larmer felt it was experience he needed. Under coach Orval Tessier, Larmer scored 38 goals and 82 points in his first pro season, and then had 12 points in 15 playoff games as his team won the Calder Cup. Larmer found himself starting for the Blackhawks the following year and scored a goal and two assists in his first game, a 3–3 tie against the Maple Leafs. The right winger would finish his rookie year with 43 goals and 90 points on a line with Al Secord and Savard. Larmer felt he was capable of scoring 50 goals in a season, and although he never hit the magic number, he did record five seasons of 40 or more. A durable performer who played in 884 consecutive games for Chicago, Larmer had terrific hands and knew how to get himself into position to score. He also took advantage of his left-hand shot playing on the right wing. In one of their many baffling moves, the Blackhawks traded Larmer away in 1993, but it turned out well for him, since he won his only Stanley Cup with the New York Rangers. He retired after the next season with more than a point-per-game average.

**CAREER STATS:** 1,006 games played; 441 goals; 571 assists; 1,012 points; 522 penalty minutes.

The Bruins had nothing left for the finals and were wiped out in four games, although one game was recorded as a 3–3 tie because a power failure in the Boston Garden forced one game to end at 16:37 of the second period. This gave the Oilers a chance to win the Cup on home ice, which they did on May 26, 1988, with a 6–3 victory. The date is relevant because it was the last game Gretzky played as an Oiler. Edmonton owner Peter Pocklington was already plotting to trade the Great One, making the on-ice team photo with the Stanley Cup one for the ages.

*Jari Kurri, Esa Tikkanen, and Wayne Gretzky of the Edmonton Oilers celebrate a goal against the Boston Bruins during the 1988 finals. Edmonton scored 21 goals in the five-game series — including one contest suspended after a power failure in the Boston Garden — while the Bruins scored 12 times.*

# WAYNE GRETZKY

## A Decade of Greatness

**AS** the 20th century came to a close, *The Hockey News* assembled a panel of 50 experts and produced a list of the greatest players of all time. At the top was none other than the Great One himself, Wayne Gretzky.

The choice may seem obvious, but strong cases can be made for at least a few of those listed below Gretzky. After all, who dominated more than Bobby Orr? Who could possibly be more durable than Gordie Howe? Can anyone say they have seen a more skilled player than Mario Lemieux, whose goals were works of art? Did anyone score more dramatic and important goals than Maurice Richard? But when one stops to think about Wayne Gretzky's career from 1979 to 1999, both on and off the ice, one thing is certain: no other player in history has had the impact and influence that Gretzky did. Even in retirement, his final legacy has yet to be written.

The funny thing about Gretzky was that he was not the physical equal of any of those who might be considered the greatest of all time. Slightly built at six feet and 185 pounds, the well-conditioned Gretzky was gifted with athletic talent, superb peripheral vision, and an indomitable drive that allowed him to survive 20 NHL seasons. His overall game was greater than the sum of its parts. He was not the fastest skater in the NHL, but he always seemed to get there in time to set up 1,963 goals. His shot was not the hardest, but he managed a record 954 goals. He was not the toughest player in the game, but he

*One of the best special team players of all-time, Wayne Gretzky scored 204 career goals on the power-play and another 73 while his team was shorthanded.*

used his tremendous instinct and guile to steer clear of trouble long enough to play in 1,487 regular-season games, plus 208 more in the playoffs. No one could have expected him to play so well for so long with such pressure on his shoulders, yet he was at his best in the play-offs, when he scored 122 goals and 260 assists for 382 points, all records for the postseason. His impressive numbers are etched in the NHL record book — many of them forever, it would appear — but Gretzky was more than the unbelievable statistics. His performance on the ice changed the way people played and viewed hockey, while his leadership off the ice made Gretzky's voice the one fans, writers, and commentators listened to most.

**Setting Up:** Gretzky was the first player to make effective use of the area behind the net. It was often termed his "office," since he liked to work behind the cage to lure defensemen to him while he feathered a perfect pass to a suddenly uncovered teammate. The main reason Gretzky was so good behind the net was his low pressure point with the puck. He would hold it, hold it, and hold it until the last possible second — much like football great Joe Montana did when he was passing the ball — before dishing the puck off to the teammate in the best spot. Others have tried to imitate Gretzky's work behind the net, but no one has come close to being as effective as he was.

**Reading the Play:** Walter Gretzky, Wayne's father, was a great influence on his son's development as a hockey player. One of Walter's mottos was "go where the puck is going to be." Gretzky took the lesson to heart, and he had a way of appearing out of nowhere to take the puck and unleash a wicked drive or set up a teammate. He was also not afraid to go against the grain to put a play in front of him. He might be carrying the puck over the blueline, looking like he would drive to the net, when suddenly he would curl back just inside the line. That move would catch defensemen by surprise, allowing Gretzky to snap off a shot or hit a late-breaking teammate for a shot on goal. By not always going straight ahead, Gretzky was able to look at the whole ice when considering which play was his best option.

**Always on the Attack:** Unlike players who let up for a variety of reasons, Gretzky was always on the attack. Even if the game was out of reach for an opponent, Gretzky knew there was still time to score another goal or set up another play. (In the eighties, this was not really a case of trying to rub it in, but a recognition that no lead was safe, especially the way the Oilers played defense.) Gretzky was not the first great player to kill penalties — Dave Keon and Marcel Dionne come to mind — but he was the first to believe he could use the extra ice offensively. It certainly helped that he was often teamed with Jari Kurri on the penalty kill, and the two worked their magic to surprise any opponent who let up because they were on the power play. It was the same at All-Star Games, which Gretzky saw as a chance to show the skill and artistry that makes hockey such a great game. For Gretzky, there was always another record to be broken, another mark to be set. He knew he would never achieve legendary status if he did

*"Wayne Gretzky has given so much to our hockey club and to this city for the past decade. I believe he has earned the right to determine his own destiny." — Peter Pocklington, Edmonton Oilers owner (The Hockey News, September 9, 1988)*

not win Stanley Cups, and he led his team to four championships. It was this attitude and approach that allowed Gretzky to ring up 61 NHL records before he retired.

**Standing Out:** When a player scores at such an extraordinary level compared with his contemporaries, it's only fitting that he look special on the ice. That was simply accomplished when Gretzky put number 99 on his back. It started as a tribute to his childhood hero, Gordie Howe (whose number nine was unavailable on Gretzky's junior team), and came to represent Gretzky's unique accomplishments. Before the 1980s, it was rare for a player to wear a number higher than 27 unless he was a goalie. But following Gretzky's lead, other great players started wearing trademark high numerals — including Lemieux with 66, Jaromir Jagr with 68, Ray Bourque with 77, and Eric Lindros with 88. All appeared larger than life, but none quite matched Gretzky, who added another distinctive touch by tucking in his jersey on one side.

**Star Player as a Manager:** Gretzky was never comfortable with the notion that he influenced management decisions — and just how much sway he actually had is debatable — but he was certainly a voice to be heard. As the best player in the game, that seemed only logical. As he got older, Gretzky was forthcoming with his opinions about player moves, especially after being dealt to Los Angeles, an organization in need of sage advice. Soon other top players would not hesitate to state their views to management — including Lindros, Lemieux, and most notably Mark Messier, Gretzky's close friend. Not everyone sees this as a positive trend, but it continued to grow as the best players started making millions of dollars and realizing the power they held. Gretzky also influenced an on-ice change starting in 1987–88, when he insisted that interference was becoming a major problem for star players who were being endlessly hooked and held, even when they did not have the puck.

**The Ambassador:** Gretzky always knew he was being scrutinized by everyone who followed hockey, even casual fans, and he was keenly aware of the responsibility that went with that attention. Remember, this was someone who had been watched since the age of 10, when he scored 378 goals! He saw it as his duty to promote the game, and that's why he hosted *Saturday Night Live!* and made a cameo on the soap

opera *The Young and the Restless*. It's also why Johnny Carson wanted him on *The Tonight Show* (he ended up missing the appearance due to snowstorm) and why he made the cover of *Sports Illustrated* more than any other hockey player. He even made the cover of *Time* magazine in 1985 with the words "Simply the Best" in large print above a painting of him and basketball's Larry Bird. While other players tired of the media spotlight, Gretzky seemed to thrive in it. For example, there is no hockey market like Toronto, and Gretzky saved some his greatest performances for the town closest to his home in Brantford, Ontario. Over his entire career, Gretzky scored more goals against the Maple Leafs (150 in 63 games) than against any other non-divisional opponent. He loved doing well on *Hockey Night in Canada*, and he

*Wayne Gretzky scored his 77th goal of the 1981–82 season against Buffalo netminder Don Edwards on January 24, 1982 to break Phil Esposito's previous mark of 76 goals in one season. He went on to score 92 times setting a new record.*

*Number 99, Wayne Gretzky was the first superstar to wear a very high sweater number.*

rarely disappointed on the national stage. Some might suggest Gretzky was a self-promoter, but the point is that he genuinely loved hockey, and he wanted to pass on his passion to others. It was a great example for media-shy players to follow — even the reluctant Lemieux finally got the message that he must help sell the game.

**Skating Away from Controversy:** Gretzky was put on the spot innumerable times during his career, so it was inevitable that a few of his ideas and opinions were controversial. But when his comments caused problems, it was only temporary, and his reputation was not harmed. For example, he attacked the New Jersey Devils organization after the Oilers had ripped them apart one game in 1983. Gretzky was right on with his review of the Devils, but he was not prepared for the reaction he received and did the right thing by apologizing. Gretzky also had strong views about fighting in hockey, saying it should be removed if the game was going to thrive in the United States. Yet he made sure he was well protected on the ice, with the likes of Dave Semenko and Marty McSorley looking after him. It seemed to be an obvious contradiction, but Gretzky was merely following the rules of the game as they were during his career.

**International Star:** Gretzky never turned down the opportunity to play for his country, no matter how tired he might have been. The hockey season kept getting longer as Gretzky's career progressed, and he usually played deep into the playoffs, but he was always there at training camp with Team Canada, looking forward to winning a Canada Cup or World Cup (he played in five such tournaments, winning three), or an Olympic medal. Other players often tried to miss these events for various reasons — some good, some pretty lame — but Gretzky always considered it an honor to play for his country, one not to be taken lightly. Whenever he did play, Gretzky performed to his usual

*Wayne Gretzky never passed up a chance to represent his country.*

high standard, setting an example for all others. Even in retirement, Gretzky manages his country's Olympic team, whom he led to a gold medal in 2002, Canada's first hockey gold since the 1950s.

**Understanding Free Agency:** One of the first players in NHL history to understand the economics of the game, Gretzky came to see that his

*The Edmonton Oilers gather for a team shot following their Stanley Cup victory on May 26, 1988. It would be Gretzky's last game as an Oiler.*

own worth was much greater than even he once imagined. His services had been bought and sold from a young age, so Gretzky was experienced in making big-money deals. When Gretzky negotiated his last contract with Edmonton owner Peter Pocklington, he reserved the right to become an unrestricted free agent at the end of the deal, thus allowing him to have the choice of where he would play out his last years. Pocklington agreed, since he was planning to sell off shares in the Oilers, and he needed his star player in the fold if those shares were to look attractive. But the new agreement set the stage for Gretzky to leave Edmonton. The need for some quick cash ($15 mil-

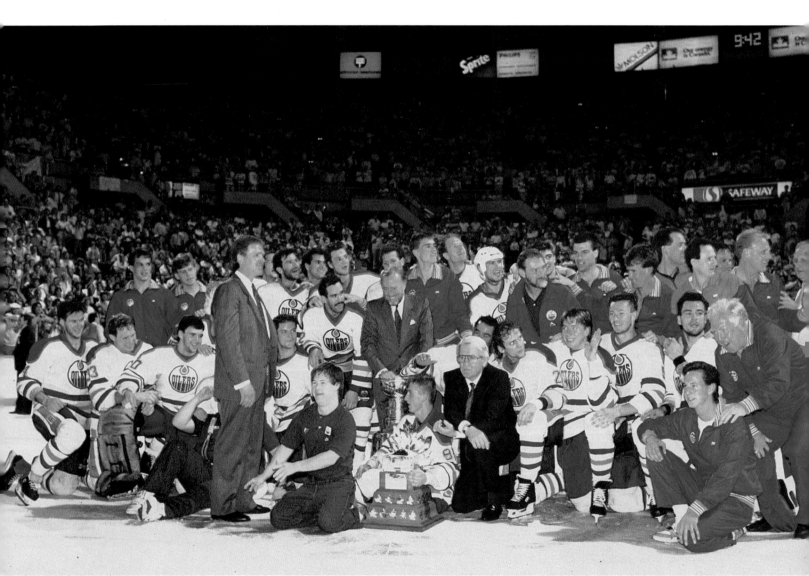

lion U.S.) and the prospect of rebuilding his team by dealing Gretzky eventually became too good for Pocklington to turn down. The Edmonton owner also realized that the free-agency clause meant Gretzky would ultimately have control over his own destiny, with the Oilers getting nothing in return. By understanding the value of his services and insisting that a player should not have choices forced upon him, Gretzky gave all hockey players more power than they had ever enjoyed. It was a far cry from the days when Gordie Howe would fill in a blank contract, give himself a tiny raise, and ask for a team jacket! Like his idol, Gretzky loved the game, but he had more business savvy, and as result, players are now treated far more equitably by the owners.

## The Biggest Trade in Hockey History

On August 9, 1988, the Edmonton Oilers traded Wayne Gretzky, Marty McSorley, and Mike Krushelnyski to the Los Angeles Kings for Jimmy Carson, Martin Gelinas, and three first-round draft choices. As difficult as it was to understand how the Oilers could trade Gretzky in his prime — there was still great potential for them to win more Stanley Cups — it really was inevitable. As the eighties were coming to an end, Edmonton was considered a "small market." The next few years would see a huge rise in salaries, and it would become impossible for the Oilers to hang on to all their stars, as they would demand more money than the team could possibly afford. Teams in larger cities could charge more for tickets, especially to corporations, and get more money from television rights. Gretzky's move out of Edmonton was merely the first of an exodus by Oilers stars.

At first, even Gretzky was taken aback by the possibility of a trade, but he soon came to see the benefits, especially when Los Angeles was the destination. He knew he could live in the fishbowl of Hollywood and fit in with its star-studded crowd. The fact that his wife already lived in Los Angeles made the move even easier. In fact, Gretzky helped Kings owner Bruce McNall complete the trade with Pocklington by coaching him along in the process. If Gretzky was going to be dealt, it was going to be on his terms. He also got a new contract out of McNall, but it typical fashion, Gretzky kept it rather modest for a player of his stature — and did a big favor for the corruptible Kings owner, who would have paid his star player whatever he asked for, even if he did not have the money!

The trade was big news all over North America, even grabbing

*"Everyone is looking for somebody to blame and the people to blame, I guess, are myself, Mr. Pocklington and Mr. McNall. We are the people who created the transaction."* Wayne Gretzky (The Hockey News, *September 9, 1988)*

*Now that he was a member of the Los Angeles Kings, Gretzky would have to play against old teammates like Mark Messier of the Edmonton Oilers. The Kings defeated the Oilers in seven games when they met in the 1989 playoffs.*

many headlines in the United States. Gretzky might have been just a hockey player, but he was one of those rare athletes who rise above the game they play. Gretzky immediately started drawing sellout crowds to Kings games — within 48 hours of the trade, the team received 2,500 new requests for season tickets. Even television and movie stars attended games. McNall improved the team, as he had promised Gretzky, and its success helped him recoup the investment he made in his prized acquisition. The Kings would make it to the Stanley Cup final by 1993, but that would be the end of the glitter and glory, as McNall was proven to be a financial fraud, ending up in jail years later. Gretzky would have to move again, as the Kings declined rapidly and needed to rebuild once again.

By the time Gretzky left Los Angeles, it was a much different NHL. The drive to expand the league came after the Gretzky trade, when many fans, especially those in the United States, started to look at hockey. Two new teams were added in California alone (San Jose and Anaheim), while two others were set up in Florida (the Lightning and Panthers). Soon the game spread to Phoenix, Nashville, Columbus, Atlanta, Colorado, and Dallas. Much of the impetus for expansion came from Gretzky bringing attention to a game previously overlooked in the U.S. (There is no doubt that hockey still ranks below football, baseball, and basketball in the States, but it is a much higher fourth now.) Helping to grow the game may have been his final achievement as a player, and he now has an opportunity to continue his work as part owner of the Phoenix Coyotes.

Two facts about Gretzky stand out. The first is that he was the most dominating player in hockey, if not all of professional sports, throughout the 1980s. (He would continue to dominate into the nineties, but certainly not to the same extent.) Second, his impact on the game was all-encompassing, from his on-ice performance to his off-ice demeanor and style. So while Orr might have been the best overall player of all time, Howe the longest lasting, Lemieux the most skilled, and Richard the flashiest, there is no doubt that the Wayne Gretzky changed hockey like no other player in the history of the game. It is unlikely fans will see such greatness again.

*"Without question, he's the most valuable player in the NHL and I intend to pay him at that level." — Bruce McNall, Los Angeles Kings owner (The Hockey News, September 9, 1988)*

# POSTSCRIPT
## A Night With Wayne Gretzky

The Minnesota North Stars were visiting the Edmonton Oilers on the night of January 4, 1984, at the Northlands Coliseum. The North Stars had a respectable 19–15–4 record at this halfway point in the season, but the Oilers were on a 8–0–1 streak that had put them first in the NHL. Wayne Gretzky had recorded a point in all 40 Oilers games so far, and already had well over 100 points to lead the scoring race, which he would go on to win by 79 points. Minnesota started Don Beaupre in net, while Edmonton countered with Grant Fuhr. Goals were expected, but neither goalie was ready for what was about to happen.

**FIRST PERIOD**
The onslaught began early as Mark Messier of the Oilers set up Glenn

Anderson, who faked out a defenseman and broke in cleanly to beat Beaupre with a snap shot just 2:05 into the contest. Dennis Maruk came back with two good chances for the North Stars, but was foiled

*Dennis Maruk joined the Minnesota North Stars for the 1983–84 season and the nifty playmaker recorded 60 points (17G, 43A) in 71 games played.*

by Fuhr. Then Gretzky made an incredible spin at the blueline and let go a slap shot that overpowered Beaupre, even thought the goalie got a piece of it. It was Gretzky's 44th goal of the season, and it gave the Oilers a 2–0 lead.

Maruk was not going to be denied, and he soon picked off a rebound from behind the Edmonton net and backhanded a shot over Fuhr to cut the Oilers lead to 2–1. Gretzky was on the prowl again, and set up Paul Coffey for a good chance that Beaupre stopped. Later, Gretzky stole a puck from between the skates of defenseman Craig Hartsburg behind the Minnesota net. He drew the attention of both North Stars defenders, which allowed him to send a perfect pass out to Jari Kurri, who made it 3–1 at 15:20 of the first. Fuhr made a save against Brian Lawton, but Dino Ciccarelli jammed a puck under the Oilers net-minder after some persistence to make it 3–2.

Oilers fans need not have worried, as Gretzky stole the puck again, this time from defenseman Brad Maxwell, and broke in with Kurri on a two-on-one. Kurri took the pass from number 99 and put it away to give Edmonton a 4–2 lead at 18:27. Gretzky was not finished yet, and 31 seconds later he potted the rebound of a Charlie Huddy drive to make it 5–2 with his 45th goal.

**SECOND PERIOD**

North Stars coach Bill Mahoney showed some mercy and replaced Beaupre with veteran Gilles Meloche. Minnesota responded with a power-play goal by Ciccarelli, who tapped in a pass from Maruk just 25 seconds into the period. The North Stars got another chance with the man advantage after Anderson was called for tripping, and they capitalized when a drive by Maxwell went off the stick of Oilers defender Kevin Lowe and past Fuhr to make it 5–4.

Gretzky then got into the act again by picking up a loose puck at the

*Edmonton goaltender Grant Fuhr (#31) may not have had his best night against the North Stars but he posted a 30–10–4 record during the 1983–84 season.*

Minnesota blueline. He quickly whipped a pass over to Kurri, who scored his third of the night to make it 6–4. But Minnesota came right back down the ice, and Neal Broten set up Steve Payne from behind the net to narrow the lead at 4:25 of the second. Fuhr had to make a good stop on Hartsburg to keep the Oilers ahead, but then the North Stars were flagged for a penalty. With referee Ron Wicks's arm in the air, the Oilers buzzed around the Minnesota net, and it seemed Gretzky had the puck on a string. He made a behind-the-back pass that caught everyone by surprise, including Jaroslav Pouzar, the intended receiver.

Once the Oilers got on the power play, Gretzky took one of the point positions and slid the puck to Coffey, who one-timed a blast past Meloche to make it 7–5 at 7:31 of the period. Gretzky then made a blind pass that ended up on the stick of North Star George Ferguson, his only errant setup of the evening. Minnesota's Brian Bellows took the pass and let go a hard drive to the short side that beat Fuhr cleanly to make it 7–6. The game got a little rough as Mark Napier of the

*Keith Acton (#12) joined the Minnesota club early in the 1983–84 season and recorded 17 goals and 38 assists for the North Stars in 62 games played.*

North Stars and Ken Linseman of the Oilers had a brief tussle, won by Napier. Gretzky picked the Oilers right back up again and deked Meloche, only to miss an open net with a backhand attempt. Oilers defenseman Randy Gregg then took on North Stars tough guy Willie Plett in a spirited fight as tempers heated up again.

Bellows was whistled off for a penalty, and the Oilers vaunted power play — clicking at 29.1 percent prior to this game — went into action again. Anderson dug a puck out from along the boards with help from Messier and threw it across the ice to a wide-open Gretzky at the edge of the crease. The captain completed his hat trick to make it 8–6 for Edmonton. Meloche then made stops against Kevin McClelland and Gretzky, while Fuhr made a good save on Broten. But Edmonton's Willy Lindstrom quickly got the scoring cranked up again when he was sprung in the clear on a long pass from Messier. Lindstrom was hooked as he broke in, but managed to beat a sprawling Meloche to make it 9–6. It was Messier's fourth assist on the night, and the nine Oilers goals to this point had come on just 19 shots.

After Maruk was robbed during a Minnesota power play, the Oilers went back to the attack. Gretzky missed on a clean breakaway, but he got set up on a tic-tac-toe passing play that went to Kurri, to Messier, then back to Gretzky for an easy tap in to make it 10–6. It was Gretzky's eighth point of the night (two away from the NHL record) and Meloche had to make two more saves on the Great One before the period came to an end. Both teams had totaled only 24 shots on goal each (12 per period) to this point in the game. Before the end of the period, Minnesota television analyst Tom Reid, a former North Stars player, said about Gretzky: "He's moving himself into position all the time." Play-by-play announcer Bob Kurtz added: "His shot is not that hard... but everything he does is so accurate."

## THIRD PERIOD

Both teams were used to high-scoring contests. The North Stars had lost 10–9 to Vancouver earlier in the season, and had been rocked 11–2 by the Quebec Nordiques. The Oilers had played the previous night in Calgary and had doused the Flames 9–6. So there was no way either team was going to coast the rest of the way.

McClelland got away with a high stick and a butt end on the same shift, with no penalty called. But the North Stars got the opening goal of the period at 2:20, when Keith Acton made a nice move in the Oilers end before firing a wrist shot past Fuhr. The goal narrowed the gap to 10–7, but Edmonton was 62–0–5 when they had the lead going into the third period, and they were not about to let the North Stars break that string. However, Hartsburg quickly drilled a shot from the slot past Fuhr after he was neatly set up by Plett to make it 10–8. The Edmonton netminder redeemed himself somewhat by making good saves on Ferguson and Maxwell to keep the two-goal lead.

Messier led the Oilers back on the attack, and his effort was followed up by a hard-charging Coffey, who made it 11–8. Fuhr had to make three excellent stops on a Minnesota power play before the Oilers went back to trying to score more goals. Gretzky — who did not get any extra ice time in the third, despite chasing the record — set up Pouzar and Anderson for a couple of good chances, but they were turned back by Meloche. However, Gregg let a shot go from the point that made it 12–8 at 15:22 of the final frame. Edmonton kept coming and Meloche had to stop Gretzky and Coffey on consecutive shots. Oilers rookie Jim Playfair got on the ice late in the contest and promptly took a slashing penalty. Edmonton killed off the penalty, and then Anderson rattled a shot off the post behind Meloche, and Playfair missed a great opportunity to knock in the rebound in the last minute. As the game ended, the Oilers skated off with a 12–8 victory to a cheer from their breathless fans.

This game marked Gretzky's second eight-point evening, his first coming just weeks before, on November 13, 1983, in a 13–4 win over New Jersey. The game's 20-goal total was just one short of the NHL record established in 1920. The contest is still one of only two 20-goal games (the Oilers were also involved in the other, an 11–9 loss to the Maple Leafs in 1986) and ranks as one of the best examples of how wild firewagon hockey was during the eighties.

# 1988–89

*Gretzky assumes the Kings' throne, Mario is magnificent, and the Flames win one for Lanny*

**WHILE** hockey fans in Canada — especially those in Edmonton — were still trying to get over the trading of Wayne Gretzky, the Los Angeles Kings were suddenly transformed into a contender. Gretzky finished tied with Mario Lemieux for the league lead in assists with 114, to along with 54 goals, but ended up second in the scoring race. He was helped out on the attack by Bernie Nicholls (70 goals and 150 points), Luc Robitaille (98 points), Steve Duchesne (75 points), Dave Taylor (63 points), and the recently acquired John Tonelli (64 points), all of whom helped the Kings score a league-high 376 goals. They were not strong on defense, allowing 335 goals, but made a deal during the season to pick up netminder Kelly Hrudey from the New York Islanders to bolster their club. It was the beginning of exciting times in Los Angeles as new uniforms and a fresh attitude, mostly supplied by Gretzky, gave a different look to a team that badly needed to be revamped. Plenty of credit for the Kings turnaround (42–31–7) went to new majority owner Bruce McNall, who was bold in his moves to change the stale nature of hockey on the West Coast. Years later, it was learned how McNall had paid for all of this, but for now he was hailed as a hero.

Another team that enjoyed success for the first time in years was the Pittsburgh Penguins, who finished second to Washington in the Patrick Division with a 40–33–7 record. Lemieux won the scoring race for the

*The Calgary Flames acquired center Doug Gilmour (#39) in a trade with St. Louis and he scored 26 goals and 85 points during the 1988–89 season. He added 22 points in the playoffs and scored the Stanley Cup–clinching goal against Patrick Roy (#33) and the Montreal Canadiens.*

*Mario Lemieux won his second straight Art Ross Trophy in 1988–89 when he had 199 points (85 goals, 114 assists) for the Pittsburgh Penguins. It was his first full season as captain of the team.*

second straight year with 199 points, and for a while it looked like he was going to challenge Gretzky's record of 215. He got help on offense from winger Rob Brown (115 points) and defenseman Paul Coffey (113 points), giving the Penguins three players among the league's top ten scorers. Dan Quinn was not much further back with 94 points, and center John Cullen supplied 49 points in his rookie season. Like the Kings, the Penguins were also weak in their own end, allowing 349 goals, but they too landed a new goaltender, getting Tom Barrasso from the Buffalo Sabres in an early-season swap. The Penguins now had a young netminder to add to their list of top players, and Barrasso's acquisition would have long-term benefits. While the Kings and Penguins were rejuvenated during 1988–89, they were both still a few years away from making any major impact in the playoffs.

### Canadian Teams on Top

While these American teams improved their status in the NHL, it was two Canadian clubs that would dominate the 1988–89 season. The

Calgary Flames recorded a league-high 117 points and 54 wins, losing just 17 games. Calgary was finally poised to take the final step to a championship, and the removal of Gretzky from Edmonton was enormously beneficial to their cause. The Flames got their season off to a good start by acquiring Doug Gilmour in a multi-player trade with the St. Louis Blues. Gilmour became available unexpectedly when he was the center of an investigation of sexual misconduct in St. Louis. Flames general manager Cliff Fletcher did his own checking and, after satisfying himself that there was nothing to the allegations, he made the trade for the feisty pivot. (For public relations reasons, and for Gilmour's own good, the Blues felt no choice but to deal him.) The only player of significance the Flames gave up was Mike Bullard, a 48-goal scorer the year before, and Gilmour more than made up for his loss with better all-around play and a 25-goal, 89-point regular season. The Flames' firepower was formidable with the likes of Joe Mullen (51 goals, 110 points), Hakan Loob (85 points), and Joe Nieuwendyk (his second 51-goal season), while defensemen Al MacInnis (74 points) and Gary Suter (62 points) were devastating from the blueline. Jamie Macoun's return after a near fatal auto acci-

*Pittsburgh defenseman Paul Coffey (#77) tries to score against Steve Weeks (#31) of the Vancouver Canucks. Coffey was the highest-scoring defenseman in the NHL in 1988–89 when he had 113 points (30 goals, 83 assists) and finished sixth in league scoring.*

dent certainly helped out on defense, while Mike Vernon and Rick Wamsley were a good combination in goal. The Flames had size, toughness and depth to go along with great offense, and on many nights it was difficult for coach Terry Crisp to decide who would play — those who sat in the press box could start for most other teams in the NHL. The only thing left for the Flames to accomplish was to win a Stanley Cup.

The second-best team in the NHL was the Montreal Canadiens with a 53–18–9 record, good for 115 points. The team was now guided by ex-cop Pat Burns, who was named coach before the season. Successful as a junior and minor-league coach, the no-nonsense Burns was confident he could do the job in a very tough hockey city. It was a little rough at first for Burns — some in the media speculated he would be gone by Christmas — but he won the confidence of veterans like Bob Gainey and Larry Robinson, and that got him over the initial difficulties all rookie coaches experience. Burns made Patrick Roy his number-one goalie (33 wins), but he also played backup Brian Hayward for 36 games (he recorded 20 wins), and they were terrific for the defensive-minded coach. Roy did not lose a game on home ice, with a 25–0–3 mark at the Montreal Forum. Mats Naslund led the attack with 33 goals and 51 assists, but the Habs had another six forwards who scored 20 or more goals. One was fleet-footed Russ Courtnall, acquired from Toronto in a ridiculous trade that only cost the Canadiens the services of tough guy John Kordic. Courtnall scored 22 goals in 64 games for the Habs, and general manager Serge Savard was congratulated for making such a lopsided deal. The heart of the club was a defensive group led by Chris Chelios, Craig Ludwig, Rick Green, and Robinson, and while the Canadiens didn't quite have the Flames' depth, they had similar size, balance, and toughness.

### Leafs and Blackhawks Battle in the Basement

In Toronto, the trading of Courtnall was the low point of another dismal season. Instead of cleaning house and bringing in experienced executives to run the club, owner Harold Ballard gave new authority to people already working for the woeful club. Gord Stellick was named the youngest general manager in NHL history, and was in no way ready for the job, despite sincere efforts to make the right moves. John Brophy returned as coach to start the year, but he lasted just 33 games (11–20–2) and was replaced by former Leafs legend George

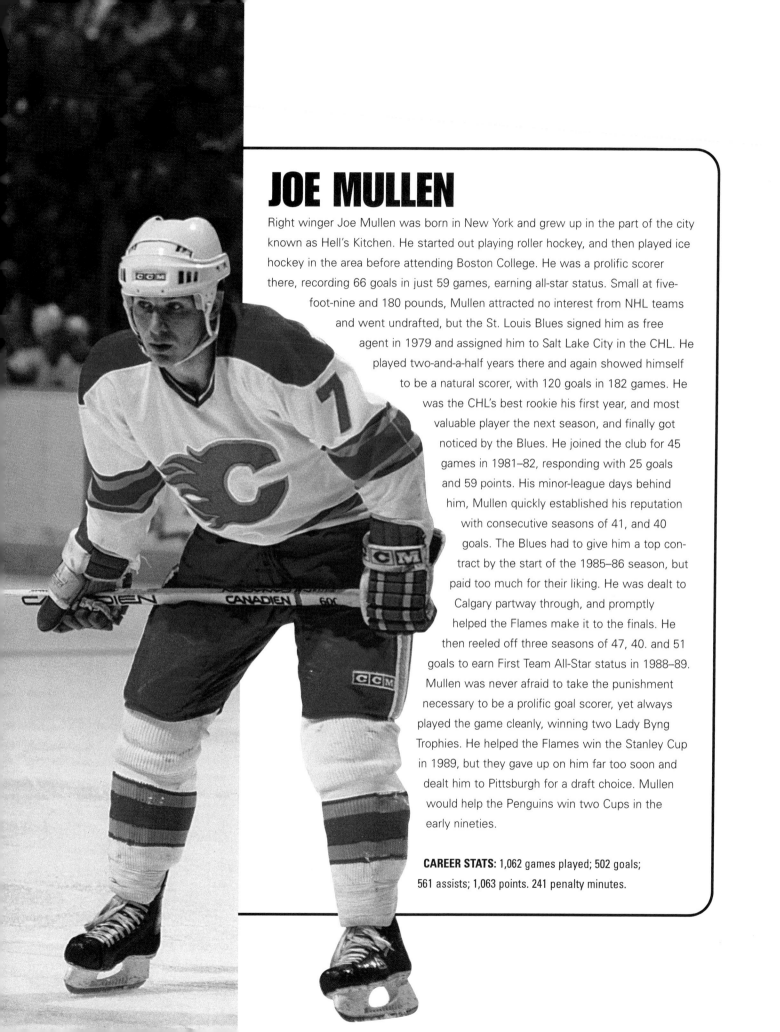

# JOE MULLEN

Right winger Joe Mullen was born in New York and grew up in the part of the city known as Hell's Kitchen. He started out playing roller hockey, and then played ice hockey in the area before attending Boston College. He was a prolific scorer there, recording 66 goals in just 59 games, earning all-star status. Small at five-foot-nine and 180 pounds, Mullen attracted no interest from NHL teams and went undrafted, but the St. Louis Blues signed him as free agent in 1979 and assigned him to Salt Lake City in the CHL. He played two-and-a-half years there and again showed himself to be a natural scorer, with 120 goals in 182 games. He was the CHL's best rookie his first year, and most valuable player the next season, and finally got noticed by the Blues. He joined the club for 45 games in 1981–82, responding with 25 goals and 59 points. His minor-league days behind him, Mullen quickly established his reputation with consecutive seasons of 41, and 40 goals. The Blues had to give him a top con-tract by the start of the 1985–86 season, but paid too much for their liking. He was dealt to Calgary partway through, and promptly helped the Flames make it to the finals. He then reeled off three seasons of 47, 40. and 51 goals to earn First Team All-Star status in 1988–89. Mullen was never afraid to take the punishment necessary to be a prolific goal scorer, yet always played the game cleanly, winning two Lady Byng Trophies. He helped the Flames win the Stanley Cup in 1989, but they gave up on him far too soon and dealt him to Pittsburgh for a draft choice. Mullen would help the Penguins win two Cups in the early nineties.

**CAREER STATS:** 1,062 games played; 502 goals; 561 assists; 1,063 points. 241 penalty minutes.

# GUY CARBONNEAU

When center Guy Carbonneau was playing junior hockey for Chicoutimi in the QMJHL, he was excellent playmaker, notching 189 assists in his last 144 games. He was also a decent goal scorer (134 over the same time) and that got him drafted 44th overall by the Montreal Canadiens in 1979. The Habs were sure he was not ready for the NHL, so he was assigned to Nova Scotia of the American Hockey League. Carbonneau adjusted well to pro hockey by scoring 66 goals and 182 points over two full seasons. The 1982–83 season saw him get full-time employment in Montreal, but coach Bob Berry used him in a defensive role. Still, he was able to produce 18 goals and 29 assists as a rookie. He also had five short-handed goals that year, second only to Wayne Gretzky, and quickly became known as one of the best two-way centers in the NHL. Over the next three seasons, Carbonneau scored 24, 23, and 20 goals to firmly establish himself on the team. His checking duties did not go unnoticed, and he won the Selke Trophy as the NHL's top defensive forward in both 1987–88 and 1988–89. It was clear by now that Carbonneau was taking over the top checking role from teammate Bob Gainey, and he would also assume the captaincy in due course. As part of a strong French-Canadian contingent that included Patrick Roy, Claude Lemieux, Stephane Richer and Eric Desjardins, Carbonneau was a two-time Stanley Cup winner (1986, 1993) with the Habs.

**CAREER STATS:** 1,318 games played; 260 goals; 403 assists; 663 points; 820 penalty minutes.

*The Maple Leafs had another terrible season in 1988–89, but one of the few bright spots was the play of center Ed Olczyk (#16), who scored 38 goals and posted a career-high 90 points.*

Armstrong. "The Chief" was little more than a figurehead behind the bench, but he stayed until the end of the season. With an ailing Wendel Clark able to play in just 15 games, the Leafs had a leadership vacuum both on and off the ice.

In spite of it all, the Leafs still had a chance to make the playoffs in the awful Norris Division. All they had to do was beat an equally weak Chicago team on the last day of the season, but they blew a two-goal lead and the Blackhawks won in overtime when Troy Murray scored on Allan Bester. It ended the eighth consecutive season in which the Leafs lost 40 or more games. The only highlights of the year were a 90-point effort from centre Ed Olczyk and a 32-goal performance from winger Gary Leeman.

It was a surprising end to the year for Chicago, who had begun the season with a new coach. Mike Keenan was named the new bench boss, even though the Blackhawks had Bob Murdoch already under contract. Chicago started slowly, and Keenan asserted his authority by having Rick Vaive (43 goals the year before) shipped to Buffalo for Adam Creighton. Veterans Denis Savard (82 points), Steve Larmer (87 points), and Doug Wilson (62 points) responded with good seasons, while Dirk Graham — the type of tough, hard-nosed competitor Keenan loved — came up with 33 goals and 78 points.

**Lafleur Returns to the NHL**

It was obvious that superstar Guy Lafleur had retired too early in 1984, and when he realized that himself, he persuaded New York Rangers GM Phil Esposito to give him a tryout. The recently inducted Hall of Famer was impressive in training camp and was signed to a one-year deal. He netted 18 goals and 45 points in 67 games, capping his return when he scored twice on Patrick Roy of the Canadiens the first time he retuned to the Forum. Esposito pulled off another stunning move when he fired coach Michel Bergeron with just two games left in the regular season. The Rangers had posted a 9–16 record prior to the dismissal, but Bergeron had another year on his contract and the team had given up a first-round draft choice to acquire him. The change did absolutely nothing to help the Rangers, and they were swept in the first round of the playoffs by the Penguins. It was little wonder that

*Even though the New York Rangers operated under much turmoil in 1988–89, captain Kelly Kisio had another fine season when he scored 26 goals and totaled 62 points. In five seasons as a Ranger, Kisio scored 110 goals and 305 points.*

Esposito was dismissed at the end of the season and replaced by Neil Smith. It would take a while, but the methodical Smith would build up the Rangers with good drafts and then make major deals to get the team to the top of the heap. One bright spot for the Rangers in '88–'89 was the play of rookie defenseman Brian Leetch, who tallied 23 goals and 71 points to take the Calder Trophy. Another top first-year player for the Rangers was Tony Granato (63 points), while other good rookies this season included Joe Sakic of Quebec (62 points), Trevor Linden of Vancouver (30 goals), and Scott Young of Hartford (40 assists).

**Top Performances**

Detroit's Steve Yzerman set team records — all of which still stand — with 65 goals, 90 assists, and 155 points, yet finished third in NHL scoring. He established the Red Wings' mark for goals in a season when he scored his 56th (John Ogrodnick held the previous high) on February 23, when the Red Wings battled back from a 6–0 deficit against Pittsburgh to earn a

6–6 tie. The club was drawing well at the gate, with an average attendance of 19,700, but could do no better than 80 points during the season, though that was still good enough to finish first in the Norris. The playoffs would prove even more disappointing.

Joe Nieuwendyk scored four goals in one period during an 8–3 victory over the Winnipeg Jets on January 11, tying an NHL record. The big Flames center scored a total of five in the contest, one of two players to score that many in a single game during 1988–89 (eight different players scored four goals in a game during the season). As good as Nieuwendyk's performance was, the show of the year was reserved for Mario Lemieux. On December 31, Lemieux scored a goal in every possible situation during an 8–6 win over the New Jersey Devils — at even strength, on a power play, while short-handed, on a penalty shot, and finally into an empty net. For good measure, Lemieux added three assists for eight points, equaling his total of October 15, when he tore apart the St. Louis Blues with two goals and six assists in 9–2 victory. These were the best two regular-season performances Lemieux put on during his entire NHL career.

The Edmonton Oilers were still a formidable team, although they certainly missed the Great One. Jimmy Carson, who was acquired in the deal for Gretzky, produced a 49-goal, 100-point season. Jari Kurri scored 44 and totaled 102 points, and Mark Messier had a 94-point campaign. But the Oilers only produced 84 points as a team and finished third in the Smythe Division, which meant they would play the Kings in the first round of the playoffs. The Oilers did win the first game Gretzky played in Edmonton, but the playoffs would prove to be a different story.

The Winnipeg Jets got great years from Dale Hawerchuk (96 points) and Tomas Steen (88 points), but they still finished 10 points out of a playoff spot. Mike Ridley led the Washington Capitals in scoring with 41 goals and 89 points, while youngster Pierre Turgeon led the Buffalo Sabres with 34 goals and 88 points in his first strong season in the NHL.

The most sentimental achievements, however, belonged to Lanny McDonald of the Calgary Flames. The man with the wild mustache recorded the 500th goal and 1,000th point of his illustrious career. The

*Vancouver's Trevor Linden (#16) enjoyed a fine rookie season in 1988–89 when he scored 30 goals and added 29 assists. He was good in the playoffs as well, with seven points in seven games.*

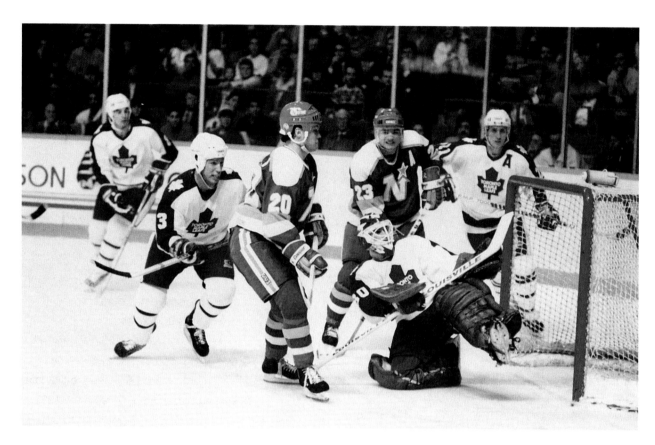

*Minnesota's Dino Ciccarelli (#20) began the 1988–89 season with 32 goals and 59 points in 65 games, but soon found himself traded to Washington. He scored 12 goals in 11 games as a Capital to finish the season.*

hard-shooting right winger was also one of three captains on the Flames that year (Jim Peplinski and Tim Hunter were the others), but he had a hard time staying in the lineup and played in only 51 games, recording 18 points. McDonald knew he playing in his last season, and looked to the playoffs to provide one more highlight before announcing his retirement.

# The PLAYOFFS

First-round series in the 1989 playoffs went to the favorites, with one exception. Detroit was knocked off by a surging Chicago team in six games. The Red Wings were riddled with troubled players such as Bob Probert and Petr Klima, and the magic they had shown over the last three years was quickly fading. The Vancouver Canucks nearly pulled off another upset, but ultimately lost to the Calgary Flames, who had to score in overtime of the seventh game to pull out the series. It was not exactly a clean goal, but Joel Otto's marker won the contest with team-

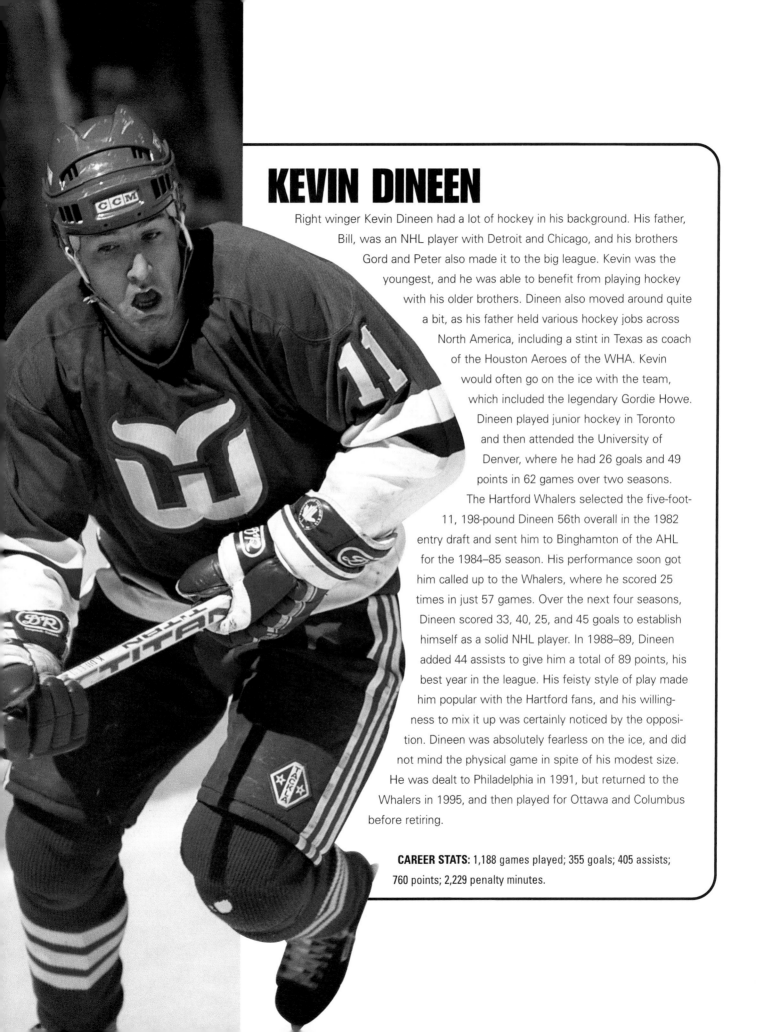

# KEVIN DINEEN

Right winger Kevin Dineen had a lot of hockey in his background. His father, Bill, was an NHL player with Detroit and Chicago, and his brothers Gord and Peter also made it to the big league. Kevin was the youngest, and he was able to benefit from playing hockey with his older brothers. Dineen also moved around quite a bit, as his father held various hockey jobs across North America, including a stint in Texas as coach of the Houston Aeroes of the WHA. Kevin would often go on the ice with the team, which included the legendary Gordie Howe. Dineen played junior hockey in Toronto and then attended the University of Denver, where he had 26 goals and 49 points in 62 games over two seasons. The Hartford Whalers selected the five-foot-11, 198-pound Dineen 56th overall in the 1982 entry draft and sent him to Binghamton of the AHL for the 1984–85 season. His performance soon got him called up to the Whalers, where he scored 25 times in just 57 games. Over the next four seasons, Dineen scored 33, 40, 25, and 45 goals to establish himself as a solid NHL player. In 1988–89, Dineen added 44 assists to give him a total of 89 points, his best year in the league. His feisty style of play made him popular with the Hartford fans, and his willingness to mix it up was certainly noticed by the opposition. Dineen was absolutely fearless on the ice, and did not mind the physical game in spite of his modest size. He was dealt to Philadelphia in 1991, but returned to the Whalers in 1995, and then played for Ottawa and Columbus before retiring.

**CAREER STATS:** 1,188 games played; 355 goals; 405 assists; 760 points; 2,229 penalty minutes.

mate Jim Peplinski crashing into the Vancouver netminder. In the most anticipated matchup of the opening round, Gretzky's Los Angeles Kings took on his old team. The Oilers looked to have the series wrapped up after a pair of wins on home ice put them up 3–1 in games, but Los Angeles bounced back to take the fifth contest 4–2 at home. The Kings then beat the Oilers 4–1 in Edmonton, and then went back home to take game seven 6–3. The series ended appropriately enough with Gretzky scoring a goal into the empty net while he was being chased by former teammate Jari Kurri.

The Kings were no competition for the Flames in the second round, especially after an opening-game loss in overtime. Calgary had learned its lesson in the first round, and wrapped up the series in four straight. The Blackhawks kept up their strong play with a 4–1 series win over the St. Louis Blues and would meet the Flames in the conference final. In the other conference, the Canadiens rolled to easy wins over the Whalers and Bruins, losing only one game, while the Philadelphia Flyers under new coach Paul Holmgren got past Washington and then edged the Penguins in seven games. The Flyers survived against the high-powered Pittsburgh team by playing good defense in the final match, coming away with a 4–1 win. Earlier in the series, Lemieux once again recorded eight points (five goals, three assists) in a 10–7 Pittsburgh win, matching the playoff record set one year before by Patrick Sundstrom.

Montreal and Philadelphia staged another nasty six-game series like

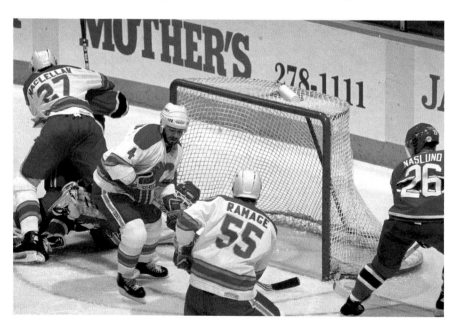

*Defenseman Brad McCrimmon (#4) was acquired by the Calgary Flames in a deal with the Philadelphia Flyers after a contract dispute. He was solid in his own end, recording a plus/minus rating of 43 in 1988–89.*

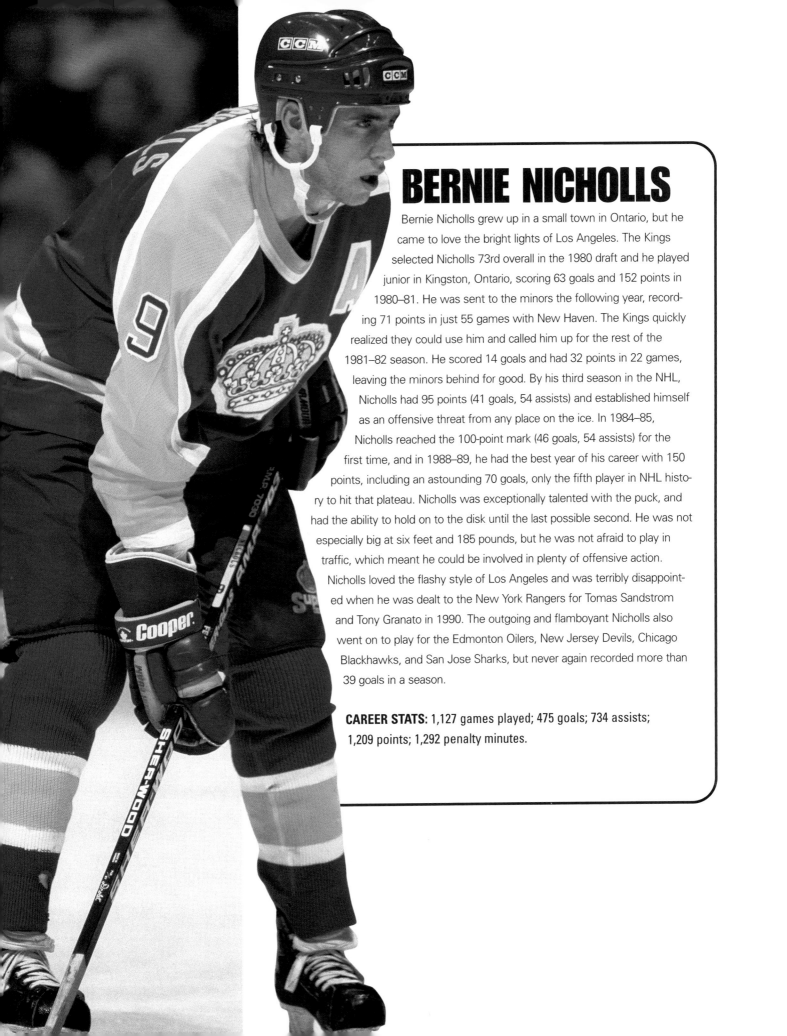

# BERNIE NICHOLLS

Bernie Nicholls grew up in a small town in Ontario, but he came to love the bright lights of Los Angeles. The Kings selected Nicholls 73rd overall in the 1980 draft and he played junior in Kingston, Ontario, scoring 63 goals and 152 points in 1980–81. He was sent to the minors the following year, recording 71 points in just 55 games with New Haven. The Kings quickly realized they could use him and called him up for the rest of the 1981–82 season. He scored 14 goals and had 32 points in 22 games, leaving the minors behind for good. By his third season in the NHL, Nicholls had 95 points (41 goals, 54 assists) and established himself as an offensive threat from any place on the ice. In 1984–85, Nicholls reached the 100-point mark (46 goals, 54 assists) for the first time, and in 1988–89, he had the best year of his career with 150 points, including an astounding 70 goals, only the fifth player in NHL history to hit that plateau. Nicholls was exceptionally talented with the puck, and had the ability to hold on to the disk until the last possible second. He was not especially big at six feet and 185 pounds, but he was not afraid to play in traffic, which meant he could be involved in plenty of offensive action. Nicholls loved the flashy style of Los Angeles and was terribly disappointed when he was dealt to the New York Rangers for Tomas Sandstrom and Tony Granato in 1990. The outgoing and flamboyant Nicholls also went on to play for the Edmonton Oilers, New Jersey Devils, Chicago Blackhawks, and San Jose Sharks, but never again recorded more than 39 goals in a season.

**CAREER STATS:** 1,127 games played; 475 goals; 734 assists; 1,209 points; 1,292 penalty minutes.

# MIKE VERNON

The Calgary Flames did something very smart with hometown hero Mike Vernon by letting him develop in the junior and minor pro systems before putting him in goal in the NHL. The Flames selected the five-foot-nine, 170-pound netminder 56th overall in 1981 after Vernon had played junior hockey with the Calgary Wranglers for a couple of years. At the end of his third season, when the Wranglers were out of the playoffs, Vernon joined the Portland Winter Hawks for the remainder of the post-season and won the Memorial Cup with his new team. He then played three years in the minors, putting together an uneven record, but the Flames called him up for good during the 1985–86 season and Vernon won nine of 18 appearances. In the playoffs, he played in 21 games and won 12 of them as the Flames made it all the way to the finals, and while they lost to Montreal, Vernon showed what a big-game goalie he was. He always relied on his quickness — his glove hand was lightning fast — and his ability to challenge the shooter. Since he was not a big goalie, he had to be strong playing the angles and moving his feet to get to as many pucks as possible. In 1988–89, he was named to the NHL's Second All-Star Team posting a league high 37 wins and only six losses. He was even better in the playoffs as the Flames beat Vancouver, Los Angeles, Chicago, and Montreal to win the Cup. His saves in the over-time session of the seventh game against the Canucks' Stan Smyl, Tony Tanti, and Petri Skriko are still talked about. Vernon also led the Detroit Red Wings to their first Cup win in 42 years when they won it all in 1997. He was awarded the Conn Smythe Trophy for his playoff performance that year.

**CAREER STATS:** 781 games played; 385 wins; 273 losses; 92 ties; 27 shutouts; 2.98 goals-against average.

*A picture-perfect ending for a great player, as Lanny McDonald of the Calgary Flames hoists the Stanley Cup after his final NHL game.*

they did two years ago, but this time the Canadiens came out the winners. The bad blood started flowing again after Chelios rammed the head of the Philadelphia's Brian Propp into the boards. Propp looked badly hurt, but the Flyers showed remarkable restraint and maintained their poise until the series was just about over. As time ran out in a 4–2 Montreal win that would end the series, goalie Ron Hextall took matters into his own hands and charged out of his net to take a swing at Chelios's head with his blocker. Chicago gave Calgary a difficult time at various points in their series, but the Flames persevered to win in five.

The finals featured the best two teams over the regular season, and it was hard-fought all the way to the end. But Calgary had too much depth for the Habs this time around, and they won the Cup in six games. They made history by clinching the series with 4–2 win in Montreal, making the Flames the only visiting team in NHL history to win the Cup in the Forum. Cliff Fletcher's work at building the Flames had finally paid off, and Lanny McDonald, in his final NHL game, scored a key goal to cap a Hall of Fame career — he had also scored his first-ever goal in Montreal. It was a perfect ending for the grateful McDonald, who accepted the Stanley Cup at center ice on behalf of the Flames

# 1989–90

The NHL sees a Russian revolution, Hull is the spirit of St. Louis, and Messier comes of age as a captain

**COMPETITION** for the Stanley Cup in 1989–90 was truly a wide-open contest. All the divisional races were extremely close, with only the Quebec Nordiques (an embarrassing 31 points) and the Vancouver Canucks (64 points) well out of playoff contention. As well, the Detroit Red Wings dropped all the way to the bottom of the Norris Division, right where they had started a just a few years ago, before Jacques Demers had taken over as coach. Their last-place finish ensured that coaching and management changes were in the works for the summer of 1990. Other teams to miss the postseason were the Pittsburgh Penguins (72 points) and the Philadelphia Flyers (71 points).

For the teams who made the playoffs, a shot at winning it all did not seem far-fetched. The Boston Bruins turned in the year's best performance with a 101-point season under coach Mike Milbury. Right winger Cam Neely led the Bruins' attack with 55 goals and 92 points, while defenseman Ray Bourque took the Norris Trophy again with 19 goals and 65 assists. Craig Janney (24 goals), Bobby Carpenter (25 goals), and Don Sweeney (22 goals) also helped out on offense, but their real strength was the superb goaltending of Reggie Lemelin and Andy Moog, who combined to win the Jennings Trophy for fewest goals against (232). Boston won a league-high 46 games, one more than division rival Buffalo, but would have a big scare in the first

*The highlight of the 1989–90 season was the night Wayne Gretzky recorded his 1,851st career point to become the NHL's all-time leader. The historic point was this goal on October 15, 1989, in Edmonton, sending the game into overtime.*

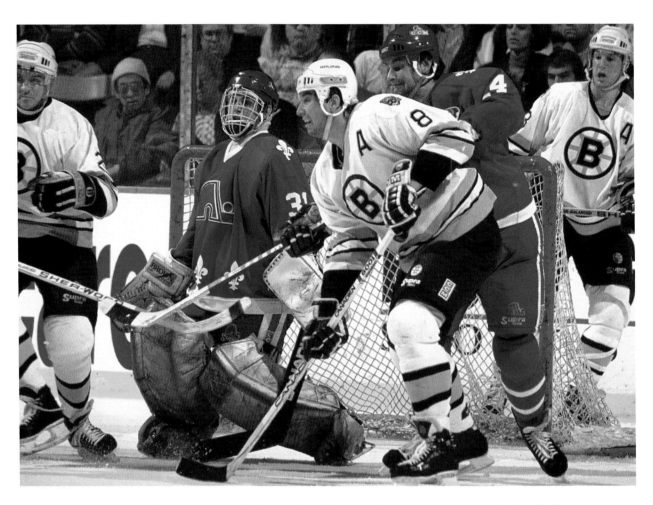

*Boston's Cam Neely (#8) had a 55-goal, 92-point regular season for the Bruins in 1989–90, and then added 12 goals and 28 points in the playoffs, helping his team to the finals.*

round of the playoffs from the surprising Hartford Whalers.

Buffalo was paced to a good season by Pierre Turgeon (40 goals, 106 points), Dave Andreychuk (40 goals) and defenseman Phil Housley (81 points). Darren Puppa had taken over as the Sabres' number-one netminder and he won 31 games during the regular season. Another interesting performer for the Sabres was Russian-born rookie Alex Mogilny, who defected to the West to play in the NHL. He scored a goal 20 seconds into his first game and totaled 15 markers in his first year.

The Montreal Canadiens were not as strong as a year ago, but still managed to win 41 games and record 92 points. Goaltender Patrick Roy had a fine year in net with a 2.53 goals-against average, but the Habs lacked offense, with only Stephane Richer having a top season, scoring 51 goals. A better balanced Boston club would prove too much for the Canadiens to handle in the postseason.

*Buffalo's Pierre Turgeon (#77) and Dave Andreychuk (#25) look for a loose puck around the Toronto net. Turgeon scored 40 goals in 1989–90 and totaled 106 points, finishing seventh in the scoring race. Andreychuk also scored 40 goals and added 42 assists.*

## Kings Decline but Gretzky Stays on Top

The Los Angeles Kings, who had finished the previous year on a good note, could not live up to higher expectations. The '89–'90 season saw the Kings record a mediocre 34–39–7 record, good for 75 points and fourth place in the Smythe Division. Despite the poor record of the team, Wayne Gretzky had a league-leading 142 points (including 102 assists). Now a Hollywood star, Gretzky showed a flair for the dramatic as he closed in on Gordie Howe's all-time point record. On October 15, in Edmonton, the Kings center scored a goal with just 53 seconds to play to tie the game with the Oilers 4–4. The goal was Gretzky's 1,851st point, moving him ahead of the legendary Howe, who was in attendance, and then to cap off his great night, Gretzky scored the game winner in overtime. The Edmonton crowd appreciated seeing the mark broken in the city where Gretzky had starred for many years. A few months later, on February 28, the Oilers and Kings set a record by combining for 85 penalties. The Oilers had 44 of those penalties, including 26 minor infractions, seven majors, six 10-minute misconducts, four game misconducts and one match penalty. The two teams would meet in the playoffs again as well.

Gretzky went on to recapture the scoring title, a position that had eluded him for the past two seasons. One of the big reasons that Gretzky was able to take the Art Ross was that Mario Lemieux missed

# ANDY MOOG

Andy Moog could have had a career as a backup goaltender to Grant Fuhr in Edmonton, and nobody would have blamed him if he had done so. But Moog wanted to be a number-one goalie and forced the Oilers to trade him in 1988. It could not have been an easy decision for the native of Penticton, British Columbia, who had played in the Edmonton organization since they drafted him 132nd overall in 1980. Moog played just seven games for the Oilers during the 1980–81 regular season, but was stellar in the playoffs when Edmonton knocked off the mighty Montreal Canadiens in the first round. The three-game sweep of the Habs was the Oilers' first shining moment and an indicator of things to come. But Moog had a poor training camp the following year and was sent to Wichita of the Central Hockey League for most of the 1981–82 season. He played very well the minors and returned to the Oilers for the next five seasons, winning 137 games over that time. He was in net in the night the Oilers won their first Stanley Cup in 1984, defeating the New York Islanders. Moog was on two other Cup-winning clubs in Edmonton before he came to the conclusion that he would never unseat Fuhr as the first-string goalie. The 1987–88 season saw Moog play for Canada's national team while he waited for a trade. The deal was finally completed in March of 1988, and Moog found himself playing for the Boston Bruins in the finals that year against the Oilers! By 1989–90, Moog was part of the top goaltending tandem in the NHL, sharing the Jennings Trophy with Reggie Lemelin and winning 24 of 46 appearances. The Oilers and Bruins met for the Cup again in 1990 and Moog was bested again, this time by Edmonton netminder Bill Ranford. Moog had three more great seasons in Boston before being traded to the Dallas Stars in 1993 and finished his career with Montreal in 1997–98.

**CAREER STATS:** 713 games played; 372 wins; 209 losses; 88 ties; 3.13 goals-against average; 28 shutouts.

21 games — undoubtedly causing Pittsburgh to miss the playoffs — though he still managed 123 points. Gretzky was also challenged for the point lead by former teammate and new Oilers captain Mark Messier (45 goals, 129 points), Detroit's Steve Yzerman (62 goals, 127 points), and the surprising new star of the NHL, Brett Hull, who scored a league-best 72 goals and totaled 113 points. Other 100-point performers were Bernie Nicholls, Pat LaFontaine, Paul Coffey, Joe Sakic, Adam Oates, Ron Francis, and Luc Robitaille. A dozen others had 90 or more points during the season, while three players — Peter Stastny, Jari Kurri and Denis Savard — each recorded their 1,000th career point during the season.

*Mario Lemieux (#66) of Pittsburgh takes the puck from Rick Tocchet (#22) of Philadelphia. Lemieux played only in 59 games during the 1989–90 season, but still managed 123 points (45 goals, 78 assists). Tocchet recorded 96 points (37 goals, 59 assists) during the regular season and had a four-goal game against Winnipeg.*

### Original Six Cities Rebound

With Floyd Smith as general manager and Doug Carpenter as coach, the revamped Toronto Maple Leafs were able to secure a 38–38–4 record, the first time the Leafs had played .500 since 1978–79. The team played an aggressive brand of hockey and could score at will, it seemed, with 337 goals, behind only Calgary and Los Angeles. One early-season contest saw Toronto goalie Mark Laforest stage a spirited fight with New Jersey netminder Sean Burke, while other fights were going on around them. The Leafs lost the game 5–4, but the brawl seemed to give the Leafs a gritty persona they carried the rest of the year. Toronto got a great year out of one trio in particular, as Gary Leeman (51 goals), Ed Olczyk (88 points), and Mark Osborne (73 points), known as the GEM line, produced high numbers. Vincent Damphousse (33 goals) and Daniel Marois (39 goals) were also rising stars on the attack, but the team's ultimate demise came about because of a lack of defense and goaltending. As well, Smith made a ridiculous trade with the Devils by sending a number-one draft choice in 1991 to New Jersey for defenseman Tom Kurvers. The American-born blueliner gave the Leafs some temporary relief (52 points in '89–'90), but the trade would have an enormous impact on the Leafs just one year later.

The New York Rangers also appeared headed in the right direction with a 36–31–13 record, good enough for first place in the Patrick Division. Phil Esposito's reign of error as Rangers general manager was terminated and his replacement was Neil Smith, the former director of scouting and player development for the Detroit Red Wings. A much more patient approach stabilized the Rangers squad, and the hiring of Roger Neilson was an inspired move, at least in the short term. By holding on to his assets a little longer, Smith would be able to wheel and deal effectively in future years, and he understood the value of making good draft selections. In '89–'90, the Rangers still made some deals and were able to secure the high-scoring Bernie Nicholls from Los Angeles and Mike Gartner from Minnesota. John Ogrodnick led the club with 43 goals, while rookie Darren Turcotte had 32 tallies. Veterans Brian Mullen (27 goals) and Kelly Kisio (22 goals) also made contributions to the Rangers' turnaround. The Madison Square Garden crowd also got a look at the future when goalie Mike Richter appeared in 23 games (12–5–5). The Rangers were not ready to challenge for the Stanley Cup, but they were able to win the first round of the playoffs.

*The St. Louis Blues' acquisition of sniper Brett Hull (#16) was looked good in 1989–90 when he scored a league-leading 72 goals and had 113 points.*

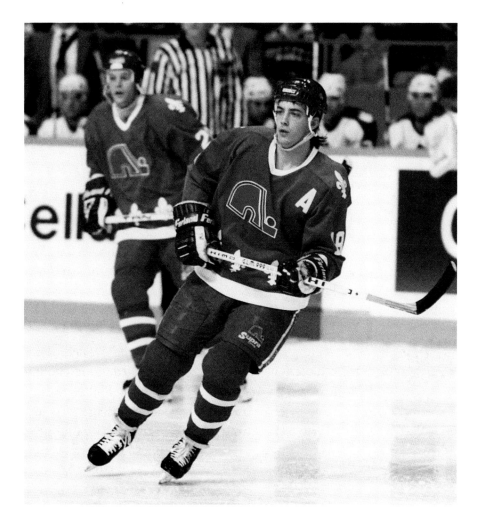

Drafted 15th overall by the Quebec Nordiques in 1987, center Joe Sakic had a breakout year in 1989–90 when he scored 39 goals and 63 assists in just his second season in the NHL.

The Chicago Blackhawks had a good season after their surprising run in the 1988 playoffs, winning 41 games and recording 88 points. Coach Mike Keenan kept a firm hand on his club and got good years from Steve Larmer (90 points), Denis Savard (80 points) and Doug Wilson (73 points). Youngsters like Steve Thomas (40 goals), Adam Creighton (34 goals), and rookie Jeremy Roenick (26 goals) added to the good mix of Chicago forwards, augmented late in the season with Michel Goulet, who came over in a trade with the Nordiques. Keenan always had his team work hard, and they had plenty of toughness with players like Dave Manson and Bob McGill on the blueline, but the team was weak in goal, with Jacques Cloutier and Alain Chevrier sharing the bulk of the work. Chicago would be a tough team in the playoffs, but they did not have enough talent on defense nor in net to go further than the conference final.

## Oilers Make More Changes

The Edmonton Oilers were still reeling from their ouster at the hands of the Los Angeles Kings the previous spring, and they got off to a poor start in '89–'90. Then they had to deal with a whining star in Jimmy Carson, who decided he did not want to play in Edmonton anymore. Luckily for the Oilers, Detroit was interested in acquiring the native of Michigan, and made a strong pitch for Carson. A deal was consummated on November 2, and the Oilers received Petr Klima, Adam Graves, Jeff Sharples, and Joe Murphy in exchange for Carson and Kevin McClelland. It was difficult for Edmonton to lose a 49-goal scorer in Carson, but the new acquisitions made the Oilers a much better team. Messier, Kurri (93 points), Glenn Anderson (34 goals), Esa Tikkanen (30 goals), Craig Simpson (29 goals), and Craig MacTavish (21 goals) were the veterans who kept the Oilers in contention and got them 90 points with a 38–28–14 record under coach John Muckler (Glen Sather concentrated on being the full-time general manager). The Oilers also had a veteran defense — led by Kevin Lowe, Charlie Huddy, and Randy Gregg — to help out young goalie Bill Ranford, acquired from Boston to replace an injured Grant Fuhr. Few predicted great things for the Oilers in the playoffs, but the revamped squad would prove to have the right combination of youth and experience.

If the Oilers were a dark horse in the playoffs, the Calgary Flames were certainly one of the favorites. They followed their Stanley Cup championship by going 42–23–15 to collect 99 points, second best in the NHL. Even though Lanny McDonald had retired and his number nine was put up in the rafters, the Flames still had enough firepower and experience to take the Cup once again. Joe Nieuwendyk (45 goals), Doug Gilmour (91 points), Al MacInnis (28 goals and 90 points), Gary Roberts (39 goals), Joe Mullen (36 goals) and Theo Fleury (31 goals) led a feared attack that saw the Flames score the most goals in the NHL. Calgary was very strong in goal with Mike Vernon and Rick Wamsley, and their defense, led by

*In both of his first two years in the NHL, Calgary's Joe Nieuwendyk (#25) scored 51 goals. In 1989–90, he scored 45 and had a career-high 95 points for the Flames.*

# ESA TIKKANEN

Forward Esa Tikkanen was one of the first players to be termed a "super pest." Undoubtedly this tag came from the opposition who could not stand the left winger's constant yapping, or his ability to get in the way of a good play. Tikkanen was a very determined player who would do just about anything to drive his opponents crazy, and he often succeeded even though it was hard to understand his English! The Edmonton Oilers drafted the six-foot-one, 190-pound native of Finland with the 82nd choice of the 1983 entry draft. He joined them in time for their 1985 Stanley Cup win, but split the next season between Nova Scotia and Edmonton. In his first full season with the Oilers, Tikkanen scored 34 goals (a career high) and proved himself a solid two-way player. He stayed with the Oilers for most of the next six seasons and scored 30 or more twice. Tikkanen was an important member of four Oilers' championships and was at his best in the postseason in 1990, when he had 24 points in 22 games. In the finals versus Boston, Tikkanen had three goals and two assists in five games as Edmonton won a final Stanley Cup with their dynasty team. The fearless Tikkanen — he was not typical of many European players, since he loved to work in the corners — was sent to the New York Rangers in a trade for Doug Weight in 1993, and he was with the Broadway club when they won the Cup in 1994. After that triumph, Tikkanen moved around the NHL, making stops in St. Louis, New Jersey, Vancouver, Florida, and Washington. He helped the Capitals make their first-ever finals appearance in 1998 and upped his playoff total to an impressive 132 points in 186 contests.

**CAREER STATS:** 877 games played; 244 goals; 386 assists; 630 points; 1,077 penalty minutes.

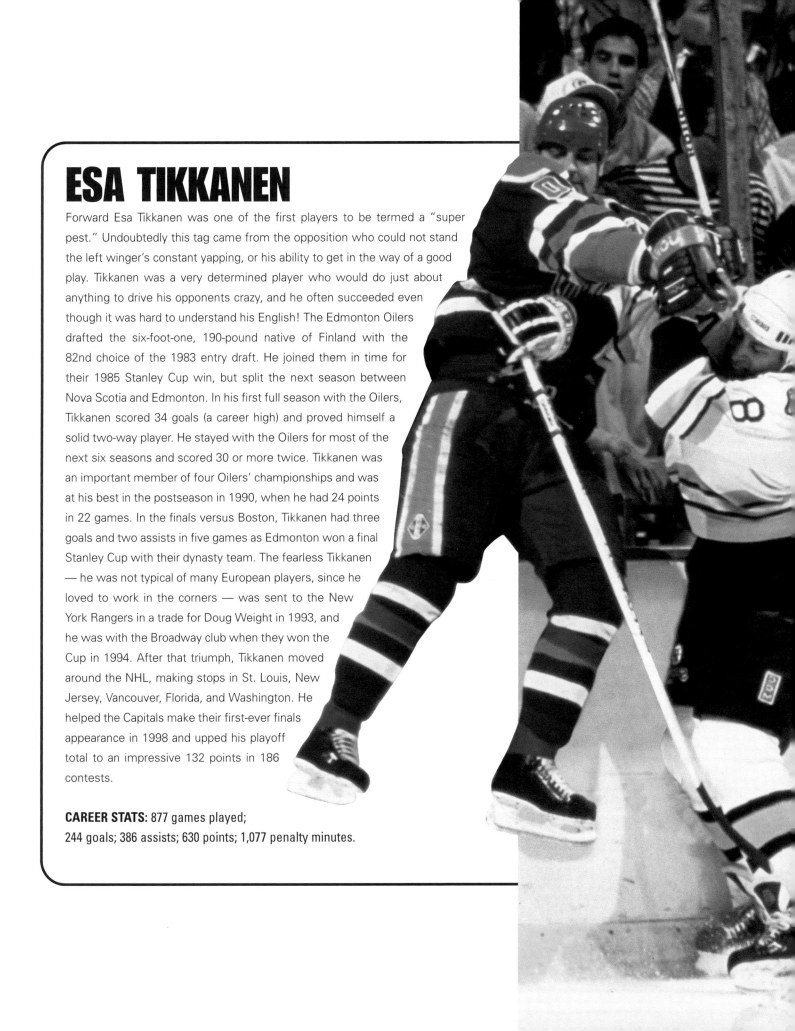

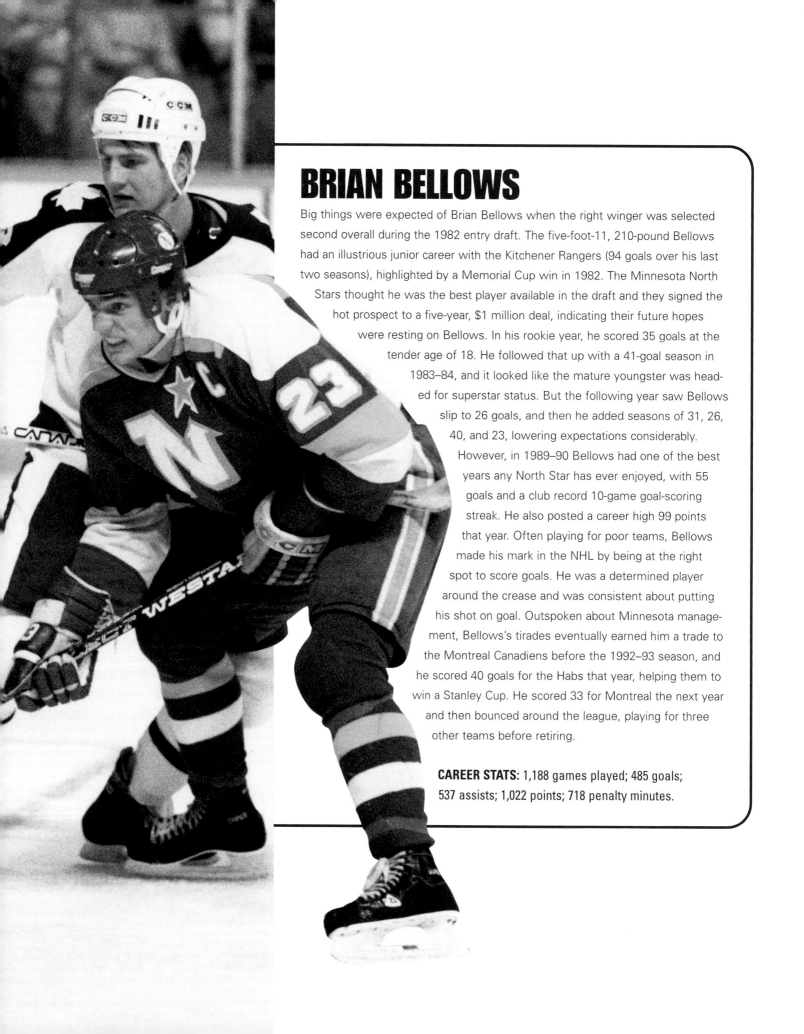

# BRIAN BELLOWS

Big things were expected of Brian Bellows when the right winger was selected second overall during the 1982 entry draft. The five-foot-11, 210-pound Bellows had an illustrious junior career with the Kitchener Rangers (94 goals over his last two seasons), highlighted by a Memorial Cup win in 1982. The Minnesota North Stars thought he was the best player available in the draft and they signed the hot prospect to a five-year, $1 million deal, indicating their future hopes were resting on Bellows. In his rookie year, he scored 35 goals at the tender age of 18. He followed that up with a 41-goal season in 1983–84, and it looked like the mature youngster was headed for superstar status. But the following year saw Bellows slip to 26 goals, and then he added seasons of 31, 26, 40, and 23, lowering expectations considerably. However, in 1989–90 Bellows had one of the best years any North Star has ever enjoyed, with 55 goals and a club record 10-game goal-scoring streak. He also posted a career high 99 points that year. Often playing for poor teams, Bellows made his mark in the NHL by being at the right spot to score goals. He was a determined player around the crease and was consistent about putting his shot on goal. Outspoken about Minnesota management, Bellows's tirades eventually earned him a trade to the Montreal Canadiens before the 1992–93 season, and he scored 40 goals for the Habs that year, helping them to win a Stanley Cup. He scored 33 for Montreal the next year and then bounced around the league, playing for three other teams before retiring.

**CAREER STATS:** 1,188 games played; 485 goals; 537 assists; 1,022 points; 718 penalty minutes.

MacInnis and Gary Suter (76 points), was as good as any in the league. While a repeat looked like it was in the offing, the Flames would have to get past an old nemesis when they faced Gretzky in the opening series of the playoffs.

### Russians Join the NHL

One of the most notable changes to the NHL during the '89–'90 campaign was the influx of Russian-born players. Previously forbidden from leaving their country legitimately, the Soviet government now allowed the New Jersey Devils to take defensemen Viacheslav Fetisov and Alexei Kasatonov, while the Flames had the rookie of the year in Sergei Makarov, who scored 24 goals and had 86 points. Calgary had the first "approved" Russian player on their squad late in the previous season, when Sergei Priakin joined the club, but he did not last long. Vancouver was able to secure the right to use Igor Larionov (44 points) and Vladimir Krutov (11 goals), and Larionov proved to be one of the finest players ever produced by the Russian hockey system. Players from the Soviet Union would demonstrate over time that they were some of the most highly skilled competitors in the world.

# The PLAYOFFS

The first round of the playoffs proved to be one of the most interesting in years. The Hartford Whalers were not supposed be an impediment to the first-place Boston Bruins, but it took seven games to subdue the club coached by former Whaler Rick Ley. The Bruins had game seven on home ice and edged out their New England rivals by a 3–1 score. Montreal handled the inexperienced Buffalo squad in six games, while the New York Rangers rolled over a weak New York Islanders team in just five contests. Washington pulled off a mild surprise by defeating the Devils in six.

Chicago had their hands full with the Minnesota North Stars, but the Blackhawks prevailed in seven games, taking the final contest 5–2 on home ice. St. Louis took out Toronto in five games, even though the Maple Leafs had beat the Blues seven out of eight times in the regular season. But the most interesting series in the West took place between Edmonton and Winnipeg. The Jets jumped out to a 3–1 lead in games, but the savvy Oilers bounced back to take the next three. Edmonton goalie Bill Ranford looked terrible early on, including an ugly 7–5 loss to the Jets

# STEPHANE RICHER

It's never easy to play in a hockey-mad city like Montreal, and it's even more difficult when you are expected to be the next French-Canadian superstar. Such was the case for the talented but enigmatic right winger Stephane Richer, an admirer of former Montreal legend Guy Lafleur. A big man at six-foot-two and 215 pounds, Richer also possessed a wicked shot that he could unleash with a half wind-up motion. When he was on his game, Richer could excite the Forum fans with his scoring exploits, but each goal would raise expectations further, and the native of Ripon, Quebec, had difficulty with the pressure. Richer starred in junior with Granby of the QMJHL, and later in Sherbrooke of the American Hockey League. A natural goal scorer, Richer joined the Habs for the 1985–86 season, when he scored 21 goals and added four more in the playoffs as the Canadiens won the Stanley Cup. He was back in the minors the next year and nearly quit the game, but came back to the big club with 20 goals in 57 games. He also patched up his differences with coach Jean Perron, and in 1987–88 he scored 50 goals. It looked like Richer had finally arrived, but the next year he dropped to 25 goals in 68 games. By this time Pat Burns was coaching the Canadiens, and he had faith in Richer's abilities. Richer responded with a 51-goal, 91-point season in 1989–90. But after a 31-goal performance the next season, he was dealt to New Jersey, where he enjoyed five years of 20 or more goals. Richer was back on a Cup winner in 1995 when the Devils won their first championship.

**CAREER STATS:** 1,054 games played; 421 goals; 398 assists; 819 points; 614 penalty minutes.

on home ice, but he got better as the series continued and eventually proved to be the difference. The Los Angeles Kings made up for a poor season by knocking off the defending champion Flames in six hard-fought games. The teams split the first two, and the Kings won the third game 2–1 in overtime before bombing Calgary 12–4 in the fourth. The Flames got back on track with a 5–1 win on home ice and appeared to have won the sixth game in overtime. But what looked like a sure goal was disallowed by referee Denis Morel, and the Kings won the series on a goal by Mike Krushelnyski. It was a shocking end to the playoffs for the Flames.

The Bruins juggernaut was still strong in the next two rounds, as they easily defeated the Canadiens in five games and then swept the Washington Capitals to make it to the finals. Edmonton had little difficulty with the Kings, who were out of miracles and lost in four straight. Chicago had edged out the Blues in seven games, but then came up against the Oilers in the conference final. The Blackhawks actually had a 2–1 lead

*Mark Messier (#11) tries to find the puck against Boston netminder Andy Moog (#35). Messier won his first Hart Trophy in 1989–90 when he scored 45 goals and had 129 points. He took his team to their fifth Stanley Cup with 31 points in 22 postseason games.*

*The Edmonton Oilers celebrate their fifth Stanley Cup after defeating the Boston Bruins in 1990. The bearded player is goalie Bill Ranford, who was named winner of the Conn Smythe Trophy.*

in games when Mark Messier, the Hart Trophy winner for the season, took over and almost single-handedly defeated Chicago in the fourth game, with two goals and two assists in a 4–2 win. It was one of the more memorable individual playoff performances in recent memory. The loss demoralized the Chicago squad, which did not win again in the series.

The finals between Boston and Edmonton seemed to turn on the first game of the series. The Bruins had a chance to take the opener on home ice, but lost 3–2 after a long overtime session in which they dominated but were not able to score on a superb Ranford. Little-used Petr Klima came off the bench for the Oilers and scored the winner against Moog after 55:13 of overtime. The Bruins never seemed to recover from the loss, winning only one game in the series (a 2–1 contest in Edmonton) while the Oilers steamrolled to 7–2, 5–1 and 4–1 victories to win the championship. Ranford was named winner of the Conn Smythe Trophy and Messier accepted the Cup for the first time as team captain. It was only fitting that the best team of the decade would walk off with their fifth Stanley Cup to close out a truly exciting ten-year period of hockey history.

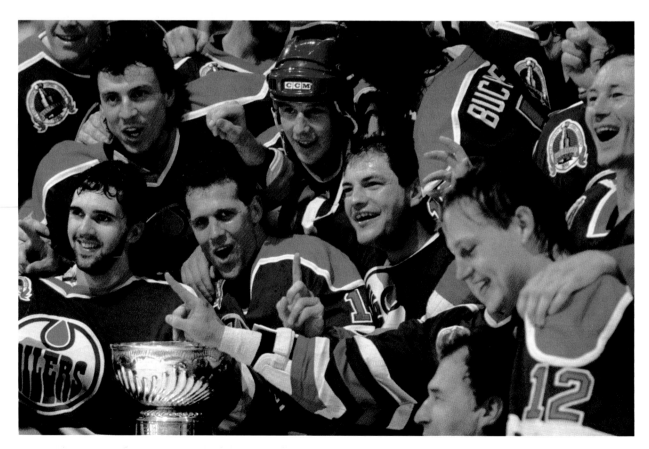

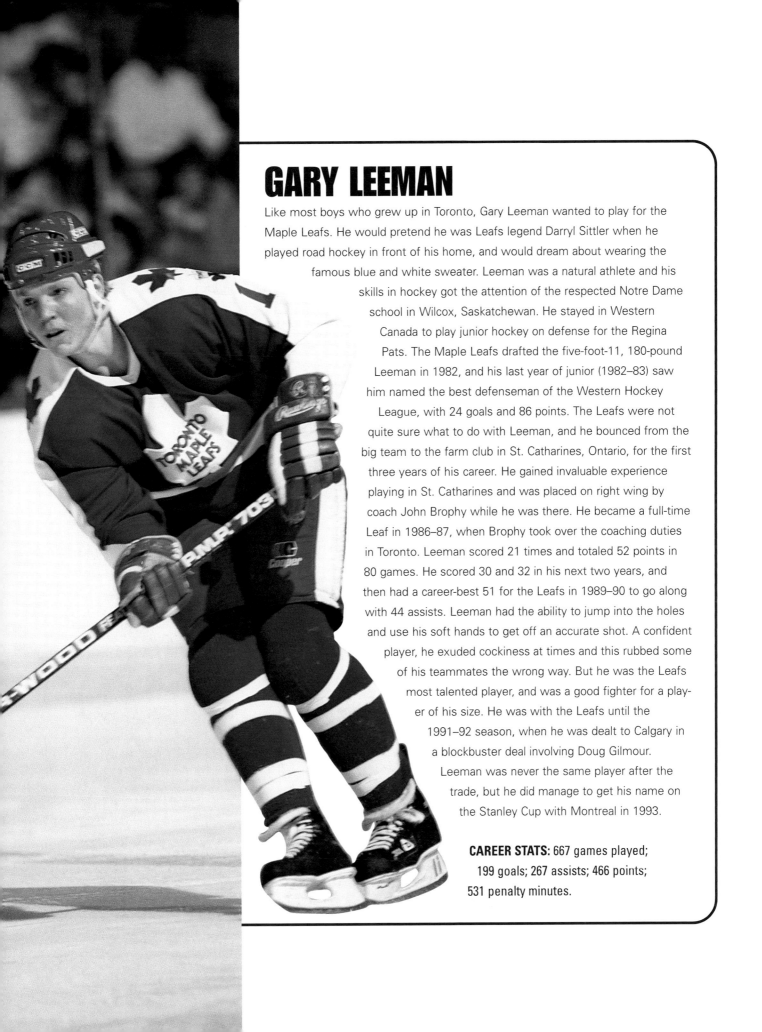

# GARY LEEMAN

Like most boys who grew up in Toronto, Gary Leeman wanted to play for the Maple Leafs. He would pretend he was Leafs legend Darryl Sittler when he played road hockey in front of his home, and would dream about wearing the famous blue and white sweater. Leeman was a natural athlete and his skills in hockey got the attention of the respected Notre Dame school in Wilcox, Saskatchewan. He stayed in Western Canada to play junior hockey on defense for the Regina Pats. The Maple Leafs drafted the five-foot-11, 180-pound Leeman in 1982, and his last year of junior (1982–83) saw him named the best defenseman of the Western Hockey League, with 24 goals and 86 points. The Leafs were not quite sure what to do with Leeman, and he bounced from the big team to the farm club in St. Catharines, Ontario, for the first three years of his career. He gained invaluable experience playing in St. Catharines and was placed on right wing by coach John Brophy while he was there. He became a full-time Leaf in 1986–87, when Brophy took over the coaching duties in Toronto. Leeman scored 21 times and totaled 52 points in 80 games. He scored 30 and 32 in his next two years, and then had a career-best 51 for the Leafs in 1989–90 to go along with 44 assists. Leeman had the ability to jump into the holes and use his soft hands to get off an accurate shot. A confident player, he exuded cockiness at times and this rubbed some of his teammates the wrong way. But he was the Leafs most talented player, and was a good fighter for a player of his size. He was with the Leafs until the 1991–92 season, when he was dealt to Calgary in a blockbuster deal involving Doug Gilmour. Leeman was never the same player after the trade, but he did manage to get his name on the Stanley Cup with Montreal in 1993.

**CAREER STATS:** 667 games played; 199 goals; 267 assists; 466 points; 531 penalty minutes.

# 1980-81

**STANLEY CUP CHAMPION:** New York Islanders

## FINAL STANDINGS

### PRINCE OF WALES CONFERENCE
**Norris Division**

| Team | GP | W | L | T | GF | GA | PTS |
|---|---|---|---|---|---|---|---|
| Montreal | 80 | 45 | 22 | 13 | 332 | 232 | 103 |
| Los Angeles | 80 | 43 | 24 | 13 | 337 | 290 | 99 |
| Pittsburgh | 80 | 30 | 37 | 13 | 302 | 345 | 73 |
| Hartford | 80 | 21 | 41 | 18 | 292 | 372 | 60 |
| Detroit | 80 | 19 | 43 | 18 | 252 | 339 | 56 |

**Adams Division**

| Team | GP | W | L | T | GF | GA | PTS |
|---|---|---|---|---|---|---|---|
| Buffalo | 80 | 39 | 20 | 21 | 327 | 250 | 99 |
| Boston | 80 | 37 | 30 | 13 | 316 | 272 | 87 |
| Minnesota | 80 | 35 | 28 | 17 | 291 | 263 | 87 |
| Quebec | 80 | 30 | 32 | 18 | 314 | 318 | 78 |
| Toronto | 80 | 28 | 37 | 15 | 322 | 367 | 71 |

### CLARENCE CAMPBELL CONFERENCE
**Patrick Division**

| Team | GP | W | L | T | GF | GA | PTS |
|---|---|---|---|---|---|---|---|
| NY Islanders | 80 | 48 | 18 | 14 | 355 | 260 | 110 |
| Philadelphia | 80 | 41 | 24 | 15 | 313 | 249 | 97 |
| Calgary | 80 | 39 | 27 | 14 | 329 | 298 | 92 |
| NY Rangers | 80 | 30 | 36 | 14 | 312 | 317 | 74 |
| Washington | 80 | 26 | 36 | 18 | 286 | 317 | 70 |

**Smythe Division**

| Team | GP | W | L | T | GF | GA | PTS |
|---|---|---|---|---|---|---|---|
| St. Louis | 80 | 45 | 18 | 17 | 352 | 281 | 107 |
| Chicago | 80 | 31 | 33 | 16 | 304 | 315 | 78 |
| Vancouver | 80 | 28 | 32 | 20 | 289 | 301 | 76 |
| Edmonton | 80 | 29 | 35 | 16 | 328 | 327 | 74 |
| Colorado | 80 | 22 | 45 | 13 | 258 | 344 | 57 |
| Winnipeg | 80 | 9 | 57 | 14 | 246 | 400 | 32 |

Photograph, page 201: *Boston's Brad Park (#22) had 14 goals and 66 points for the Bruins in 1980–81. Park was named winner of the Masterton Trophy in 1984, when he was with the Detroit Red Wings.*

## LEADING SCORERS

| Player | Team | GP | G | A | PTS | PIM |
|---|---|---|---|---|---|---|
| Wayne Gretzky | Edmonton | 80 | 55 | 109 | 164 | 28 |
| Marcel Dionne | Los Angeles | 80 | 58 | 77 | 135 | 70 |
| Kent Nilsson | Calgary | 80 | 49 | 82 | 131 | 26 |
| Mike Bossy | NY Islanders | 79 | 68 | 51 | 119 | 32 |
| Dave Taylor | Los Angeles | 72 | 47 | 65 | 112 | 130 |
| Peter Stastny | Quebec | 77 | 39 | 70 | 109 | 37 |
| Charlie Simmer | Los Angeles | 65 | 56 | 49 | 105 | 62 |
| Mike Rogers | Hartford | 80 | 40 | 65 | 105 | 32 |
| Bernie Federko | St. Louis | 78 | 31 | 73 | 104 | 47 |
| Jacques Richard | Quebec | 79 | 52 | 51 | 103 | 39 |

## NHL AWARD WINNERS

| | |
|---|---|
| Hart (MVP) | Wayne Gretzky |
| Art Ross (leading scorer) | Wayne Gretzky |
| Calder (rookie of the year) | Peter Stastny |
| Vezina (fewest goals against) | Richard Sevigny, Denis Herron, Michel Larocque |
| Lady Byng (gentlemanly conduct) | Rick Kehoe |
| Norris (best defenseman) | Randy Carlyle |
| Conn Smythe (playoff MVP) | Butch Goring |
| Masterton (perseverance) | Blake Dunlop |
| Pearson (NHLPA MVP) | Mike Liut |
| Adams (coach of the year) | Red Berenson |
| Selke (best defensive forward) | Bob Gainey |

# 1981-82

**STANLEY CUP CHAMPION:** New York Islanders

## FINAL STANDINGS

### CLARENCE CAMPBELL CONFERENCE
**Norris Division**

| Team | GP | W | L | T | GF | GA | PTS |
|---|---|---|---|---|---|---|---|
| Minnesota | 80 | 37 | 23 | 20 | 346 | 288 | 94 |
| Winnipeg | 80 | 33 | 33 | 14 | 319 | 332 | 80 |
| St. Louis | 80 | 32 | 40 | 8 | 315 | 349 | 72 |
| Chicago | 80 | 30 | 38 | 12 | 332 | 363 | 72 |
| Toronto | 80 | 20 | 44 | 16 | 298 | 380 | 56 |
| Detroit | 80 | 21 | 47 | 12 | 270 | 351 | 54 |

**Smythe Division**

| Team | GP | W | L | T | GF | GA | PTS |
|---|---|---|---|---|---|---|---|
| Edmonton | 80 | 48 | 17 | 15 | 417 | 295 | 111 |
| Vancouver | 80 | 30 | 33 | 17 | 290 | 286 | 77 |
| Calgary | 80 | 29 | 34 | 17 | 334 | 345 | 75 |
| Los Angeles | 80 | 24 | 41 | 15 | 314 | 369 | 63 |
| Colorado | 80 | 18 | 49 | 13 | 241 | 362 | 49 |

### PRINCE OF WALES CONFERENCE
**Adams Division**

| Team | GP | W | L | T | GF | GA | PTS |
|---|---|---|---|---|---|---|---|
| Montreal | 80 | 46 | 17 | 17 | 360 | 223 | 109 |
| Boston | 80 | 43 | 27 | 10 | 323 | 285 | 96 |
| Buffalo | 80 | 39 | 26 | 15 | 307 | 273 | 93 |
| Quebec | 80 | 33 | 31 | 16 | 356 | 345 | 82 |
| Hartford | 80 | 21 | 41 | 18 | 264 | 351 | 60 |

**Patrick Division**

| Team | GP | W | L | T | GF | GA | PTS |
|---|---|---|---|---|---|---|---|
| NY Islanders | 80 | 54 | 16 | 10 | 385 | 250 | 118 |
| NY Rangers | 80 | 39 | 27 | 14 | 316 | 306 | 92 |
| Philadelphia | 80 | 38 | 31 | 11 | 325 | 313 | 87 |
| Pittsburgh | 80 | 31 | 36 | 13 | 310 | 337 | 75 |
| Washington | 80 | 26 | 41 | 13 | 319 | 338 | 65 |

Photograph, page 203: *John Tonelli (#27) celebrates his overtime winner against the Pittsburgh Penguins during the 1982 playoffs. The goal eliminated the Penguins and the Islanders went on to win their third straight Stanley Cup.*

## LEADING SCORERS

| Player | Team | GP | G | A | PTS | PIM |
|---|---|---|---|---|---|---|
| Wayne Gretzky | Edmonton | 80 | 92 | 120 | 212 | 26 |
| Mike Bossy | NY Islanders | 80 | 64 | 83 | 147 | 22 |
| Peter Stastny | Quebec | 80 | 46 | 93 | 139 | 91 |
| Dennis Maruk | Washington | 80 | 60 | 76 | 136 | 128 |
| Bryan Trottier | NY Islanders | 80 | 50 | 79 | 129 | 88 |
| Denis Savard | Chicago | 80 | 32 | 87 | 119 | 82 |
| Marcel Dionne | Los Angeles | 78 | 50 | 67 | 117 | 50 |
| Bobby Smith | Minnesota | 80 | 43 | 71 | 114 | 82 |
| Dino Ciccarelli | Minnesota | 76 | 55 | 51 | 106 | 138 |
| Dave Taylor | Los Angeles | 78 | 39 | 67 | 106 | 130 |

## NHL AWARD WINNERS

| | |
|---|---|
| Hart (MVP) | Wayne Gretzky |
| Art Ross (leading scorer) | Wayne Gretzky |
| Calder (rookie of the year) | Dale Hawerchuk |
| Vezina (best goaltender) | Bill Smith |
| Jennings (fewest goals against) | Rick Wamsley, Dennis Herron |
| Lady Byng (gentlemanly conduct) | Rick Middleton |
| Norris (best defenseman) | Doug Wilson |
| Conn Smythe (playoff MVP) | Mike Bossy |
| Masterton (perseverance) | Glenn Resch |
| Pearson (NHLPA MVP) | Wayne Gretzky |
| Adams (coach of the year) | Tom Watt |
| Selke (best defensive forward) | Steve Kasper |

# 1982-83

**STANLEY CUP CHAMPION:** New York Islanders

## FINAL STANDINGS

### CLARENCE CAMPBELL CONFERENCE
#### Norris Division

| Team | GP | W | L | T | GF | GA | PTS |
|------|-----|-----|-----|-----|-----|-----|-----|
| Chicago | 80 | 47 | 23 | 10 | 338 | 268 | 104 |
| Minnesota | 80 | 40 | 24 | 16 | 321 | 290 | 96 |
| Toronto | 80 | 28 | 40 | 12 | 293 | 330 | 68 |
| St. Louis | 80 | 25 | 40 | 15 | 285 | 316 | 65 |
| Detroit | 80 | 21 | 44 | 15 | 263 | 344 | 57 |

#### Smythe Division

| Team | GP | W | L | T | GF | GA | PTS |
|------|-----|-----|-----|-----|-----|-----|-----|
| Edmonton | 80 | 47 | 21 | 12 | 424 | 315 | 106 |
| Calgary | 80 | 32 | 34 | 14 | 321 | 317 | 78 |
| Vancouver | 80 | 30 | 35 | 15 | 303 | 309 | 75 |
| Winnipeg | 80 | 33 | 39 | 8 | 311 | 333 | 74 |
| Los Angeles | 80 | 27 | 41 | 12 | 308 | 365 | 66 |

### PRINCE OF WALES CONFERENCE
#### Adams Division

| Team | GP | W | L | T | GF | GA | PTS |
|------|-----|-----|-----|-----|-----|-----|-----|
| Boston | 80 | 50 | 20 | 10 | 327 | 228 | 110 |
| Montreal | 80 | 42 | 24 | 14 | 350 | 286 | 98 |
| Buffalo | 80 | 38 | 29 | 13 | 318 | 285 | 89 |
| Quebec | 80 | 34 | 34 | 12 | 343 | 336 | 80 |
| Hartford | 80 | 19 | 54 | 7 | 261 | 403 | 45 |

#### Patrick Division

| Team | GP | W | L | T | GF | GA | PTS |
|------|-----|-----|-----|-----|-----|-----|-----|
| Philadelphia | 80 | 49 | 23 | 8 | 326 | 240 | 106 |
| NY Islanders | 80 | 42 | 26 | 12 | 302 | 226 | 96 |
| Washington | 80 | 39 | 25 | 16 | 306 | 283 | 94 |
| NY Rangers | 80 | 35 | 35 | 10 | 306 | 287 | 80 |
| New Jersey | 80 | 17 | 49 | 14 | 230 | 338 | 48 |
| Pittsburgh | 80 | 18 | 53 | 9 | 257 | 394 | 45 |

Photograph, page 205: *Buffalo's Dave Andreychuk (#25) was a rookie in 1982–83 when he scored 14 goals and 37 points in 43 games. New York's Mike Rogers (#17) had three straight seasons of more than 100 points between 1979–80 and 1981–82.*

## LEADING SCORERS

| Player | Team | GP | G | A | PTS | PIM |
|---|---|---|---|---|---|---|
| Wayne Gretzky | Edmonton | 80 | 71 | 125 | 196 | 59 |
| Peter Stastny | Quebec | 75 | 47 | 77 | 124 | 78 |
| Denis Savard | Chicago | 78 | 35 | 86 | 121 | 99 |
| Mike Bossy | NY Islanders | 79 | 60 | 58 | 118 | 20 |
| Marcel Dionne | Los Angeles | 80 | 56 | 51 | 107 | 22 |
| Barry Pederson | Boston | 77 | 46 | 61 | 107 | 47 |
| Mark Messier | Edmonton | 77 | 48 | 58 | 106 | 72 |
| Michel Goulet | Quebec | 80 | 57 | 48 | 105 | 51 |
| Glenn Anderson | Edmonton | 72 | 48 | 56 | 104 | 70 |
| Kent Nilsson | Calgary | 80 | 46 | 58 | 104 | 10 |

## NHL AWARD WINNERS

| | |
|---|---|
| Hart (MVP) | Wayne Gretzky |
| Art Ross (leading scorer) | Wayne Gretzky |
| Calder (rookie of the year) | Steve Larmer |
| Vezina (best goaltender) | Pete Peeters |
| Jennings (fewest goals against) | Roland Melanson, Billy Smith |
| Lady Byng (gentlemanly conduct) | Mike Bossy |
| Norris (best defenseman) | Rod Langway |
| Conn Smythe (playoff MVP) | Billy Smith |
| Masterton (perseverance) | Lanny McDonald |
| Pearson (NHLPA MVP) | Wayne Gretzky |
| Adams (coach of the year) | Orval Tessier |
| Selke (best defensive forward) | Bobby Clarke |

# 1983–84

**STANLEY CUP CHAMPION:** Edmonton Oilers

## FINAL STANDINGS

### CLARENCE CAMPBELL CONFERENCE
**Norris Division**

| Team | GP | W | L | T | GF | GA | PTS |
|------|----|----|----|----|----|----|----|
| Minnesota | 80 | 39 | 31 | 10 | 345 | 344 | 88 |
| St. Louis | 80 | 32 | 41 | 7 | 293 | 316 | 71 |
| Detroit | 80 | 31 | 42 | 7 | 298 | 323 | 69 |
| Chicago | 80 | 30 | 42 | 8 | 277 | 311 | 68 |
| Toronto | 80 | 26 | 45 | 9 | 303 | 387 | 61 |

**Smythe Division**

| Team | GP | W | L | T | GF | GA | PTS |
|------|----|----|----|----|----|----|----|
| Edmonton | 80 | 57 | 18 | 5 | 446 | 314 | 119 |
| Calgary | 80 | 34 | 32 | 14 | 311 | 314 | 82 |
| Vancouver | 80 | 32 | 39 | 9 | 306 | 328 | 73 |
| Winnipeg | 80 | 31 | 38 | 11 | 340 | 374 | 73 |
| Los Angeles | 80 | 23 | 44 | 13 | 309 | 376 | 59 |

### PRINCE OF WALES CONFERENCE
**Adams Division**

| Team | GP | W | L | T | GF | GA | PTS |
|------|----|----|----|----|----|----|----|
| Boston | 80 | 49 | 25 | 6 | 336 | 261 | 104 |
| Buffalo | 80 | 48 | 25 | 7 | 315 | 257 | 103 |
| Quebec | 80 | 42 | 28 | 10 | 360 | 278 | 94 |
| Montreal | 80 | 35 | 40 | 5 | 286 | 295 | 75 |
| Hartford | 80 | 28 | 42 | 10 | 288 | 320 | 66 |

**Patrick Division**

| Team | GP | W | L | T | GF | GA | PTS |
|------|----|----|----|----|----|----|----|
| NY Islanders | 80 | 50 | 26 | 4 | 357 | 269 | 104 |
| Washington | 80 | 48 | 27 | 5 | 308 | 226 | 101 |
| Philadelphia | 80 | 44 | 26 | 10 | 350 | 290 | 98 |
| NY Rangers | 80 | 42 | 29 | 9 | 314 | 304 | 93 |
| New Jersey | 80 | 17 | 56 | 7 | 231 | 350 | 41 |
| Pittsburgh | 80 | 16 | 58 | 6 | 254 | 390 | 38 |

Photograph, page 207: *New York's Bryan Trottier (#19) struggles for position with Toronto's Borje Salming. Trottier had 111 points (40 goals, 71 assists) for the Islanders in 1983–84, while Salming had 43 points (five goals, 38 assists) in 68 games.*

## LEADING SCORERS

| Player | Team | GP | G | A | PTS | PIM |
|---|---|---|---|---|---|---|
| Wayne Gretzky | Edmonton | 74 | 87 | 118 | 205 | 39 |
| Paul Coffey | Edmonton | 80 | 40 | 86 | 126 | 104 |
| Michel Goulet | Quebec | 75 | 56 | 65 | 121 | 76 |
| Peter Stastny | Quebec | 80 | 46 | 73 | 119 | 73 |
| Mike Bossy | NY Islanders | 67 | 51 | 67 | 118 | 8 |
| Barry Pederson | Boston | 80 | 39 | 77 | 116 | 64 |
| Jari Kurri | Edmonton | 64 | 52 | 61 | 113 | 14 |
| Bryan Trottier | NY Islanders | 68 | 40 | 71 | 111 | 59 |
| Bernie Federko | St. Louis | 79 | 41 | 66 | 107 | 43 |
| Rick Middleton | Boston | 80 | 47 | 58 | 105 | 14 |

## NHL AWARD WINNERS

| | |
|---|---|
| Hart (MVP) | Wayne Gretzky |
| Art Ross (leading scorer) | Wayne Gretzky |
| Calder (rookie of the year) | Tom Barrasso |
| Vezina (best goaltender) | Tom Barrasso |
| Jennings (fewest goals against) | Al Jensen, Pat Riggin |
| Lady Byng (gentlemanly conduct) | Mike Bossy |
| Norris (best defenseman) | Rod Langway |
| Conn Smythe (playoff MVP) | Mark Messier |
| Masterton (perseverance) | Brad Park |
| Pearson (NHLPA MVP) | Wayne Gretzky |
| Adams (coach of the year) | Bryan Murray |
| Selke (best defensive forward) | Doug Jarvis |

# 1984–85

**STANLEY CUP CHAMPION:** Edmonton Oilers

## FINAL STANDINGS

### CLARENCE CAMPBELL CONFERENCE
#### Norris Division

| Team | GP | W | L | T | GF | GA | PTS |
|------|----|----|----|----|----|----|----|
| St. Louis | 80 | 37 | 31 | 12 | 299 | 288 | 86 |
| Chicago | 80 | 38 | 35 | 7 | 309 | 299 | 83 |
| Detroit | 80 | 27 | 41 | 12 | 313 | 357 | 66 |
| Minnesota | 80 | 25 | 43 | 12 | 268 | 321 | 62 |
| Toronto | 80 | 20 | 52 | 8 | 253 | 358 | 48 |

#### Smythe Division

| Team | GP | W | L | T | GF | GA | PTS |
|------|----|----|----|----|----|----|----|
| Edmonton | 80 | 49 | 20 | 11 | 401 | 298 | 109 |
| Winnipeg | 80 | 43 | 27 | 10 | 358 | 332 | 96 |
| Calgary | 80 | 41 | 27 | 12 | 363 | 302 | 94 |
| Los Angeles | 80 | 34 | 32 | 14 | 339 | 326 | 82 |
| Vancouver | 80 | 25 | 46 | 9 | 284 | 401 | 59 |

### PRINCE OF WALES CONFERENCE
#### Adams Division

| Team | GP | W | L | T | GF | GA | PTS |
|------|----|----|----|----|----|----|----|
| Montreal | 80 | 41 | 27 | 12 | 309 | 262 | 94 |
| Quebec | 80 | 41 | 30 | 9 | 323 | 275 | 91 |
| Buffalo | 80 | 38 | 28 | 14 | 290 | 237 | 90 |
| Boston | 80 | 36 | 34 | 10 | 303 | 287 | 82 |
| Hartford | 80 | 30 | 41 | 9 | 268 | 318 | 69 |

#### Patrick Division

| Team | GP | W | L | T | GF | GA | PTS |
|------|----|----|----|----|----|----|----|
| Philadelphia | 80 | 53 | 20 | 7 | 348 | 241 | 113 |
| Washington | 80 | 46 | 25 | 9 | 322 | 240 | 101 |
| NY Islanders | 80 | 40 | 34 | 6 | 345 | 312 | 86 |
| NY Rangers | 80 | 26 | 44 | 10 | 295 | 345 | 62 |
| New Jersey | 80 | 22 | 48 | 10 | 264 | 346 | 54 |
| Pittsburgh | 80 | 24 | 51 | 5 | 276 | 385 | 53 |

*Photograph, page 209: Brent Sutter (#21) of the New York Islanders had the best year of his career in 1984–85 when he had 102 points (42 goals, 60 assists) in 72 games.*

## LEADING SCORERS

| Player | Team | GP | G | A | PTS | PIM |
|--------|------|----|----|----|-----|-----|
| Wayne Gretzky | Edmonton | 80 | 73 | 135 | 208 | 52 |
| Jari Kurri | Edmonton | 73 | 71 | 64 | 135 | 30 |
| Dale Hawerchuk | Winnipeg | 80 | 53 | 77 | 130 | 74 |
| Marcel Dionne | Los Angeles | 80 | 46 | 80 | 126 | 46 |
| Paul Coffey | Edmonton | 80 | 37 | 84 | 121 | 97 |
| Mike Bossy | NY Islanders | 76 | 58 | 59 | 117 | 38 |
| John Ogrodnick | Detroit | 79 | 55 | 50 | 105 | 30 |
| Denis Savard | Chicago | 79 | 38 | 67 | 105 | 56 |
| Bernie Federko | St. Louis | 76 | 30 | 73 | 103 | 27 |
| Mike Gartner | Washington | 80 | 50 | 52 | 102 | 71 |

## NHL AWARD WINNERS

| | |
|---|---|
| Hart (MVP) | Wayne Gretzky |
| Art Ross (leading scorer) | Wayne Gretzky |
| Calder (rookie of the year) | Mario Lemieux |
| Vezina  (best goaltender) | Pelle Lindbergh |
| Jennings (fewest goals against) | Tom Barrasso, Bob Sauve |
| Lady Byng (gentlemanly conduct) | Jari Kurri |
| Norris (best defenseman) | Paul Coffey |
| Conn Smythe (playoff MVP) | Wayne Gretzky |
| Masterton (perseverance) | Anders Hedberg |
| Pearson (NHLPA MVP) | Wayne Gretzky |
| Adams (coach of the year) | Mike Keenan |
| Selke (best defensive forward) | Craig Ramsay |

# 1985–86

**STANLEY CUP CHAMPION:** Montreal Canadiens

## FINAL STANDINGS

### CLARENCE CAMPBELL CONFERENCE
#### Norris Division

| Team | GP | W | L | T | GF | GA | PTS |
|------|----|----|----|----|----|----|----|
| Chicago | 80 | 39 | 33 | 8 | 351 | 349 | 86 |
| Minnesota | 80 | 38 | 33 | 9 | 327 | 305 | 85 |
| St. Louis | 80 | 37 | 34 | 9 | 302 | 291 | 83 |
| Toronto | 80 | 25 | 48 | 7 | 311 | 386 | 57 |
| Detroit | 80 | 17 | 57 | 6 | 266 | 415 | 40 |

#### Smythe Division

| Team | GP | W | L | T | GF | GA | PTS |
|------|----|----|----|----|----|----|----|
| Edmonton | 80 | 56 | 17 | 7 | 426 | 310 | 119 |
| Calgary | 80 | 40 | 31 | 9 | 354 | 315 | 89 |
| Winnipeg | 80 | 26 | 47 | 7 | 295 | 372 | 59 |
| Vancouver | 80 | 23 | 44 | 13 | 282 | 333 | 59 |
| Los Angeles | 80 | 23 | 49 | 8 | 284 | 389 | 54 |

### PRINCE OF WALES CONFERENCE
#### Adams Division

| Team | GP | W | L | T | GF | GA | PTS |
|------|----|----|----|----|----|----|----|
| Quebec | 80 | 43 | 31 | 6 | 330 | 289 | 92 |
| Montreal | 80 | 40 | 33 | 7 | 330 | 280 | 87 |
| Boston | 80 | 37 | 31 | 12 | 311 | 288 | 86 |
| Hartford | 80 | 40 | 36 | 4 | 332 | 302 | 84 |
| Buffalo | 80 | 37 | 37 | 6 | 296 | 291 | 80 |

#### Patrick Division

| Team | GP | W | L | T | GF | GA | PTS |
|------|----|----|----|----|----|----|----|
| Philadelphia | 80 | 53 | 23 | 4 | 335 | 241 | 110 |
| Washington | 80 | 50 | 23 | 7 | 315 | 272 | 107 |
| NY Islanders | 80 | 39 | 29 | 12 | 327 | 284 | 90 |
| NY Rangers | 80 | 36 | 38 | 6 | 280 | 276 | 78 |
| Pittsburgh | 80 | 34 | 38 | 8 | 313 | 305 | 76 |
| New Jersey | 80 | 28 | 49 | 3 | 300 | 374 | 59 |

Photograph, page 211: *Montreal rookie netminder Patrick Roy (#33) stunned the hockey world by winning 15 postseason games and leading the Canadiens to a surprising Stanley Cup win in 1986.*

## LEADING SCORERS

| Player | Team | GP | G | A | PTS | PIM |
|---|---|---|---|---|---|---|
| Wayne Gretzky | Edmonton | 80 | 52 | 163 | 215 | 46 |
| Mario Lemieux | Pittsburgh | 79 | 48 | 93 | 141 | 43 |
| Paul Coffey | Edmonton | 79 | 48 | 90 | 138 | 120 |
| Jari Kurri | Edmonton | 78 | 68 | 63 | 131 | 22 |
| Mike Bossy | NY Islanders | 80 | 61 | 62 | 123 | 14 |
| Peter Stastny | Quebec | 76 | 41 | 81 | 122 | 60 |
| Denis Savard | Chicago | 80 | 47 | 69 | 116 | 111 |
| Mats Naslund | Montreal | 80 | 43 | 67 | 110 | 16 |
| Dale Hawerchuk | Winnipeg | 80 | 46 | 59 | 105 | 44 |
| Neal Broten | Minnesota | 80 | 29 | 76 | 105 | 47 |

## NHL AWARD WINNERS

| | |
|---|---|
| Hart (MVP) | Wayne Gretzky |
| Art Ross (leading scorer) | Wayne Gretzky |
| Calder (rookie of the year) | Gary Suter |
| Vezina (best goaltender) | John Vanbiesbrouck |
| Jennings (fewest goals against) | Bob Froese, Darren Jensen |
| Lady Byng (gentlemanly conduct) | Mike Bossy |
| Norris (best defenseman) | Paul Coffey |
| Conn Smythe (playoff MVP) | Patrick Roy |
| Masterton (perseverance) | Charlie Simmer |
| Pearson (NHLPA MVP) | Mario Lemieux |
| Adams (coach of the year) | Glen Sather |
| Selke (best defensive forward) | Troy Murray |

# 1986–87

**STANLEY CUP CHAMPION:** Edmonton Oilers

## FINAL STANDINGS

### CLARENCE CAMPBELL CONFERENCE
#### Norris Division

| Team | GP | W | L | T | GF | GA | PTS |
|---|---|---|---|---|---|---|---|
| St. Louis | 80 | 32 | 33 | 15 | 281 | 293 | 79 |
| Detroit | 80 | 34 | 36 | 10 | 260 | 274 | 78 |
| Chicago | 80 | 29 | 37 | 14 | 290 | 310 | 72 |
| Toronto | 80 | 32 | 42 | 6 | 286 | 319 | 70 |
| Minnesota | 80 | 30 | 40 | 10 | 296 | 314 | 70 |

#### Smythe Division

| Team | GP | W | L | T | GF | GA | PTS |
|---|---|---|---|---|---|---|---|
| Edmonton | 80 | 50 | 24 | 6 | 372 | 284 | 106 |
| Calgary | 80 | 46 | 31 | 3 | 318 | 289 | 95 |
| Winnipeg | 80 | 40 | 32 | 8 | 279 | 271 | 88 |
| Los Angeles | 80 | 31 | 41 | 8 | 318 | 341 | 70 |
| Vancouver | 80 | 29 | 43 | 8 | 282 | 314 | 66 |

### PRINCE OF WALES CONFERENCE
#### Adams Division

| Team | GP | W | L | T | GF | GA | PTS |
|---|---|---|---|---|---|---|---|
| Hartford | 80 | 43 | 30 | 7 | 287 | 270 | 93 |
| Montreal | 80 | 41 | 29 | 10 | 277 | 241 | 92 |
| Boston | 80 | 39 | 34 | 7 | 301 | 276 | 85 |
| Quebec | 80 | 31 | 39 | 10 | 267 | 276 | 72 |
| Buffalo | 80 | 28 | 44 | 8 | 280 | 308 | 64 |

#### Patrick Division

| Team | GP | W | L | T | GF | GA | PTS |
|---|---|---|---|---|---|---|---|
| Philadelphia | 80 | 46 | 26 | 8 | 310 | 245 | 100 |
| Washington | 80 | 38 | 32 | 10 | 285 | 278 | 86 |
| NY Islanders | 80 | 35 | 33 | 12 | 279 | 281 | 82 |
| NY Rangers | 80 | 34 | 38 | 8 | 307 | 323 | 76 |
| Pittsburgh | 80 | 30 | 38 | 12 | 297 | 290 | 72 |
| New Jersey | 80 | 29 | 45 | 6 | 293 | 368 | 64 |

*Photograph, page 213: In 1986–87, Edmonton's Jari Kurri (#17) scored 54 goals and 54 assists. He then had 25 points (15 goals, 10 assists) in 21 playoff games as the Oilers recaptured the Stanley Cup.*

## LEADING SCORERS

| Player | Team | GP | G | A | PTS | PIM |
|---|---|---|---|---|---|---|
| Wayne Gretzky | Edmonton | 79 | 62 | 121 | 183 | 28 |
| Jari Kurri | Edmonton | 79 | 54 | 54 | 108 | 41 |
| Mario Lemieux | Pittsburgh | 63 | 54 | 53 | 107 | 57 |
| Mark Messier | Edmonton | 77 | 37 | 70 | 107 | 73 |
| Doug Gilmour | St. Louis | 80 | 42 | 63 | 105 | 58 |
| Dino Ciccarelli | Minnesota | 80 | 52 | 51 | 103 | 92 |
| Dale Hawerchuk | Winnipeg | 80 | 47 | 53 | 100 | 54 |
| Michel Goulet | Quebec | 75 | 49 | 47 | 96 | 61 |
| Tim Kerr | Philadelphia | 75 | 58 | 37 | 95 | 57 |
| Ray Bourque | Boston | 78 | 23 | 72 | 95 | 36 |

## NHL AWARD WINNERS

| | |
|---|---|
| Hart (MVP) | Wayne Gretzky |
| Art Ross (leading scorer) | Wayne Gretzky |
| Calder (rookie of the year) | Luc Robitaille |
| Vezina (best goaltender) | Ron Hextall |
| Jennings (fewest goals against) | Brian Hayward |
| Lady Byng (gentlemanly conduct) | Joey Mullen |
| Norris (best defenseman) | Ray Bourque |
| Conn Smythe (playoff MVP) | Ron Hextall |
| Masterton (perseverance) | Doug Jarvis |
| Pearson (NHLPA MVP) | Wayne Gretzky |
| Adams (coach of the year) | Jacques Demers |
| Selke (best defensive forward) | Dave Poulin |

# 1987–88

**STANLEY CUP CHAMPION:** Edmonton Oilers

## FINAL STANDINGS

### CLARENCE CAMPBELL CONFERENCE
**Norris Division**

| Team | GP | W | L | T | GF | GA | PTS |
|------|----|----|----|----|----|----|----|
| Detroit | 80 | 41 | 28 | 11 | 322 | 269 | 93 |
| St. Louis | 80 | 34 | 38 | 8 | 278 | 294 | 76 |
| Chicago | 80 | 30 | 41 | 9 | 284 | 328 | 69 |
| Toronto | 80 | 21 | 49 | 10 | 273 | 345 | 52 |
| Minnesota | 80 | 19 | 48 | 13 | 242 | 349 | 51 |

**Smythe Division**

| Team | GP | W | L | T | GF | GA | PTS |
|------|----|----|----|----|----|----|----|
| Calgary | 80 | 48 | 23 | 9 | 397 | 305 | 105 |
| Edmonton | 80 | 44 | 25 | 11 | 363 | 288 | 99 |
| Winnipeg | 80 | 33 | 36 | 11 | 292 | 310 | 77 |
| Los Angeles | 80 | 30 | 42 | 8 | 318 | 359 | 68 |
| Vancouver | 80 | 25 | 46 | 9 | 272 | 320 | 59 |

### PRINCE OF WALES CONFERENCE
**Adams Division**

| Team | GP | W | L | T | GF | GA | PTS |
|------|----|----|----|----|----|----|----|
| Montreal | 80 | 45 | 22 | 13 | 298 | 238 | 103 |
| Boston | 80 | 44 | 30 | 6 | 300 | 251 | 94 |
| Buffalo | 80 | 37 | 32 | 11 | 283 | 305 | 85 |
| Hartford | 80 | 35 | 38 | 7 | 249 | 267 | 77 |
| Quebec | 80 | 32 | 43 | 5 | 271 | 306 | 69 |

**Patrick Division**

| Team | GP | W | L | T | GF | GA | PTS |
|------|----|----|----|----|----|----|----|
| NY Islanders | 80 | 39 | 31 | 10 | 308 | 267 | 88 |
| Washington | 80 | 38 | 33 | 9 | 281 | 249 | 85 |
| Philadelphia | 80 | 38 | 33 | 9 | 292 | 292 | 85 |
| New Jersey | 80 | 38 | 36 | 6 | 295 | 296 | 82 |
| NY Rangers | 80 | 36 | 34 | 10 | 300 | 283 | 82 |
| Pittsburgh | 80 | 36 | 35 | 9 | 319 | 316 | 81 |

Photograph, page 215: *New Jersey winger John MacLean (#15) scored one the biggest goals of his career when he notched an overtime winner on the last night of the 1987–88 season to get the Devils into the playoffs. MacLean had 23 goals during the regular season and added seven more in the postseason.*

## LEADING SCORERS

| Player | Team | GP | G | A | PTS | PIM |
|---|---|---|---|---|---|---|
| Mario Lemieux | Pittsburgh | 77 | 70 | 98 | 168 | 92 |
| Wayne Gretzky | Edmonton | 64 | 40 | 109 | 149 | 24 |
| Denis Savard | Chicago | 80 | 44 | 87 | 131 | 95 |
| Dale Hawerchuk | Winnipeg | 80 | 44 | 77 | 121 | 59 |
| Luc Robitaille | Los Angeles | 80 | 53 | 58 | 111 | 82 |
| Peter Stastny | Quebec | 76 | 46 | 65 | 111 | 69 |
| Mark Messier | Edmonton | 77 | 37 | 74 | 111 | 103 |
| Jimmy Carson | Los Angeles | 80 | 55 | 52 | 107 | 45 |
| Hakan Loob | Calgary | 80 | 50 | 56 | 106 | 47 |
| Michel Goulet | Quebec | 80 | 48 | 58 | 106 | 56 |

## NHL AWARD WINNERS

| | |
|---|---|
| Hart (MVP) | Mario Lemieux |
| Art Ross (leading scorer) | Mario Lemieux |
| Calder (rookie of the year) | Joe Nieuwendyk |
| Vezina (best goaltender) | Grant Fuhr |
| Lady Byng (gentlemanly conduct) | Mats Naslund |
| Jennings (fewest goals against) | Patrick Roy, Brian Hayward |
| Norris (best defenseman) | Raymond Bourque |
| Conn Smythe (playoff MVP) | Wayne Gretzky |
| Masterton (perseverance) | Bob Bourne |
| Pearson (NHLPA MVP) | Mario Lemieux |
| Adams (coach of the year) | Jacques Demers |
| Selke (best defensive forward) | Guy Carbonneau |
| Clancy (leadership) | Lanny McDonald |

# 1988-89

**STANLEY CUP CHAMPION:** Calgary Flames

## FINAL STANDINGS

### CLARENCE CAMPBELL CONFERENCE
**Norris Division**

| Team | GP | W | L | T | GF | GA | PTS |
|---|---|---|---|---|---|---|---|
| Detroit | 80 | 34 | 34 | 12 | 313 | 316 | 80 |
| St. Louis | 80 | 33 | 35 | 12 | 275 | 285 | 78 |
| Minnesota | 80 | 27 | 37 | 16 | 258 | 278 | 70 |
| Chicago | 80 | 27 | 41 | 12 | 297 | 335 | 66 |
| Toronto | 80 | 28 | 46 | 6 | 259 | 342 | 62 |

**Smythe Division**

| Team | GP | W | L | T | GF | GA | PTS |
|---|---|---|---|---|---|---|---|
| Calgary | 80 | 54 | 17 | 9 | 354 | 226 | 117 |
| Los Angeles | 80 | 42 | 31 | 7 | 376 | 335 | 91 |
| Edmonton | 80 | 38 | 34 | 8 | 325 | 306 | 84 |
| Vancouver | 80 | 33 | 39 | 8 | 251 | 253 | 74 |
| Winnipeg | 80 | 26 | 42 | 12 | 300 | 355 | 64 |

### PRINCE OF WALES CONFERENCE
**Adams Division**

| Team | GP | W | L | T | GF | GA | PTS |
|---|---|---|---|---|---|---|---|
| Montreal | 80 | 53 | 18 | 9 | 315 | 218 | 115 |
| Boston | 80 | 37 | 29 | 14 | 289 | 256 | 88 |
| Buffalo | 80 | 38 | 35 | 7 | 291 | 299 | 83 |
| Hartford | 80 | 37 | 38 | 5 | 299 | 290 | 79 |
| Quebec | 80 | 27 | 46 | 7 | 269 | 342 | 61 |

**Patrick Division**

| Team | GP | W | L | T | GF | GA | PTS |
|---|---|---|---|---|---|---|---|
| Washington | 80 | 41 | 29 | 10 | 305 | 259 | 92 |
| Pittsburgh | 80 | 40 | 33 | 7 | 347 | 349 | 87 |
| NY Rangers | 80 | 37 | 35 | 8 | 310 | 307 | 82 |
| Philadelphia | 80 | 36 | 36 | 8 | 307 | 285 | 80 |
| New Jersey | 80 | 27 | 41 | 12 | 281 | 325 | 66 |
| NY Islanders | 80 | 28 | 47 | 5 | 265 | 325 | 61 |

Photograph, page 217: *Detroit's Steve Yzerman (#19) had the best year of his career in 1988–89 when he scored 65 goals and 155 points. Yzerman had three consecutive seasons of more than 100 points to close out the eighties.*

## LEADING SCORERS

| Player | Team | GP | G | A | PTS | PIM |
|---|---|---|---|---|---|---|
| Mario Lemieux | Pittsburgh | 76 | 85 | 114 | 199 | 100 |
| Wayne Gretzky | Los Angeles | 78 | 54 | 114 | 168 | 26 |
| Steve Yzerman | Detroit | 80 | 65 | 90 | 155 | 61 |
| Bernie Nicholls | Los Angeles | 79 | 70 | 80 | 150 | 96 |
| Rob Brown | Pittsburgh | 68 | 49 | 66 | 115 | 118 |
| Paul Coffey | Pittsburgh | 75 | 30 | 83 | 113 | 195 |
| Joe Mullen | Calgary | 79 | 51 | 59 | 110 | 16 |
| Jari Kurri | Edmonton | 76 | 44 | 58 | 102 | 69 |
| Jimmy Carson | Edmonton | 80 | 49 | 51 | 100 | 36 |
| Luc Robitaille | Los Angeles | 78 | 46 | 52 | 98 | 65 |

## NHL AWARD WINNERS

| | |
|---|---|
| Hart (MVP) | Wayne Gretzky |
| Art Ross (leading scorer) | Mario Lemieux |
| Calder (rookie of the year) | Brian Leetch |
| Vezina (best goaltender) | Patrick Roy |
| Jennings (fewest goals against) | Patrick Roy, Brian Hayward |
| Lady Byng (gentlemanly conduct) | Joe Mullen |
| Norris (best defenseman) | Chris Chelios |
| Conn Smythe (playoff MVP) | Al MacInnis |
| Masterton (perseverance) | Tim Kerr |
| Pearson (NHLPA MVP) | Steve Yzerman |
| Adams (coach of the year) | Pat Burns |
| Selke (best defensive forward) | Guy Carbonneau |
| Clancy (leadership) | Bryan Trottier |

# 1989-90

**STANLEY CUP CHAMPION:** Edmonton Oilers

## FINAL STANDINGS

### CLARENCE CAMPBELL CONFERENCE
**Norris Division**

| Team | GP | W | L | T | GF | GA | PTS |
|------|----|----|----|----|----|----|----|
| Chicago | 80 | 41 | 33 | 6 | 316 | 294 | 88 |
| St. Louis | 80 | 37 | 34 | 9 | 295 | 279 | 83 |
| Toronto | 80 | 38 | 38 | 4 | 337 | 358 | 80 |
| Minnesota | 80 | 36 | 40 | 4 | 284 | 291 | 76 |
| Detroit | 80 | 28 | 38 | 14 | 288 | 323 | 70 |

**Smythe Division**

| Team | GP | W | L | T | GF | GA | PTS |
|------|----|----|----|----|----|----|----|
| Calgary | 80 | 42 | 23 | 15 | 348 | 265 | 99 |
| Edmonton | 80 | 38 | 28 | 14 | 315 | 283 | 90 |
| Winnipeg | 80 | 37 | 32 | 11 | 298 | 290 | 85 |
| Los Angeles | 80 | 34 | 39 | 7 | 338 | 337 | 75 |
| Vancouver | 80 | 25 | 41 | 14 | 245 | 306 | 64 |

### PRINCE OF WALES CONFERENCE
**Adams Division**

| Team | GP | W | L | T | GF | GA | PTS |
|------|----|----|----|----|----|----|----|
| Boston | 80 | 46 | 25 | 9 | 289 | 232 | 101 |
| Buffalo | 80 | 45 | 27 | 8 | 286 | 248 | 98 |
| Montreal | 80 | 41 | 28 | 11 | 288 | 234 | 93 |
| Hartford | 80 | 38 | 33 | 9 | 275 | 268 | 85 |
| Quebec | 80 | 12 | 61 | 7 | 240 | 407 | 31 |

**Patrick Division**

| Team | GP | W | L | T | GF | GA | PTS |
|------|----|----|----|----|----|----|----|
| NY Rangers | 80 | 36 | 31 | 13 | 279 | 267 | 85 |
| New Jersey | 80 | 37 | 34 | 9 | 295 | 288 | 83 |
| Washington | 80 | 36 | 38 | 6 | 284 | 275 | 78 |
| NY Islanders | 80 | 31 | 38 | 11 | 281 | 288 | 73 |
| Pittsburgh | 80 | 32 | 40 | 8 | 318 | 359 | 72 |
| Philadelphia | 80 | 30 | 39 | 11 | 290 | 297 | 71 |

Photograph, page 219: *The Edmonton Oilers celebrate at their bench as the 1990 Stanley Cup finals comes to an end. The Oilers defeated the Boston Bruins in five games.*

## LEADING SCORERS

| Player | Team | GP | G | A | PTS | PIM |
|---|---|---|---|---|---|---|
| Wayne Gretzky | Los Angeles | 73 | 40 | 102 | 142 | 42 |
| Mark Messier | Edmonton | 79 | 45 | 84 | 129 | 79 |
| Steve Yzerman | Detroit | 79 | 62 | 65 | 127 | 79 |
| Mario Lemieux | Pittsburgh | 59 | 45 | 78 | 123 | 78 |
| Brett Hull | St. Louis | 80 | 72 | 41 | 113 | 24 |
| Bernie Nicholls | L.A./NYR | 79 | 39 | 73 | 112 | 86 |
| Pierre Turgeon | Buffalo | 80 | 40 | 66 | 106 | 29 |
| Pat LaFontaine | NY Islanders | 74 | 54 | 51 | 105 | 38 |
| Paul Coffey | Pittsburgh | 80 | 29 | 74 | 103 | 95 |
| Joe Sakic | Quebec | 80 | 39 | 63 | 102 | 27 |

## NHL AWARD WINNERS

| | |
|---|---|
| Hart (MVP) | Mark Messier |
| Art Ross (leading scorer) | Wayne Gretzky |
| Calder (rookie of the year) | Sergei Makarov |
| Vezina (best goaltender) | Patrick Roy |
| Jennings (fewest goals against) | Andy Moog, Reggie Lemelin |
| Lady Byng (gentlemanly conduct) | Brett Hull |
| Norris (best defenseman) | Raymond Bourque |
| Conn Smythe (playoff MVP) | Bill Ranford |
| Masterton (perseverance) | Gord Kluzak |
| Pearson (NHLPA MVP) | Mark Messier |
| Adams (coach of the year) | Bob Murdoch |
| Selke (best defensive forward) | Rick Meagher |
| Clancy (leadership) | Kevin Lowe |

# Acknowledgments

I would like to thank the following writers, whose works I consulted for this book: Michael Berger, Dan Diamond, Ken Dryden, Shirley Fischler, Stan Fischler, Walter Gretzky, Wayne Gretzky, Zander Hollander (editor of *The Complete Handbook of Pro Hockey*, 1982 edition), Douglas Hunter, Jeff Z. Klein, Kevin Lowe, Roy MacGregor, Andrew Podnieks, Jim Proudfoot, Karl-Eric Reif, Lew Stubbs, Jim Taylor, and Sheila Wawanash (editor of *Kings of the Ice*).

Statistical information was complied with the help of the *Official NHL Guide and Record Book* (every season during the eighties), *Total Hockey* (second edition), *Total NHL* (2003 edition), *Stanley Cup Playoff Guide* (1996 issue), *Hockey Almanac* (issued by *The Hockey News* in 2000), and *Sporting News Player Register* (various editions).

Anecdotal material came from the following magazines: *The Hockey News* (every year of the eighties), *The Hockey News – The Top 50*, *The Hockey News – The Best of Everything in Hockey*, *Inside Hockey*, *Hockey Digest*, *Hockey Illustrated*, *Hockey Scene*, *Superstar Hockey*, and *Sports Illustrated*.

Thanks to the following people for their invaluable assistance in helping to put this book together: Paul Patzkou, Tyler Wolosewich, Craig Campbell, Phil Pritchard, Dennis Miles, Bruce Bennett and his staff, Jason Kay, and Brad Wilson. I would also like to thank my editor, Dan Bortolotti, whose sharp eye and technique made the text much stronger, and Kimberley Young, who created the colorful design.

A special word of thanks for my wife, Maria, and my son, David.

# Photo Credits